China in the World

China in the World

An Anthropology of Confucius Institutes, Soft Power, and Globalization

Jennifer Hubbert

University of Hawai'i Press
Honolulu

Printed in the United States of America
25 24 23 22 21 20   6 5 4 3 2 1

Library of Congress Cataloging-in-Publication Data
Names: Hubbert, Jennifer Ann, author.
Title: China in the world : an anthropology of Confucius Institutes, soft
power, and globalization / Jennifer Hubbert.
Description: Honolulu : University of Hawai'i Press, [2019] | Includes
bibliographical references and index.
Identifiers: LCCN 2018036238 | ISBN 9780824878207 (cloth ; alk. paper)
Subjects: LCSH: Kongzi xue yuan. | Chinese language—Study and
teaching—Foreign speakers. | Chinese language—Globalization. |
Cultural diplomacy—China.
Classification: LCC PL1069.K66 H83 2019 | DDC 306.441/951—dc23
LC record available at https://lccn.loc.gov/2018036238

ISBN 978-0-8248-8426-0 (pbk.)

Cover photo: Statue of Confucius at the Imperial College
(Guozijian) in Beijing, China (October 18, 2015).
beibaoke / Shutterstock.com

Contents

Acknowledgments

I scarcely know where to begin in acknowledging the intellectual and personal sources of inspiration amassed over the years spent researching and writing this book, although I must begin with the hundreds of students, parents, teachers, and administrators in the Confucius Institute programs I have interviewed over the years and the schools that have hosted me. By necessity these educational institutions and interlocutors remain anonymous, but my heartfelt thanks to those who patiently explained the Chinese programs to me, shared their joys and concerns, hopes and sorrows, cannot be overexpressed.

I first conceptualized this project over a long writing retreat weekend with two other anthropologists who have over the past twenty-plus years become central to my intellectual endeavors and general well-being. Lisa Hoffman and I met when my oldest child, who graduated from college the year this book went to press, was not yet walking, and we began writing our dissertations together. We added Monica DeHart to our mix a few years later and spent the next several decades meeting at roadside truck stops, bed-and-breakfast inns, remote cabins, and anthropology conferences to swap manuscripts and ponder the curveballs of life. Their imprint rests on each page of this book and my debt to their collaborations over the years knows no bounds.

Others over the years have read and provided vital commentary on various pieces of this manuscript. Jennifer Hsu, Oren Kosansky, Dawn Odell, and Eileen Otis offered sound suggestions on different chapters, and David Campion reined in my vocabulary excesses. A special thank-you goes to Anne Grossman, who dragged me out of my office (not often enough) to work in brighter venues. I am pretty sure that over the years we lugged our computers to every coffee shop and wine bar in town. The gracious anonymous reviewers of this manuscript similarly deserve recognition and gratitude for pointing out my theoretical inconsistencies and directing me to potential reader misunderstandings. All remaining imperfections are, of course, my own.

I have long felt as if I won the job lottery with my position at Lewis & Clark College. My colleagues have been intellectually stimulating and always supportive and my students inspiring in their enthusiasm for knowledge; collectively they have listened to numerous talks on the subject of Confucius Institutes, have provided excellent feedback, and are mercifully consistent in sending me links to news media on the subject that I might have missed. I would also like to express my gratitude to Lewis & Clark's Office of the Dean, which supplied research money over the years, and to Lorry Lokey, whose Faculty Excellence Award provided much of the financial support needed to complete this project.

Portions of this book were presented at the University of Oregon, the University of Southern California, and assorted annual meetings sponsored by the Association for Asian Studies, the American Anthropological Association, and the International Union of Anthropological and Ethnological Sciences, and my deliberations on the subject have benefited from audience feedback at these venues. Chapter 5 has been published in slightly different form in *PoLAR: Political and Legal Anthropology Review* (2014), and sections of chapter 4 were published by the University of Southern California's Center on Public Diplomacy working paper series (2014).

Lastly, my foremost and most heartfelt thanks belong to my family, who over the years of research and writing this book have suffered through long periods of both physical absence and mental absentmindedness. My two children, Nathan and Isabelle, now young adults off on adventures of their own, have been models for me of intellectual curiosity and compassion, and Jay, who was instrumental in encouraging me to pursue my interest in anthropology way back when, has always been a stimulating intellectual companion, gentle critic, staunch supporter, and very, very patient spouse. Your pesto pastas have nurtured my appetite and my soul.

China in the World

CHAPTER 1

An Anthropology of International Relations

In December 2014, I attended the American Anthropological Association meeting in Washington, DC, to present a paper on Confucius Institutes as a form of globalization. Confucius Institutes (CIs) are Chinese culture and Mandarin Chinese language programs that are funded by the government of the People's Republic of China (PRC), staffed by Chinese nationals, and exported around the world. According to their mission statement, CIs were created to answer the interest of the global community in learning Chinese and to use educational and cultural exchange to promote global friendship. By ultimately establishing language and culture programs in all corners of the globe, CIs hope to reach two lofty goals: "the development of multiculturalism" and the construction of "a harmonious world" (Hanban n.d., "Constitution").

Confucius Institutes, however, are not simply language exchange programs, but also the centerpiece of China's soft power policies—that is, its attempts to win the hearts and minds of target constituencies through attraction to its culture and ideals rather than coercion or force.[1] The aim of Confucius Institutes is thus not only to teach the Chinese language to foreigners, but also to build a more favorable image of the Chinese nation—in effect, to export Chinese culture in the interest of furthering China's foreign policy and economic development goals.[2] Although CIs are language exchange programs in name and practice, they are also an instrument of China's public diplomacy, and arguably the most controversial of those instruments (Barr 2011, 62).[3]

The timing of my Washington visit could not have been more fortuitous, for the day after my arrival, the House of Representatives Subcommittee on Africa, Global Health, Global Human Rights, and International Organizations held a congressional hearing to discuss China's soft power projects. According to the chair of the committee, Representative Chris Smith (Republican, New Jersey), the hearing was the first in a series intended to investigate whether China's "soft power initiatives are undermining academic freedom at U.S. schools and universities." In particular, he announced, the committee would examine the "myriad outposts of Chinese soft power that have opened on campuses throughout the United States and the world, the so-called Confucius Institutes," whose curriculum "integrates Chinese Government policy on contentious issues such as Tibet and Taiwan" and whose "hiring practices explicitly exclude Falun Gong practitioners," a spiritual organization the Chinese state considers a threat to national security. The central question facing the committee, he announced, was whether American education is for sale: "Are U.S. colleges and universities undermining the principle of academic freedom in exchange for China's education dollars?" (US Congress 2014, 1–2). Smith's question mirrored broader debates among scholars, journalists, educators, parents, students, school administrators, and government officials about propaganda, national interests, and freedom of thought and expression in US classrooms that have raged since the very establishment of CIs in 2004. Yet the congressional hearing also made evident that critics of the CIs were responding to the institutes not only as language programs but also as a reflection of China's changing place in the world and perceived threat to extant global hierarchies of national power, and hence, by default, of the changing relative place of the United States.[4] China, as manifest in the CIs, these hearings and debates suggested, was attempting to become a new model of modernity and globalization for the world and was posing a symbolic challenge not only to US education but also to US hegemony and the nation's ideals for and ideologies of globalization, modernity, and the global order.

□ *China in the World* thus turns an anthropological eye on China's most globally visible, ubiquitous, and controversial soft power projects to offer a different perspective on international relations and the production of power, demonstrating how ethnography can illuminate the mechanisms of power, how it works, and to what goals.[5] To that end, it combines critical perspectives from international relations and political science research with those of anthropology to examine soft power policy—the concept that a nation-state, through the appeal and attraction of its cultural products, political values, and foreign policies, can shape the preferences, opinions, and actions of other nations. Unlike most previous studies of CIs, which have focused primarily on their founding policy makers, policy documents, and official policy goals, this book is based on original in-depth research on soft power policy in practice through a focus on those who people those policies and the cultures in which those policies are embedded.[5] Based on five years (2011–2016) of transnational, multiscalar, and multisited ethnographic and archival research in CIs in the United States, and on CI-sponsored travel-study trips to China, this book examines the experiences of teachers, administrators, students, and parents to understand how soft power policy plays out among diverse audiences and leads to complex and sometimes contradictory soft power goals and effects. In so doing, it considers not only how China uses culture and educational exchange to influence relations between nation-states, but also how the relations between states that manifest in the CIs are culturally constituted. Moving beyond the binary question of whether CIs are a pernicious threat to liberal education or benevolent foreign language programs, *China in the World* investigates what actually takes place in CI classrooms. It examines the ways in which China attempts to exercise soft power and produce new forms of globalization and modernization and how those attempts are met and negotiated by the targets of those policies.

The research for this book was inspired by the dearth of actual ethnographic inquiry inside Confucius Institute classrooms, particularly at the K–12 level, and the intensity of the debates among scholars, parents, school administrators, and the general public that nonetheless spoke on behalf of what politicians, parents, and scholars presumed was happening there. Most of the academic studies of Confucius Institutes have been published by scholars in international relations and political science whose investigations are largely based upon textual analysis of policy documents and address the subject at the level of state-to-state engagement and soft power policy goals rather than their implementation and effect. These studies largely understand the language programs as part of a zero-sum game in which the growth of China's soft power, assumed to be evinced by the rapid expansion of the Confucius Institutes, represents a corresponding decrease in American power—both soft and hard. Similarly, most of the journalistic studies have mirrored this focus on the Chinese state and the potential for conflict, with the most attention-grabbing headlines accusing the programs of being spy outposts and gateways for communist propaganda. When I began this research, few journalists or scholars had ventured into the actual spaces of pedagogical engagement, and this general absence of empirical knowledge on the subject, in combination with a desire to move beyond a macrolevel perspective, sent me into the Confucius Institute classroom and motivated the production of this book.

Based on this extensive research, *China in the World* offers the stories of US students seeking admission to college and successful careers, parents concerned with propaganda in the classroom, teachers struggling with stereotypes about China, and administrators frustrated with institutional bureaucracy who recount the details of their involvement with China's attempts to globalize its language. In other words, *China in the World* interrogates CIs not only as objects of study in and of themselves, but also as outcomes of relations between actors and among nation-states and as spaces of engagement and exchange, where soft power is produced and challenged through the globalization of the Chinese language. As it demonstrates, the CI language classrooms and exchange programs constitute a setting in which we can observe globalization, modernity, and the global order being defined and produced in the United States and China through complicated and contingent assemblages of historical and contemporary experiences and relations of power.

While I wholeheartedly agree with many educational analysts who advise caution when accepting funding from ideologically motivated organizations and actors, be they the Chinese government or any other outside funding source that expresses a sociopolitical agenda, this book does not center on the common question of whether the programs are positive forms of global communication or bastions of socialist propaganda. Rather, it asks why these "good" versus "bad" binaries remain the dominant frameworks for understanding the Confucius Institutes and ultimately contends that the debates and controversies over the programs say as much about American ideological preconceptions of the changing global order—what "should" count for a superpower in the twenty-first century (How should the status of a superpower be evaluated? What is expected conduct for a superpower?)—as they do about the empirical nature of the Confucius Institute programs themselves.

China Goes Global: Globalization, Modernity, and the Global Order

As its title suggests, this book views Confucius Institutes as a direct reflection and manifestation of China's history of globalization over the last three decades, albeit in this case as an example of the Chinese government's newfound attempts to offer the nation as a model for rather than target of globalization, in effect to be the agent of cultural and political influence rather than the passive recipient.[6] Since their debut in 2004, Hanban, the colloquial name for the CI governing body, has established nearly sixteen hundred CI programs around the world.[7] This figure includes more than one thousand Confucius Classrooms (CCs), which are located in K–12 schools, and more than five hundred Confucius Institutes (located in colleges and universities).[8] By 2016, Hanban claimed to have provided those programs with more than forty-six thousand CI teachers, taught more than 2 million students, and attracted 13 million participants to its forty-one thousand cultural activities.[9] Of those, approximately a quarter million were enrolled in five hundred K–12 and college programs in the United States alone, where their reach extended to all but three states in the nation.[10]

China's recent globalization practices are, like much else in present-day China, massive, broad ranging, and highly diverse. The government framed its initial post-Mao globalization efforts as "inviting the world in" (*yinjinlai*) by encouraging international investment in domestic financial, manufacturing, and infrastructure endeavors and seeking the advice of foreign experts.[11] This period of globalization set the stage for China's emergence as the "world's factory," when the consumer goods stocked by Western merchandisers, from microchips to running shoes to air conditioners, seemed invariably to be labeled "made in China."[12]

In the later 1990s and early 2000s, China's globalization practices began to take an explicit turn toward "going out" (*zouchuqu*) and "going global" (*zouxiang shijie*), processes that exemplified a different rationale for national globalization, including not only the rapidly growing need for natural resources and investment opportunities for sustained growth but also a desire for what the Chinese government refers to as the "comprehensive national power" appropriate to its status as a rising international player.[13] Much of this shift was initially led by financial outreach overseas, including Chinese corporate investments in such global enterprises as vineyards in France's Bordeaux region, purchase of IBM's personal computer division and New York's Waldorf Astoria hotel, and infrastructure development projects in Africa and Latin America.[14] This going-out process has also included increased participation in global multilateral organizations such as the United Nations, joining negotiations on global climate change, participating in conferences on gender equity, and committing troops to international peacekeeping forces.[15] China's growing engagement with the international community became particularly prominent in 2001 through its admission to the World Trade Organization and through Beijing's being awarded the 2008 Summer Olympics, a highly symbolic event that was widely touted as China's "coming out party" and a validation of its presence as a legitimate player at the global table.[16]

As a result of these and other economic and political strategies during the last several decades, China has averaged double-digit economic growth on a nearly annual basis, built the fastest computer and the most extensive subway and high-speed rail systems in the world, and hosted the most expensive Olympic Games and world's fair ever. It also witnessed the growth of per capita GDP from $193 in 1980 to $8,123 in 2016 and the emergence of its economy as second only to that of the United States in size and first in terms of purchasing power (World Bank n.d.). This massive growth has vaulted it into the ranks of global superpowers and led media pundits to dub the current era the beginning of the "China Century," a neologistic paean to its rapid economic growth, poverty reduction, low-cost labor, manufacturing potential, and sheer bigness. No wonder Michael Yahuda has called China "a World Bank poster child for successful globalization" (Yahuda 2003).

In many ways, China's recent participation in the globalization process has mirrored and reproduced dominant Western understandings of how globalization is presumed to work. *New York Times* columnist Thomas Friedman, arguably the most well-known US public face of this discussion, defines globalization as "the inexorable integration of markets, nation-states, and technologies to a degree never witnessed before—in a way that is enabling individuals, corporations and nation-states to reach around the world farther, faster, deeper and cheaper than ever before." From his perspective, "globalization means the spread of free-market capitalism to virtually every country in the world" (Friedman 1999, 9), a process that he sees as "enabling" and "empowering" (Friedman 2007, 10) for countries, corporations, and individuals alike. This "more is better" and "big is better" assessment of globalization, according to Marjorie Ferguson, presupposes that "increased competition, unfettered by ownership or trading restrictions . . . equals increased benefits for all; QED, increased profits, consumer choice and satisfaction" (Ferguson 2005, 27). Although there was always some domestic opposition to this model of globalization (Garrett 2001, 415), in a 2000 address at the Asia-Pacific Economic Cooperation, Chinese president Jiang Zemin noted his approval, stating that this model of globalization was an "objective requirement" for economic development and that China had "no alternative but to march full-steam ahead" (cited in Garrett 2001, 409).[17]

Anthropologists have long been interested in examining the effects of globalization and often critical of the kinds of theorizations of globalization that assume inevitability and progress, sometimes focusing on local communities' resistance to processes of globalization, other times focusing on cultural homogenization and economic domination.[18] In the case of China, this has entailed a highly productive focus on a broad range of topics related to the effects of globalization, including the consumption and reproduction of global products (Lozada 2005; Yan 1997; Yang 2015), resistance to the cultural whitewashing often born of globalization and modernization (Wu 2015) and to the appropriation of labor (Pun 2005), informal trade (Mathews, Ribeiro, and Vega 2012), and urbanization (Chu 2014).

While these studies rarely assume that globalization is either a homogenous process or uniformly beneficial, they have historically and typically shared a common sense of globalization's direction and spatiality. Unlike most anthropological studies of Chinese globalization, *China in the World* examines China as a new *source* of globalization rather than as its recipient—that is, as a site for theorizing globalization rather than merely for studying globalization's effects. It asks why, if globalization forms a set of known and predictable practices, would we need to study it (Tsing 2000a)? Drawing upon recent work in globalization studies that rethinks concepts of local and global,[19] *China in the World* questions the categories of global and local and examines CIs for how they challenge assumptions about the directionality and spatiality of globalization. Based upon analysis of student, parent, and teacher experiences with the CI program, whether with official texts, in the classroom, or on study tours that offer China as a different model for global modernity, this approach allows us not only to examine the practices and products of globalization, but also to reconceptualize the concept itself, moving away from a "reductive globalism" in favor of theorizing the routes of globalization that "take many unexpected turns, burst at the seams, and carve out new landscapes while recharting old ones" (Zhan 2009, 6, 7). Through critically assessing globalization as a category of analysis rather than taking its practices and suppositions for granted, *China in the World* offers a conceptual intervention into the way we think about globalization and the global order. China in this case is examined for what it can offer us theoretically—indeed as a method of inquiry—rather than merely as a subject of study (Eng, Ruskola, and Shen 2012, 6).[20]

Confucius Institutes have also troubled dominant assumptions about the conceptualizations and practices of modernity, particularly those that pertain to configurations of the state and state-society relations and to issues of human rights. At the same time, they also challenge dominant assumptions about China's own engagements with modernity.[21] Because of the CIs' embeddedness within formal state structures of power and because they are promoted and funded by the government as an important mechanism for the realization of state policy goals, they are logically interpreted as an embodiment of state practice and aspiration. However, at the same time, most soft power analyses also take for granted a unified monolithic Chinese state as the producer of its soft power projections that ignores the diversity of state agencies and actors. Akhil Gupta urges scholars doing analyses of the state to accept state partiality for what it is and as the starting point for analysis, beginning by accepting contradictions and contrasts in the constitution of the state as inherent and inevitable (2012, 53).[22] This, he argues, is less dangerous analytically than assuming the state acts as a unified entity, because it allows us to grasp how the state is a "congeries of institutions" and to move beyond analysis of the state through its spectacular displays of power (2012, 55). Accordingly, the analysis in *China in the World* disaggregates the Chinese state to reveal the multiple types of agents that embody China and Chinese culture within soft power projects, and whose actions thus produce complex and even contradictory goals and effects.[23]

Free speech, in particular the freedom to criticize the practices of the state, is a second aspect of governance that has long been framed conceptually in Western philosophical literature as a marker of modernity (Lee and LiPuma 2002, Taylor 2002). As such, from the very beginning there has been a great deal of controversy over the CIs' presence on US campuses, and the current increasingly widespread and repressive crackdown on free speech within China has reinforced concerns about censorship in the CI classroom. Many CI watchers are thus concerned that China's language programs may engage in similar censorial practices on US campuses because, as the American Association of University Professors (AAUP) suggests, they "advance a [Chinese] state agenda" and "sacrifice the integrity of the university" through suppressing academic freedom (AAUP 2014). Similarly, anthropologist Marshall Sahlins has labeled CIs "malware" and notes that they facilitate "the global spread of academic and intellectual principles contrary to those upon which they are founded—human knowledge in the interest of human welfare" (Sahlins 2015, 62).[24] *China in the World* interrogates conversations surrounding the constitution of free speech at CIs, not to question the value of freedom of speech, but to question how the concept is used to evaluate CIs in ways that can lead to uncritical assessments of modernity. This book offers ethnographic detail about what actually happens in the classroom, finding examples of both censorship and critique, not only to provide empirical evidence of soft power image management, but also to interrogate how "speech" within the context of the CIs is understood in a manner that threatens to diminish the usefulness of the concept of freedom of speech as an analytical tool for examining human rights and the function of a liberal education. How, I ask, does the discourse of free speech both reproduce *and* "misrecognize and distort the experience of policy by its targets and their political claims" (Tate 2015, 7)? This book thus analytically explores how human rights are defined and used in debates over CIs to reproduce global hierarchies of power that understand China as performing modernity incorrectly.[25] Expanding the register of inquiry allows us to think more broadly about questions of global agency, specifically how we recuperate and register agency when, for global others, only one form of modernity is deemed acceptable. Ultimately this book questions assumptions about reactivity to power to gain a sense of the reception and effects of soft power strategies among the populations within which they are deployed, thus attending not only to the Chinese government's goals and strategies for augmenting global power, but also to the context of their reception in the United States, a long-dominant nation grappling with challenges to its ideals for globalization and modernity and facing a changing global order.

Soft Power Policy: China Responds to Perceptions of Threat

China's challenges to Western norms of and expectations for globalization and modernity have not been universally well received by the already globalized and modernized West. Historically, the arrival of new global powers has brought tension and conflict, and China's arrival as a player at the global table has occasioned not only praise but also considerable criticism and resistance.[26] Political campaign advertisements in the United States, for example, have exploited fears of China's growing power by employing threatening, essentialized images of China such as fire-breathing dragons, portraits of Mao Zedong, and red flags to place blame for the supposed growing financial disadvantages of the United States occasioned by China's rise to power. This blame placing and fearmongering were common in political discourse during the 2010 campaign season, when, for example, one CNN commentator claimed, "As much as the products in the aisles at Wal-Mart, this recession was made in China" (Frum 2010). And during the 2016 election season, presidential candidates targeted China for such offenses as having perpetuated the "hoax" of global warming, driving down US wages, and triggering massive job losses. While perhaps exaggerated, such claims and portrayals are part of a wider discourse about China called the "China threat" or the "China threat theory," which maintains that China's growth endangers international stability.[27] According to the zero-sum conception of power implicit in this theory, as China's power rises, that of other nations must necessarily fall (Glaser and Murphy 2009; Houlden and Schmidt 2014).

Many in China argue that the discursive hegemony of Europe and the United States and their frequent "demonization" of China has given China little opportunity to explain itself and express its own opinions (Hongying Wang 2011, 45). In response to this perceived lack of control over a Western global narrative that presents the Chinese nation as a threat, the Chinese government has launched a massive international soft power campaign, of which the CIs are the most extensive and most future-oriented components, and have the greatest long-term potential impact.[28] The study and promotion of soft power have become something of a cottage industry in China, and high-level Chinese politicians and officials have been explicit about their intention to promote soft power to counteract perceptions of threat and to transform economic might into a more enduring and welcome phenomenon accompanied by greater political and cultural authority.[29] Du Ruiqing, former president of Xi'an International Studies University, has argued that "it's high time to make ourselves better understood by the world's people" (quoted in Lahtinen 2015, 205–206) and urged the use of soft power "to quench misunderstanding and hostility between people of different races" (quoted in Starr 2009, 66). Scholars have similarly argued that China perceives soft power as a critical mechanism for realizing global status as a great power (Ding 2008), and that how China is perceived by other nations that are the targets of its soft power efforts will greatly determine its future (Xie and Page 2013).[30]

The assumption behind these soft power engagements, according to policy speeches by Chinese officials and many of the CI teachers and administrators I interviewed, is that if foreigners understood the "real" China, they would view China's rise to power less skeptically.[31] The stated purpose of soft power projects such as the CIs, therefore, is to reveal China's "true" nature to the world by promoting and providing global access to its cultural products, philosophies, and practices.[32] In an article titled "China Threat Fear Countered by Culture," for instance, the *People's Daily*, the dominant media voice of the government in China, argued that "when people know China better, they will find out that harmony is an essential part of China's tradition, and a country that values harmony poses no threat to the world" (cited in Niquet 2014, 79). By virtue of its "harmonious" cultural tradition, so this theory goes, China's engagement in global politics will be a responsible and productive process, and providing foreigners with knowledge of this tradition will help lessen their fears of an ascendant China.

Accordingly, the Chinese Communist Party (CCP) has massively invested in soft power ventures all over the world. Among its short-term soft power activities are the 2008 Beijing Olympics, the 2010 Shanghai world's fair, and advertising blitzes in New York's Times Square, such as the sixty-second promotional video called *Experience China*, which played three hundred times a day for a month in 2011 and featured images of former Houston Rockets NBA player Yao Ming, renowned pianist Lang Lang, and fifty-nine "ordinary" Chinese citizens (Aldrich, Lu, and Kang 2015).[33] Longer-term soft power projects include a Peace Corps–like volunteer program in Africa (the China Youth Volunteers Organization), a $6.6 billion global launch of the English-language *Global Times*, published by the *People's Daily* (Canaves 2009), and the creation of foreign language channels for China Central Television (CCTV), the predominant state broadcaster, which have been included in many cable television packages in Europe, the United States, and the Middle East. These soft power projects also include, of course, the CIs, which, despite a price tag that pales in comparison with that of the *Global Times*, the Olympics, or the Shanghai Expo, have come to be labeled by multiple scholars and journalists as the "centerpiece" of China's efforts to empower itself through attraction rather than through coercion, force, or financial incentives.[34]

Many scholars will argue that for soft power to be most effective, it must arise from what we might call "organic" features of a nation-state; that is, when soft power policy targets perceive governments as engaging in self-promotion, they tend toward skepticism of the messaging. In contrast, when attraction derives through the products and actions of a society rather than the state, nations are more likely to accrue soft power benefits.[35] For example, the United States has historically amassed soft power through the spread of its popular culture, private technological innovation, and commercial brands, to mention a few, whereas its government-sponsored image management efforts are often received with controversy (Albro 2015). In contrast, China's soft power endeavors are explicitly and deeply embedded within Communist Party structures of power. CIs, for example, are on the one hand officially sponsored by the government's Ministry of Education. On the other hand, while as one reporter has noted, CIs may not necessarily be covers for espionage (Mattis 2012), they remain conceptually if not officially part and parcel of the Communist Party's "united front work," what Mao called one of the "three secret weapons" that seek to strengthen CCP authority and legitimacy (Groot 2016, 167). The United Front Work Department's labors involve both domestic efforts to quell dissent within China through clamping down on political ideals and social philosophies that might threaten CCP control and international efforts to improve China's public image. Perhaps the most telling link between the CIs and the United Front is that the chair of the Confucius Institutes Headquarters council, Liu Yandong, also chaired the CCP's United Front Work Department from 2002 to 2007. Chinese officials do not routinely link the two programs directly but have been explicit about their intentions for the CIs to play an important role in China's international propaganda efforts. As such, China's soft power efforts face an uphill battle to win the hearts and minds of global citizens.

Confucius Institutes: The Centerpiece of China's Soft Power Policy

Confucius Institutes have come to be China's most widespread and systematically planned soft power project. As of 2017, they have been established in 1,742 educational institutions in more than 140 nations around the world. Chinese state officials have been explicit about the diplomatic justification for their investment in CIs. According to Hu Youqing, a deputy in the National People's Congress, "Promoting the use of Chinese among overseas people has gone beyond purely cultural issues" to be recognized as a way to "help build up our national strength" and "to develop our country's soft power" (cited in Kurlantzick 2007, 67). Although CIs may not offer the effervescent buzz of an Olympics or the shock-and-awe value of a massive video screen in Times Square, I would argue that their soft power influence is potentially far greater. This is true for both individual and structural reasons. On the one hand, CIs target citizens who are arguably the world's most impressionable—its children and young adults—investing in their educations with the long-term goal of creating a generation of global power brokers who hold favorable opinions about China and the Chinese state.[36] On the other hand, public schools in the United States have suffered debilitating budget cuts in the last several decades and may be particularly susceptible to the pressures that accompany external, ideologically motivated funding.

The first Confucius Institute opened in South Korea in 2004, followed later that year by the first US CI at the University of Maryland, College Park.[37] Falk Hartig reports that the initiative for the formation of the CI program arose from Lu Qiutian, who, as a result of his career as Chinese ambassador to Germany (1997–2001), "deeply understood the cultural differences between East and West" and realized that "the failure to know the differences always leads to unnecessary misunderstandings" (quoted in Hartig 2016, 99). Lu further explained that in efforts to attenuate these misunderstandings, he proposed to the Chinese Foreign Ministry establishing cultural centers modeled on Europe's language programs, such as the Goethe-Institut and the British Council, and suggested naming them after Confucius (Hartig 2016, 99). At the same time, Jiang Feng, also a former Chinese diplomat in Germany, noted the existence of "numerous requests from abroad" for assistance in establishing Chinese language studies, which, he argued, prompted the Chinese Ministry of Education to establish the CIs (Hartig 2016, 99). As is discussed at length through the book, such conceptual and philanthropic rationales discount the more ideological and practical motivation, also frequently promoted by Chinese political figures, of the "rectification" of global perceptions of China in the interest of the production of soft power.

In response to these goals, in 2004, China formulated a five-year plan to cultivate Chinese language programs abroad and an initial goal of establishing one hundred CIs around the world (Zhe 2012, 2–3). At the height of its expansion, Hanban launched a new CI an average of every four days (Li 2007), a pace that by 2014 had slightly slowed to one every six days (Ruan 2014).[38] CIs are headquartered in Beijing under the direct financial and managerial aegis of one of China's most important government bureaus, the Ministry of Education, and managed by Hanban. In addition to its best-known and most extensive CI project, Hanban runs a number of programs related to Chinese language acquisition, including certification programs for teaching Chinese as a foreign language, Chinese proficiency competitions, and summer camps for secondary school students.

Hanban typically provides CI host institutions with initial funding of between $100,000 and $150,000 annually for a period of five years, with the expectation that the programs will eventually become self-funded, although this latter has yet to happen.[39] Program support provided by Hanban includes recruiting and training teachers in China, airfare and salaries for teaching and administrative staff sent abroad from China, cultural programming, and free curricular materials for students and reference libraries. Host programs typically have a "sister" university in China that is involved with teacher recruitment and training and draws its teaching staff largely from a pool of recent graduates who most commonly majored in either teaching Chinese as a foreign language or English. Host institutes are responsible for supplying classroom facilities, office space and supplies, and support staff, and for locating teacher housing. Each CI has an in-house program director, some of whom are US staff members of the host institution, while others are sent from the Chinese home institution. Hanban also provides summer training programs for teachers and hosts an annual conference in Beijing for CI host-school principals and administrators from around the world.

The route to establishing a CI program generally follows one of two paths, the first being that schools seek out and apply directly to Hanban. In much of its promotional literature, Hanban links the growth of CIs around the world to China's rapid economic growth and the consequent international desire—what it describes as a "China fever"—to communicate and cooperate with this growing powerhouse. In 2015, Hanban claimed that in addition to its growing roster of established programs, two hundred educational institutions in more than eighty countries were on a wait list to establish a CI (Hanban 2015). For representatives from schools and school districts interested in hosting a CI, Hanban offers ten-day informational visits to Beijing, where they are wined and dined and bused around to visit national historical monuments and contemporary architectural wonders. Upon returning home, interested administrators fill out an extensive application in both English and Chinese that includes information on CI bylaws and the requirements and obligations of both sides of the agreement.[40]

While Hanban's claims about a global desire for increased communications with China are in part backed by a rapid increase in demand for

Chinese language skills (Tsung and Cruikshank 2010), a second path to establishing a CI is through Hanban preemptively approaching specific educational and cultural institutions with proposals to establish programs on their campuses. And Hanban is sometimes willing to go to great lengths to establish footholds. The targets of these Hanban pursuits tend to be elite universities in Europe and the United States whose collaboration, many teachers told me, is perceived by the government as increasing prestige for the nation and sanctioning its political objectives. In the case of the CI at Stanford University, an oft-cited example of Hanban's attempt to legitimate its international presence by forging connections with elite Western institutions, *Bloomberg News* reported that Hanban offered Stanford $4 million to establish a CI and fund an endowed professorship but insisted that the selected professor not be permitted to engage in classroom discussions of what China considered sensitive issues (Golden 2011). When Stanford refused to comply with this caveat, Hanban endowed a position in classical Chinese poetry, a topic unlikely to lead to "uncomfortable" conversations about Tibet, Tiananmen, or Taiwan, and the CI was established without further impediment. Hanban has proactively reached out to other elite US institutions, including Cornell University, which rejected the funding, and Columbia University, which initially declined a professorship but ultimately accepted Hanban's offer to establish a CI that came with $1 million over five years to support research projects and campus programming (Von Mayrhauser 2011). Hanban's practice of seeking legitimation through association with elite Western structures of power was also evident in its Beijing headquarters displays, such as one featuring the Middle Tennessee State University CI, which said little about the university itself but showcased a framed image of the school's three Nobel laureates.

Targeting institutions such as Stanford and Columbia is part of the CCP's efforts to counteract growing antipathy in places that arguably have the greatest ability to counteract its rising global power—in the United States and Europe.[41] Although China has opened CIs and CCs in more than 140 countries on six continents, more than 60 percent of these programs are in Europe and North America, with nearly a third in the United States alone. The growth has been particularly marked at the secondary level; Hanban recently collaborated with the College Board (the administrator of the SAT college entrance exam) to teach Chinese language and culture in twenty large school districts across the United States and subsidized half the cost of developing the high school Advanced Placement program in

Chinese (Austin 2004). Although the growth of CIs in Western nations is partially a result of those countries having more capital to invest in educational programming (Kluver 2014), distrust of China in that part of the world is a greater impediment to its nascent rise to superpower status. From the Chinese government's perspective, therefore, these countries are in greater need of "proof" that China does not intend to upset the global status quo.[42]

Chinese language and culture offerings at CIs in the United States are varied and depend upon the specific agreements with the sister university in China, the training and skills of the individual teachers, and the needs of the host institution.[43] At one university where I observed classes, CI offerings included traditional language classes ranging from the beginner level to more advanced levels that used feature films to teach language skills or focused on business language. This CI also routinely offered an array of "culture" courses in topics such as tai chi, cooking, and traditional handicrafts. Both kinds of courses cost around $100 per semester per class, and none were credit bearing.[44] Hanban funding similarly supports a wide range of extracurricular activities that include academic conferences, teacher-training workshops, film festivals, Chinese medicine workshops, and lectures on a broad spectrum of topics from environmental concerns to economic development and foreign trade. Hanban has also recently begun to fund research projects by doctoral students on such topics as comparative studies of Chinese and Western music or politics, Buddhist art, classical Chinese philosophy, and Confucianism outside of China.[45]

Although Confucius Institutes at universities and colleges around the world have attracted the majority share of critical attention, as noted earlier, two-thirds of Hanban's Chinese language programs are located in Confucius Classrooms at the K–12 level. Confucius Classrooms provide similar programming to that of CIs, but at a level more appropriate for younger students. One of the CCs I researched, for example, offered beginning through intermediate Chinese classes at both the middle school and high school levels, but incorporated culture lessons within the language classes rather than as separate programming. Perhaps the most notable and important difference between the CCs and the CIs, besides the age of the students, is that CC classes are taken for credit, appear on official transcripts, and count for graduation requirements. Similar to the CI university situations, Hanban provides extracurricular programs at CCs that include visitors from Chinese cultural organizations, such as Shaolin monks and song and dance troupes from art institutes, language and culture competitions, and cultural festivals. Hanban also sponsors the annual Chinese Bridge summer program for high school students, which sends between five hundred and seven hundred US high school students to China every summer for seventeen days of study and travel.

Confucius Institutes are structured in several specific ways to provide maximum soft power impact. First, they have been explicitly modeled on philanthropic and culture-centric language exchange programs in Europe, such as France's Alliance Française, Germany's Goethe-Institut, and Spain's Instituto Cervantes. Through its overt comparisons with these programs, Hanban has clearly hoped to frame the CIs as noncontroversial language exchange programs that would "normalize" China as just one power among others (Niquet 2014, 83).[46] Second, in hopes of promoting a kinder and gentler image of China among future power brokers, Hanban has targeted the programs toward youth who, at least in the United States, are facing tightening job markets and cuts in education funding for foreign languages and other subjects perceived as nonessential and may be grateful for the opportunities provided by the programs. Third, the CIs are embedded in existing educational institutions that provide the necessary physical and administrative infrastructure to run the programs in a cost-effective manner. This also provides greater opportunity to dominate representations of China in smaller institutions that may have a dearth of China scholars and alternative perspectives.[47] Fourth, the CI curriculum focuses on the study of traditional Chinese culture, drawing upon a repertoire of globally recognized and well-regarded practices and values that are less threatening to the West than China's military and economic strength.

Despite their advantages for Hanban's soft power mission, these same features of the Chinese language programs have also sparked concerns about their growing presence and scale and suspicions about their pedagogical mission. Unlike the emulated European language programs, which are independent institutions, housed and managed separately from extant educational structures, CIs are directly embedded within host schools, colleges, and universities. While embedding programs in existing institutions provides cost savings for the government, that CI students may receive grades and credit for attendance (unlike those enrolled in European language programs, which are non–credit bearing, nongraded, and wholly voluntary) occasions fear among some critics and parents that students' ability or willingness to be critical of China or to explore research topics that might diverge from acceptable CI representations might be hampered.

Similarly, because Hanban provides curricular and extracurricular programming and materials that focus predominantly on traditional rather than contemporary Chinese culture, ideologies, and practices, critics have expressed concern that these lessons mask what amounts to state propaganda that presents a distorted image of China and potentially undermines Western academic and philosophical values of freedom of inquiry and speech, human rights, and democracy. In addition, because CIs are administered in part by Hanban supervisors, there are concerns that host universities become dependent upon the funding (which must be reapplied for every year) to support their Chinese language offerings and avoid pedagogical programming on topics critical of CCP policy or engage in indirect self-censorship to protect their funding (Chey 2008; Churchman 2011).[48]

The methods for assigning CI teaching staff also exacerbate the trepidations of critics. Unlike teachers in the European programs, who are frequently fluent members of the host community, known and vetted locally, CI teachers (except in rare instances) are hired and trained in China with little to no input from the host institution.[49] Although this is partly a matter of expediency, the knowledge that CI teaching staff are appointed by a Chinese state agency created for the purposes of generating soft power has led critics to distrust their philosophical perspectives and intentions. Some critics have gone so far as to view CI teachers as vehicles "for infiltration and spying into the campuses to find out what's going on hostile to [China's] interest" (Steffenhagen 2008). The concern here is that soft power emerges as what has recently come to be called "sharp power," power that does not merely seek to "win the hearts and minds" of policy targets but that "pierce[s], penetrate[s], or perforate[s] the information environments in the targeted countries" in ways that manipulate or poison the information that reaches target audiences (Walker and Ludwig 2017, 13).[50] Clearly, although the Ministry of Education established the CI program to ameliorate global concerns about China's rise to power, the very presence of a CI at a US school has the potential to also be understood contradictorily as a symbol of political domination, its invocations of culture having the paradoxical effect of augmenting rather than diminishing perceptions of threat and distrust.[51]

Studying International Relations through Ethnography: Methods and Organization

While *China in the World* engages with these concerns, instead of taking the existence and nature of this "threat" for granted or assuming that CIs are effective instruments for projecting power, it moves into the space of classroom encounters to understand how concepts of threat are produced through encounters among teachers, students, and parents and how power is established and perceived through texts and pedagogy and negotiated by policy targets. As we shall see, Confucius Institutes offer rich and complex places for exploration and analysis of the changing global order and its attendant discontents as they provide students with a purposefully crafted and packaged experience that offers tangible examples of China's soft power policy intentions, strategies, and practices intended to enhance its place in the world. As this analysis will demonstrate, however, making and implementing policy are complex processes that incorporate policy makers, actors, and targets, each embedded in their own material, social, economic, and political realities, and how we study policy has important repercussions for how we understand its implementation and effect.

By examining these interactions, engagements, and strategies as they occur "on the ground" in CI classrooms, this study differs from most previous studies of CIs and soft power, which have focused on the politics and political intentions of official state policy and drawn data from textual examination of official policy documents and promotional materials, interviews with administrative officials, and public opinion polls on attitudes about China.[52] While these analyses have provided valuable information on the soft power goals and discourses of policy makers and the political intentions of the state, they have provided less insight into the nature and practice of policy implementation. As previous scholars of soft power policy have discovered, measuring the effects of soft power is a notoriously difficult and slippery process.[53] Relying on opinion polls as a form of assessment, for instance, tells us very little about how soft power actually works, for it does not operate through the social and political categories utilized by polls, but through differently situated individuals who respond to policy technologies in ways that reflect their unique positions. Likewise, while discursive analysis of policy documents illuminates policy goals, it reveals little about what actually happens in the CI classroom. These kinds of studies fall prey to what Gritt Nielsen calls the rationality-technology-subjectivity problem of policy analysis, in which "politics and policies are reduced to a mentality of rule or a practice of thinking. . . . The persons toward whom a policy directs its efforts are construed in the image of, and as mere effects of, a political rationality" (2011, 69), an approach that assumes that policy holds hegemony over the subject and that implementation occurs through a "world of rule-following subordinates" (Mosse 2005, 3, 103).[54] Ethnographic approaches, in contrast, possess the ability to identify the elephant in the room (Stambach 2014, 122), which in this case means the ability to understand how culture mediates between these assumed transfers of power from the West to China and challenges us to rethink critically the manner in which Chinese "culture" is summoned and reconstituted in diverse and meaningful ways as a form of soft power.[55] To evaluate soft power ethnographically, *China in the World* draws upon an anthropology of policy approach that focuses not only on the official intention but also on the concrete implementation of soft power projects to understand how policies result in practice outcomes and in meanings that are often beyond the control of state desire (Shore and Wright 1997; Shore, Wright, and Però 2011). It approaches the models and language of these policy makers as data that require scrutiny (Shore and Wright 1997, xiii), emphasizes that intention and effect are not necessarily equivalent, and recognizes that policy objectives do not automatically correspond with the actual capabilities of the policies to achieve their desired outcomes.

Although this study investigated CIs at both the university and secondary levels—institutions whose purpose, as Ritty Lukose observes (2009), is to produce the citizens of modern nation-states—most of the encounters featured in this book, as noted earlier, took place at the middle and high school levels for several reasons.[56] For one, CCs at the middle school and high school levels have until now been a deeply under-researched subject, even though almost eleven hundred of the nearly sixteen hundred Hanban Chinese language programs around the world are at the K–12 level. And given that middle and high school students are less likely than college students to have been exposed to other information or viewpoints about China, the potential influence of CIs on their understanding of China is presumably greater.[57] The on-site research for this book was conducted between 2011 and 2016. At the college level, I attended CI classes and CI-sponsored lectures, culture competitions, teacher training sessions, symposia, and conferences at a large public university. At the middle and high school levels, this research included three extended site visits at a private sixth-through-twelfth-grade college-preparatory school and multiple visits to two public high schools and two public middle schools with affiliated CI programs. One of these CC organizations also offered a distance-learning program where I observed teachers conduct online courses and accompanied them on campus visits.

The primary data for this book were collected by participant observation at these K–12 schools, in focus groups, in semi- and unstructured interviews, and in everyday conversations with students, parents, administrators, board members, and teachers. I observed Chinese instruction classes offered to students from seventh through twelfth grades and ranging from introductory to advanced levels; I sometimes actively engaged in lesson plans and assisted with Chinese homework and at other times sat in the back of the classroom or off to the side and observed. Outside of the classroom, I also attended Hanban-sponsored cultural performances, Chinese language and culture competitions, local receptions for Chinese delegates visiting CI programs across the United States, and US congressional hearings, and held conversations about the CI program with members of Congress, state-level representatives, human rights activists, journalists, and documentary filmmakers. In China, I chaperoned high school students on the annual seventeen-day Chinese language Chinese Bridge summer program, visited Hanban headquarters, and interviewed CI teachers and administrators. To maintain the anonymity of the participants and programs, I have been purposefully vague about the locations and specific details of these educational institutions and used pseudonyms for the teachers, students, and parents with whom I interacted. This is particularly important for the Chinese teachers who participated in this study and who potentially could suffer adverse ramifications for their critiques of the programs when they return to China.

The archival research conducted for the project spanned a broad array of texts related to policy engagement and production, including memorandums of understanding, mission statements, public relations documents and videos, Hanban annual reports, administrative and political speeches, Chinese media reports, individual school agreements, teacher training materials, and textbooks. At the level of policy engagement, I observed and evaluated student work, including essays, presentations, and artistic creations. I also examined US congressional reports, transcripts of public debates over the CIs, and local reportage. While the "official" Chinese materials were revealing for how they constituted the goals and intentions of soft power policy, both for what they say outright and for what they avoid enunciating, so was the work of the students. Teachers offered specific guidelines to students for what they were to research and present, and these documents thus reflected what we might call the "correct" production of knowledge about China as envisioned by official policy, equally telling for the forms of knowledge that were excluded.

Recognizing that the implementation of policy is rarely a strictly linear process, this study, by attending to different scales of experience and following Kay Warren's (1998) approach to multisited research, explores the interconnections among individual stories, broader institutional practices and ideologies, and practices and political transformations at local and global hierarchies of power. In so doing, it views soft power not merely as a political phenomenon but also as a cultural practice, spanning both the macrolevel of geopolitical engagement and policy intention and the domestic cultural level of classroom micropolitics. By examining these transnational cultural exchanges as responses to concerns and pressures in political agendas on both sides of the Pacific, it demonstrates that the processes of cultural translation are anything but the seamless projection of power that policy makers and critics often envision.

The chapters that follow explore not only how power is imagined, but also how it is produced, mediated, and challenged through policy engagement to understand how CIs have emerged in the contemporary era as a focal point for debates over globalization, modernity, and the global order. Chapter 2, "The Culture of Cultures," begins this analysis by situating the growth of CIs within the broader context of China's soft power engagements, including the 2008 Olympics and 2010 world's fair, exploring the forms of culture featured in China's soft power projects, and considering Confucius as a branding mechanism for China. In doing so, it examines the nature of "culture" as invoked in China's soft power endeavors and how it mediates assumed transfers of power. Chapter 3, "Coolness and Magic Bullets," explores student experiences in the Confucius classroom and identifies student rationales for studying Chinese and their production of "China" as an object of knowledge and source of personal authority. Both coolness and magic bullets are analyzed for their invocations of long-term orientalist ideologies of Asian "exoticness" and through US-based pressures to brand the youthful self. Chapter 4, "Conjuring Commensurability and Particularity," explores the CC program's attempts to offer China as a new model for the global through an examination of a Hanban-sponsored travel-study program in China, the Chinese Bridge program, and of how students "misrecognize" the China offered by the program because of their own entrenched expectations for "globalization" and "authenticity." Through probing the hybrids of modernity, this chapter highlights the self-exoticizations of the CI program alongside the paradoxical notions of authenticity of the students. Chapter 5, "Imagining the State," focuses on how US parent and student perceptions of the Chinese state are formed through their CC experiences, both deconstructing concepts of the monolithic state and exploring debates over universal values that simultaneously construct China as both modern and lacking in modernity.

The final two chapters examine the public debates over the CIs and their abstractions of China. Chapter 6, "Rethinking 'Free' Speech," looks specifically at how some Western scholars, parents, school administrations, and concerned members of the public have understood these language programs as a threat to freedom of expression and inquiry in the classroom and how dominant American conceptions of free speech can paradoxically diminish its usefulness as an analytical tool for examining human rights. Lastly, chapter 7, "The Sites and Struggles of Global Belonging," returns to the often-binary nature of the debates over CIs to examine the ways in which CIs challenge the categories of analysis through which Western publics, broadly speaking, typically understand international relations and global belonging and think through the effects of culture and policy on a nation's place in the world. Together, these chapters offer a cultural critique of power that engages public policy debates through exploring a diversity of experiences that reveal how CIs engage and highlight different processes and meanings of globalization and modernity in ways that underscore the multivalent nature of culture and its relationship to equally multivalent constructions of power.

CHAPTER 2

The Culture of Cultures

In September 2014, at Hanban's first global Confucius Institute Day and in commemoration of the tenth anniversary of the founding of the CI program, the vice president of China's State Council read aloud a letter from President Xi Jinping expressing Xi's appreciation for the CIs' "tireless efforts for world peace and international cooperation" and central role in disseminating cultural knowledge about China throughout the world (cited in Ding 2014).[1] According to Xinhua News, more than four hundred school principals, university deans, and various agencies and institutions from more than one hundred countries around the world had also sent congratulatory letters in honor of the day.[2] In contrast to this celebration of what Hanban (2014, 2) labeled the "solidarity and influence of the Confucius Institute big family," just a day earlier, on the other side of the world, the University of Chicago had announced that it was terminating its agreement with Hanban and closing the Confucius Institute located on its campus. This followed a petition signed earlier in the year by more than one hundred faculty members objecting to the "political constraints on free speech and belief" they believed to be occurring in the CI Chinese language classroom (Leavenworth 2014).[3] US news reporting on the decision in Chicago referred to the reading of Xi's letter at the Beijing event and bolstered the perception of China's political repression by noting that foreign reporters had not been invited or permitted to attend the celebration (Leavenworth 2014).

The coincidence and cross-referencing of these two events reinforce a global experience in which both the production and consumption of power function within the realm and language of culture.[4] Whereas President Xi invoked Chinese culture as an essential national resource, within the US context, that same Chinese culture, in the configuration of foreign language programs, was viewed as a threat to liberal education.[5] Both the events also revealed how one's relationship to this culture emerged as a form of empowerment, in one case as a potential means of directing global politics and in the other as a potential means of promoting moral authority.[6] And deploying culture in the interest of national power, sovereignty, and moral authority is indeed the objective of soft power. Yet, perhaps because Chinese officials have been so forthright about efforts to instrumentalize culture as a form of patriotic ritual and render it profitable to the production of power, few studies of China's soft power engagements have taken seriously the type of culture CIs promote or the role it plays in policy formation, implementation, and outcomes, instead more commonly dismissing it as simply poorly disguised propaganda to increase China's national power.[7] This chapter embraces these interstices, scrutinizing the implications of the CI use and configuration of culture for understanding China's perceptions of its place in the world. Precisely because the CIs have adopted culture as a central tool in the production of soft power, understanding what counts as culture and why it is defined as such, how the government deploys it as an instrument of state power, and why policy targets or representatives of the state themselves may or may not challenge the meanings ascribed to it provides new insight into how China assesses its assets and shortcomings and its position in global hierarchies of power.

Any argument about culture confronts enduring debates over its definition and capaciousness. While popular vernacular conceptions of culture frequently configure it as a dichotomy of "popular" culture and "high" culture—current trends versus opera, for example—anthropological conceptions offer a more expansive understanding of culture that, despite skepticism over its potential to reify human practice and fall prey to cultural determinism, includes these material manifestations but also that "complex whole" (Tylor [1871] 1920, 1), of tangled, messy, and inconsistent human behaviors, philosophies, meanings, and symbolic systems.[8] Among the most important of these symbolic systems, many anthropologists would argue, is that of language, clearly a prominently positioned form of culture in the Confucius Institutes. Language as a form of cultural power is explored at greater length in chapter 3. Also left to later chapters are the central ways in which the cultural behaviors, philosophies, meanings, and symbolic systems of policy targets run roughshod over China's attempts to use culture to the end of national power and sovereignty. This chapter addresses "official" CI culture—what I have come to call patriotic state culture and is more simply often referred to in CI materials and conversations as "traditional" culture—that complex and sometimes paradoxical fusion of Confucian thought, elite material culture, and popular folk art that the language programs and the CCP have advocated as representative of China's contemporary significance. The chapter begins with a discussion of the official state rejection of Maoist forms of revolutionary culture through the embrace of traditional forms of cultural belonging and examines how they are constituted in recent soft power projects such as the 2008 Beijing Olympics and the 2010 Shanghai Expo. It then explores how the CIs' invocation of Confucius, specifically, as a cultural model is rooted in the production of national identity and China's rise to power. Throughout, the chapter interrogates why this particular amalgamation of ideals and practices has arisen as a politically sponsored paean to national value, who benefits from it, and what it discounts and conceals through its production.

Culture as a Patriotic State Ritual

The salience of culture in China's soft power engagements reflects the specific historical context of China's own state-society relations, in which the state has long invoked culture as central to the practices and values of ruling. During the imperial era, for instance, citizens seeking positions in the government sat for an arduous exam that was based upon the Confucian classics and commentary on this oeuvre, and the comprehensiveness and ferocity with which Mao Zedong exploited culture as a mechanism of power remain legendary. Despite the various post-Mao administrations' more recent rejection of both the "feudalism" of the imperial era and the excesses of Mao's Cultural Revolution, they, too, have continued to deploy Chinese culture as a form of patriotic ritual. If anything, the PRC president from 2002 to 2012, Hu Jintao, declared, "Culture has become a more and more important source of national cohesion and creativity and a factor of growing significance in the competition in overall national strength," making it therefore incumbent upon China, he argued, to "enhance culture as part of the soft power of our country to better guarantee the people's basic cultural rights and interests" (Hu 2007).

What Counts as Culture

While space precludes an extended discussion of the Maoist era's manipulation and deployment of culture in the interest of state politics, the maneuverings remain central to an understanding of similar operations in the contemporary era, for that culture Mao sought to destroy is precisely what current administrations have sought to elevate seemingly to the level of state religion.[9] Mao set the stage for his cultural policy early in his rise to power in a 1942 series of talks in Yan'an, a city in north-central China controlled by communist forces prior to their gaining hegemony over the remainder of geopolitical China in 1949. Codifying the role of culture in concrete and visual terms, Mao proclaimed, "In our struggle for the liberation of the Chinese people, there are various fronts, among which there are the fronts of the pen and of the gun, the cultural and the military fronts. To defeat the enemy . . . the army alone is not enough; we must also have a cultural army, which is absolutely indispensable for uniting our own ranks and defeating the enemy" (Mao 1967, 69). Mao declared that art and literature were to "serve the people" through reflecting the common citizens' lived experiences and inspiring them to foment revolution and promote socialism.[10] This policy regarding appropriate art and literature was part of a broader state strategy of cultural control that, at its most dogmatic and violent during the Cultural Revolution, promulgated the destruction of the "four olds": old ideas, old customs, old habits, and old culture (including ideologies, practices, and material culture deemed "Confucian"). While this movement prompted some relatively benign reforms, such as replacing existing store and street names with more revolutionary ones, it also inspired the rampant destruction of classical Chinese temples, libraries, artworks, furniture, and many other "old" objects and edifices to the end of reformulating Chinese culture to align more closely with communist ideology.[11]

Even though political reformers abandoned many of Mao's more radical policies after his death, much of Mao's notion of the intended role and importance of culture as an instrument of governance and national identity continues to flourish. As Liu Kang (2012) has noted, this has especially been the case since the technocratic administrations of the immediate post-Mao era gave way to a series of leaders determined to augment cultural production by increasing educational and research funds as a strategy for wielding and augmenting power. Indeed, President Xi, in language decidedly and perhaps somewhat unnervingly reminiscent of Mao's Yan'an talks, has recently proclaimed a "Confidence Doctrine," declaring that "confidence in our culture" is as essential to the political well-being of the Chinese state as faith in China's communist political system, and committing the state to efforts to "consolidate the confidence in Chinese culture and use art to inspire . . . serve and praise the people" (quoted in Chen 2016).

What is this "culture" in which Xi has expressed such confidence? China's current focus lauds and promotes, as did its predecessor, a highly circumscribed vision of culture. In 2004, which was decreed the "*Jia Shen* Cultural Declaration Year," a group of "Seventy-Two Prominent Scholars in the Field of Chinese Culture" put forth a "cultural declaration" that formalized the general constitution of this Chinese culture in the official realm (Chang 2016, 115–116). The term *jia shen* refers literally to the traditional naming system of the Chinese lunar calendar and figuratively to an idiosyncratic array of traditional cultural practices and ideologies that have become the central component of the CCP's broader promotion of culture as a mechanism of governance. The declaration asserted the "dignity and humanistic spirit of the East" and, in a break with Mao's cultural policies, promoted the same "traditional" Chinese culture (including Confucianism) that the Cultural Revolution had targeted for destruction as a contemporary model for ameliorating the troubles that beset the modern world (Chang 2016, 115; Guo-qiang Liu 2012). In public addresses, then premier Wen Jiabao and then president Hu Jintao urged the promotion of traditional Chinese culture to heighten the nation's reputation in the global arena, and the declaration was followed by a series of official and popular projects and movements intended to encourage classical Chinese studies and the revival of Confucianism.[12] Over the next decade, for example, the Ministry of Education revised the textbooks used in the nation's schools to feature traditional Chinese culture, and the CCP began to hold related study sessions for officials. This promotion of traditional/patriotic state culture also emerged as the most common strategy for China's soft power initiatives, including the Confucius Institutes.[13]

Rather than attempt to destroy the four olds, as did the Mao regime, recent political regimes in China have promulgated their own version. To this end, they have defined the culture of this millennia-old civilization as a set of globally recognizable ideologies and practices that draw upon Confucian, Daoist, and Buddhist traditions and material objects and applications from its long history of art, culinary practices, and architectural production. In this configuration, traditional Chinese material culture includes such arts as calligraphy, cuisine, opera, literature, and brush painting and such archaeological and architectural wonders as the terra-cotta warriors, the Great Wall, the Potala Palace, and the Forbidden City in addition to more common architectural examples such as temples and courtyard housing. The cultural practices defined as epitomizing this civilization include martial arts, drinking tea, and making dumplings, among many others. Accordingly, these are also the material products and artistic practices that dominate Confucius Institute projections of culture, where Chinese language instruction is inevitably accompanied by exposure to China's cultural glories and historical ideologies, from lessons on Beijing opera to documentaries on Ming dynasty art forms and classroom texts replete with images of China's vast system of temples and historical architectural splendors.[14] As we shall see in coming chapters, students in the CIs and CCs I observed attended presentations by kung fu artists from China and enacted Chinese culture through practicing their hands at calligraphy, painting opera masks, and dressing up in elaborate Qing dynasty costumes. Ideologically, traditional Chinese culture is expressed in these soft power campaigns most often through the Confucian concepts of benevolence, filial piety, peace, and harmony. Together, these images, ideals, and practices present the Chinese nation as historically stable, artistically rich, community and family oriented, and peace loving. Indeed, the CI logo incorporates a white dove, a common Western symbol of peace, whose wings encircle the globe and which is meant to suggest a peaceful Confucian tradition that offers a very different visual image than the ubiquitous fire-breathing dragon that is often chosen to represent China by Western media, and to vastly different effect.[15]

Five Thousand Years of Civilization at the Beijing Olympics and the Shanghai Expo

Chinese state promotion of this anodyne traditional culture as a patriotic mechanism of image management can be readily seen in two of the state's most prominent soft power projects, the 2008 Beijing Summer Olympics and the 2010 Shanghai world's fair. As one student remarked to me about the Chinese culture and history featured at the 2008 Olympics, "This is how China is different from the world. This is the biggest fortune China can give to the world." Indeed, this gift to humanity was made explicit in the slogan on the T-shirts worn by volunteers at an Olympics-related conference I attended in Beijing: "The world gives us 16 days, we give back to the world 5,000 years." Culture was one of the official themes of the 2008 Olympics, and presentations of Chinese traditional culture graced nearly every aspect of the games, from the accompanying cultural festivals and opening ceremony to the architectural styles of exhibits and design of official logos. And culture was the dominant discursive medium through which Olympic organizers asserted China's national identity and attempted to magnify and reproduce its splendor on the global stage offered by the Olympics.

Through offering this "gift to the world," Olympic organizers hoped to make Chinese traditional culture relevant to contemporary life and pressing international concerns. The opening ceremony of the 2008 Olympics offers a well-analyzed example of these essentialized customs and cultural forms and how they have been invoked in China's soft power endeavors as a mechanism for cultural governance, what Elizabeth Perry defines as the strategic "deployment of cultural symbols as an instrument of political authority" (2013, 2). From LED-lit reproductions of brush-painted scrolls and inventive paeans to early literacy, to the weaving of Confucian aphorisms throughout a variety of scenes, the ceremony invoked a cultural background that both located historical China in the forefront of cultural innovation and positioned contemporary China as the logical culmination of Chinese culture's moral and political values and practices. Less well-known are other distinctive ways in which the Olympics provided a venue for this cultural governance, including, for example, the publicizing and marketing of traditional Chinese products called *laozihao,* which some Beijing residents described to me as the "essence of Chinese culture" and deemed important because they "represent [China's] history and culture."[16] These *laozihao* ranged from Beijing roast duck and mandarin-style clothing to dumplings and Chinese medicine and were described in Olympic ad campaigns and by one of my interviewees as "business cards" for the nation-state. As one Beijing graduate student explained to me, "They remind us of cultural China, [that] people respect history and their ancestors. Through the Olympics, China will take this opportunity to express its culture, history, tradition, and modernization to the world. We are very proud of this."[17]

During the time of the Olympics, as I analyzed China's use of *laozihao* and other forms of culture broadcast by the Olympics, it became clear that official patronage of traditional culture was intended not only to inspire domestic pride and hence reinforce national identity but also to address China's position in the global order: *laozihao* brokered not only China's cultural essence but also its potential for garnering a larger share of the worldwide commodity market. As the previously quoted graduate student also noted, "These precious products can help with China's economic development and bring China economic profit." Through such soft power endeavors, Charlotte Bruckermann notes, "culture" in China has become "heralded as an untapped resource to be excavated, appropriated, and marketed for profit" (2016, 189). Yet "pride" here derives not only from market endeavors but also through an identifiable and specific linkage of historical grandeur, captured and fostered so thoroughly during the Olympics, with a capitalist modernity and proffered as an alternative to its homogenizing demands.

The 2010 Shanghai world's fair offered a similar and massive example of how the Chinese state has deployed traditional culture for the purpose of wielding soft power, in this case by offering Chinese culture as a solution to some of the world's most intractable environmental problems. The China-specific exhibits at the expo—the biggest (5.28 square kilometers), most visited (73 million attendees), and most expensive ($45 billion) world's fair in history—repeatedly alluded to Chinese philosophical, aesthetic, and mythological traditions and histories to attest to China's current and future exceptionalism (Hubbert 2015, 2017). These exhibits and the built environment both offered seemingly endless examples of these messages, from a monumental central pavilion that replicated the shape of an imperial-era vessel used to make offerings to the gods to promotional films that linked Confucian wisdom to appropriate development and multicultural diversity.

The expo, like the Olympics, sought to promote core values of traditional Chinese culture, in this case specifically by promoting select cultural ideals as the answer to the environmental devastation wrought upon the globe by decades of industrialization, resource extraction, and urbanization. Throughout the Chinese exhibits, references to Chinese traditional culture posed ideal-type portrayals of how it could offer a model and guide for a less destructive relationship between humans and nature.[18] These portrayals most commonly referred to the Confucian concepts of *tianren heyi,* the unity between humans and nature, and *hexie,* or harmony. Among these, the urban utopias section of the Urban Future Pavilion offered *hexie* as the path to ecological sustainability, albeit without providing specific examples. And against a backdrop of images of the highly urbanized city, a movie about Shanghai in the Shanghai Corporate Pavilion stressed the need for humans to be "in balance with nature, in harmony." Visitor comments likewise often drew upon these concepts. As we meandered through an exhibit that chronicled the massive 2008 Sichuan earthquake, for example, one visitor described the disaster to me as an example of "the earth telling us that we are not following the ideals of *tianren heyi.*"[19] "People and heaven are the same," she explained. "We cannot take too much from nature. We have to live in harmony [*hexie*] with nature." And as another visitor summarized the message of these exhibits, "*Tianren heyi* is the most important philosophy for these problems. If we are good to the environment, it will treat us better."

Motivations and Exclusions

This schematic representation of culture offers a prime example of what William Callahan labels the "new orientalism" employed by China to justify its rise to global power (2012, 50). The term implies both a reification of culture and a form of discursive power, or a "complex hegemony," as Edward Said put it (1978, 5), that seeks to convince its subjects of the legitimacy and fertility of its rule. As such, and to comprehend the challenges to "culture" that inhabit the CI landscape, it is valuable to understand both the motivations behind the comprehensive promotion of culture as a form of power and what forms of culture remain outside the wake of its formidable path.

As these Olympics and expo examples demonstrate, the Chinese government has been strategic about what it promotes as culture as it attempts to leverage that culture to close the gap between its global economic power and its global welcome. Even as China has emerged on the global stage as an economic powerhouse, its political ideals and practices have rarely been consistent objects of global admiration, particularly in the West. Given the CCP's perhaps implicit recognition that its political ideology has little currency in a largely postcommunist global system (Fallows 2016), its soft power efforts to influence global opinion positively have largely avoided references to its political system and practices and—even as policy makers insist that contemporary Chinese culture also has soft power value (d'Hooghe 2011, 25)—have focused almost entirely on traditional Chinese culture.[20] The traditional culture packaged in China's soft power projects is presented as having endured for thousands of years, as outwardly apolitical, and as genuinely "Chinese,"[21] and is specifically designed to ignore less positive moments and aspects of Chinese history, politics, and culture (Jian Wang 2011b, 6).[22] After all, who could argue with the value of learning about calligraphy, the Great Wall, respect for one's elders, or family orientation? This strategy presents China as a vast but united nation, with diversity but without dissent, struggle, or, above all, contentious politics.[23] Tiananmen Square appears solely as a central tourist attraction, Tibet and Taiwan as integral provinces of a harmonious nation, and Xinjiang as a source of natural resources and example of the nation's religious pluralism.

Ingrid d'Hooghe argues that while China's leaders promote certain forms of national culture as the predominant source of global soft power, they simultaneously engage in crackdowns on other forms of culture considered to be subversive, even if those forms of culture "dazzle the world"

[margin note: focus on traditional]

(2011, 25) and might as a result be effective tools of soft power.[24] These include, for example, a new generation of artists, filmmakers, writers, and other cultural actors whose works have won global acclaim for both their artistry and their resistance to a disempowering state. As d'Hooghe suggests, many of these artists face domestic denunciation by Chinese officials who do not regard them as positive examples of public diplomacy, instead disparaging Nobel Prize winners as derivative and critiquing Oscar winners as pandering to Western audiences.

The diversity that does exist in these representations arrives in as select a form as the broader official cultural history that contains it. Minority culture, for example, is rarely included in China's soft power productions other than as different sartorial practices and architecture, or is invoked to highlight China's officially endorsed multiculturalism. The inclusion of the Tibetan Potala Palace in these iconic representations sheds light not only on the expansive definition of what exactly the CCP is trying to promote as constituting Chinese essence, since the original occupants would not necessarily have considered themselves Chinese, but also on China's efforts to suggest the nation as inclusive and welcoming. Minorities took the stage during the Olympic opening ceremony when Han children, dressed in domestically recognizable minority clothing, marched in formation across the arena toward a massive flag, ending their promenade by handing control over to members of the People's Liberation Army. At the Shanghai Expo, portrayals of diversity constructed similar hierarchies of power with minority "victims" of the 2008 earthquake shown thanking their CCP Han "saviors" for providing them with a new modernity following the devastation of natural disaster (Hubbert 2017).

Scholars have hypothesized a broad range of explanations for the promotion of these patriotic forms of culture invoked in China's soft power endeavors, vacillating between the most cynical of rationalizations and the more sympathetic. One explanation for the mobilization of this particular amalgamation of culture concerns the disenfranchisement that was a response to the 1989 Tiananmen Square massacre and to the more general decline in beliefs in communism and socialism in China. Linda Walton, for example, argues that through promoting "public identification with unifying cultural symbols" (2017, 6) the government sought to both quell dissent and instill a domestic identity with a vaunted heritage as a form of national uniqueness. Such recognizable cultural traditions provide what Jeremy Page calls "a fresh source of legitimacy [for the state] by reinventing the party as inheritor and savior of a 5,000-year-old civilization" (Page 2015). Others have similarly argued that the "traditional" nationalism assembled through these cultural symbols provided new foundations of political legitimacy for the state, tying the CCP less to specifically repressive acts such as in 1989 and more to a rapid Western-style modernization and economic growth that has led to "money worship" and a consequent "moral vacuum" (Zheng 1999, 71). The *jia shen* declaration, mentioned earlier, which helped to formalize traditional culture as a form of national identity, was in part motivated by a desire to neutralize what the government considered to be the negative influences of these modernization practices (Guo-qiang Liu 2012).

Alongside these more domestically oriented rationales for the promotion of traditional culture rests a more globally situated explanation and strategy, the hope for which was described by President Hu Jintao: "If a country has an admirable culture and ideological system, other countries will tend to follow it. . . . It does not have to use its hard power which is expensive and less efficient" (cited in Glaser and Murphy 2009, 12). Numerous state officials have explicitly argued that China's cultural legacy offers a legitimate model for international relations and globalization, and thus insight into how culture is deployed can also illuminate the workings of international relations, particularly throughout East Asia, where the CCP is increasingly claiming a leadership role based upon a shared common cultural legacy. The ideologies and philosophies summoned through these traditional cultural symbols resonate with historical approaches to global diplomacy, drawing upon classical Chinese thinkers such as Confucius, Mencius, and Sun Tzu, who envisioned ideal-type politics as a "harmonious" rather than an ineluctably competitive process (Hayden 2012, 171; Zhang 2010).[25] As such, this suggests a manner through which both Chinese domestic and global citizens might be encouraged to envision China as in possession of understandings and practices of global engagement that challenge what Isaac Kamola calls an "asymmetrical political economy of knowledge production" in which North America and Europe dominate how the world is understood (2013, 41). The "Confucian" values that are part of this package of traditional culture promoted in China's soft power packages, as discussed later in this chapter, are also touted globally as a source of the family orientation, educational proficiency, and business acumen and are often understood to have engendered East Asia's economic growth "miracle" and to provide a moral force linking China to the rest of East Asia (Niquet 2012; Ong 1999). Dirlik (1995) argues that within a perceived

Confucian realm of engagement, Japan and South Korea may thus be thought of not only as competing economic "tigers" but also as compatible and like-minded "alternative capitalisms" of common cultural heritage and descent.[26] This allows the Chinese government to promote a supposedly "Asian" version of modernity to its geopolitical neighbors as a counterweight to Western power (Dirlik 1995).

Even if, as Heather Schmidt argues, China's soft power focus on traditional culture purposely detracts from the nation's contemporary problems (2014, 356), its discursive protestations to diversity reinforce the structural disenfranchisement of national minorities, and its "official culture" is promoted in the interests of state legitimacy, dismissing these soft power cultural forms as purely propaganda fails to grasp or illuminate the specific ways in which the state deploys them as a rationale for political behavior and consequently diminishes the diagnostic possibilities for analyzing soft power culture as a guide for both global and domestic engagements with the state. Furthermore, understanding this culture solely as indoctrination ignores that culture is always contested and unstable, including the official culture presented in these soft power endeavors. As discussed later in this chapter, even Confucius himself, despite his global renown and a massive export of the eponymous institutions, is not universally lauded in China. Accordingly, understanding ways in which official patriotic culture is sometimes challenged by the very representatives of the state who promote it can help us better understand the nature of the state as a governing institution and its relations with the society it governs.[27] As we shall see, soft power policy targets also often actively respond to culture in ways that shape state-society relations and that reveal how the production of soft power is rarely linear, one-directional, or uncontested. To assume otherwise, that these soft power efforts convert automatically into authority, is to assume a totalitarian model of power that rarely obtains in practice.

Why Confucius? Branding and Cultural Ideals

The most widely recognized embodiment of this traditional culture is undoubtedly Confucius, who is arguably China's most famous historical figure and whose writings have profoundly influenced Chinese society and those of its Asian neighbors. This alone may seem enough to explain why Hanban officials decided to name their government-sponsored Chinese culture and language institutes after him.[28] When, however, one considers that Confucius was also ferociously vilified as the "arch-villain of feudalism" during the Mao years (Murray 2009, 264), remains a sometimes contentious symbolic figure within contemporary China, and is rarely even referred to in CI classrooms, the question of why Hanban chose Confucius as the eponymous symbol becomes a more evident one.

The embrace and sponsorship of Confucian philosophy by China's ruling regimes has had an uneven history, despite global perceptions of the sage as an incontrovertible symbol of China and Chineseness. During Confucius's lifetime, in the sixth century BCE, his philosophy was largely ignored by rulers, many of whom feared his critiques of their political practices and sought to undermine his authority. Confucius Institute texts have highlighted the forms of adversity Confucius encountered in his life, particularly during his travels though China to spread his philosophy and advice, and compared them to China's current efforts to modernize. The comparisons these hagiographic stories make with contemporary China are clearly meant to symbolize the current nation's own ability to persevere and eventually triumph over hardship and disparagement. *China Today,* a government-sponsored monthly magazine directed toward a global audience, has accordingly labeled the contemporary Confucius Institute program an "ambassador" projecting China to the world and has compared it to its namesake, who left his home to travel around the country, suffering hardships, promoting his philosophy, and seeking new political opportunities (Dong 2014). The "revival" of Confucius is not therefore of a Confucianism that had lapsed because of popular apathy or a lack of historical memory but rather of a culture destroyed by earlier deliberate government campaigns against it.

Confucian ideals began to flourish in earnest during the Han dynasty (206 BCE to 220 CE) and gained particular and lasting prominence in the Tang dynasty (618 CE to 907 CE). China's civil service exams testing candidates' knowledge of the Confucian classics were instituted during the Tang dynasty and remained in place as the route to official positions and prominence into the early part of the twentieth century. And, although Confucian political regimes in China showed little interest in global exploration and political conquest through trade and other forms of exchange, Confucianism as a moral philosophy and guideline for governance spread throughout East Asia and created a zone of cultural familiarity that, as many scholars have argued, has continued through the present era. Confucius Institute historical materials often mention this cultural spread of Confucian ideology to elevate China to the position of "natural" leader of a diverse group of nation-states with a presumed common cultural heritage and concomitant development goals and values. Similarly, CI history texts and documentaries celebrate these historical periods of cosmopolitan effervescence as precursors to China's current economic and cultural blossoming, utilizing Confucius as a cultural reference to high points in Chinese history that the materials assess as having characteristics in common with today.

Despite the high regard in which Confucius and Confucian ideals had been held for centuries in China and throughout Asia, China's shift to communism in the twentieth century led China's leaders to reject the highly hierarchal and patriarchal Confucian model of society and governance. Confucius's ideas, Mao proclaimed in 1951, were "not democratic" and "lacked a spirit of self-criticism." "There is a good bit of the work-style of the bully in Confucius," Mao charged, and "something of a fascistic flavor" (cited in Kau and Leung 1986, 401). Through the years of his rule, Mao continued to denounce the "feudalism" he associated with Confucianism, most vociferously and mercilessly during the "Criticize Lin, Criticize Confucius" campaign, when fervent cadres and Red Guards destroyed Confucian temples, vilified scholars, and sought to rid China of remnants of Chinese culture associated with Confucian values and practices.[29]

Yet Confucius has been making a comeback as a cultural icon in post-Mao China, despite this relatively recent period of anti-Confucian fervor. In the 1990s, the state began to launch Confucian education campaigns in which newspaper articles and public billboards praised the attributes of "Confucian values," which they commonly defined as filial piety, loyalty, education, industriousness, and thrift.[30] Two decades later, Confucius has become a ubiquitous figure in the Chinese cultural and political landscape.[31] Television shows feature popular university professors explaining his philosophy in laical terms, and books about Confucianism that read like how-to manuals for living the good life line the shelves at the nation's largest bookstores. Ching-Ching Ni reports, for instance, that when Beijing professor Yu Dan "turned dusty old Confucian teachings into a Chinese version of 'Chicken Soup for the Soul,'" her book outsold Harry Potter (2007). An elaborate state-sponsored biographical film about Confucius's life starring Hong Kong's Chow Yun-Fat filled theaters in the summer of 2010, and in 2011 a thirty-one-foot, seventeen-ton bronze statue of Confucius was installed in the sacred civic space of Tiananmen Square, literally staring down upon Mao's mausoleum. Parents can now opt to send their young children to Confucian kindergartens or Camp Confucius summer activities; for the older crowd, some businessmen are adding "Confucian entrepreneur" to the list of titles under their names on their business cards (Yao 2011). President Xi himself frequently dots his political speeches with references to Confucian classics and was the first communist leader to attend celebrations in honor of the sage's birthday (Page 2015). The state has also invested millions in the renovation of Confucius's hometown of Qufu in Shandong Province, now included as a stop on the high-speed train between Beijing and Shanghai.

China's massive soft power campaigns have similarly promoted Confucius as the essence of Chinese traditional culture and model for global progress. In addition to providing the name for the Confucius Institutes, the Confucian notion of harmony exemplified in the phrase *he er bu tong*, meaning harmony without uniformity, took center stage at the 2008 Beijing Olympics, where, for instance, the torch relay was dubbed the "Journey of Harmony." Similarly, at the 2010 Shanghai Expo, each section of *Harmonious China,* the three-screen film that was the main attraction at the central Chinese national pavilion, opened with a quote attributed to Confucius, and numerous references to his philosophies were included in pavilions across the massive fairgrounds.[32]

The reasons behind the current revitalization of Confucius are numerous, multifaceted, and rarely agreed upon. When I lived in southwest China from 1994 to 1995, Communist Party appeals to Confucianism steadily began to gain prominence, often accompanied by reference to economic (capitalist) success stories of more authoritarian states such as Singapore as evidence of the inherent worth of the Confucian system and the Chinese cultural heritage.[33] Yet, despite these ostensibly positive invocations, many of the more skeptical Chinese citizens I interviewed then viewed the party's about-face regarding Confucius as an attempt to instill a sense of blind obedience in the population and fill the vacuum left by the demise of faith in the ideologies of socialism, not as homage to an "authentic Confucian philosophy."[34] Rather than see such efforts as an example of China's continued search for a *tiyong* (Chinese essence and Western practical use) form of modernity, they perceived the government's promotion of Confucius as an implicit recognition that its Maoist revolutionary philosophies were bankrupt and that the state was merely blindly searching for an alternative ideological system to shore up its rapidly diminishing moral authority, especially in the aftermath of the 1989 massacre in Tiananmen Square.

In recent years, scholarship on the origins and rationales for the Confucian revival has expanded beyond this cynical explanation, sometimes retaining a dose of skepticism and at others seeing an indigenous logic that preempts an explanatory reduction to state legitimacy. Daniel Bell sees the official revival of Confucianism as a conscious attempt to fill the moral vacuum left by the rejection of Maoist forms of socialism but also sees legitimate "advantages" for the state in its promotion of such values as harmony, filial piety, and unity that continue to resonate with the broader population (2006). Dirlik's assessment of the Confucian renaissance suggests that it has been employed globally as a postcolonial discursive critique that both asserts a powerful and common East Asian identity and also glorifies "Orientalized subjectivities as a universal model for emulation" (Dirlik 1995, 231).[35] Scholars in China are more likely to assess the revival as a constructive foundation for moral endeavor, whether seeing Confucian philosophy as a basis for thinking through relationships between family, filial piety, and economic modernization or as a foundation for augmenting psychological well-being (Bell 2009).[36]

These diverse explanations for the growing ubiquity of Confucius express clearly that the contemporary revitalization of Confucius's legacy has not been without controversy, demonstrating the potentially fragile nature of any cultural campaign that has received such extensive state backing. Indeed, the expensive state-funded biopic about Confucius mentioned earlier met with widespread critical disapproval in China. According to one blogger, "Chinese people tend to feel that the theme of the movie and the thoughts of Confucius are so old-fashioned and pedantic that they do not fit into China's current social needs" (Chen 2010)—although the film's disappointing reception was undoubtedly also affected by the government's decision to pull the popular *Avatar* from theaters to accommodate the two-plus-hour *Confucius*. And four months following its installation, the statue of Confucius in Tiananmen Square, which the *Shanghai Daily* called "the government's most visible endorsement yet of the ancient sage, and, selectively, his teachings" (Chang 2011), was suddenly removed in the dark of night, without comment by either the sculptor or government officials (Jacobs 2011), giving expression to how the state itself is not a monolithic entity and how Confucius—as an embodiment of Chinese values—even among officials has yet to achieve full approval.[37]

As these controversies over the Confucian revival also reveal, China's citizenry, even those who are political agents of the state—like those of other countries targeted by its soft power initiatives—cannot be depended upon to consume state propaganda in an uncritical manner, even with massive investment on the part of the government. Even certain high-level Chinese political insiders, according to a *Wall Street Journal* article, have viewed President Xi Jinping's proclivity to quote Confucius and attendance at the birthday celebration for Confucius as a cynical and reactive attempt to "inoculate Chinese people against the spread of Western political ideas of individual freedom and democracy" (Page 2015) rather than as a proactive engagement with historical cultural assets. At the same time, while Chinese state officials are willing to invoke Confucius on a regular basis, they remain unwilling to address the complex history of his thought and obfuscate the contradictions of the Confucian ethos over the centuries (Lee 2010, 276). While Confucian ideals of benevolence and moderation may be meant to suggest a nonaggressive international relations policy to global China watchers, when domestic dissidents are routinely jailed and migrant laborer housing torn down in the interests of "safety" and the "China Dream," the obfuscations of the contradictions of history *and* present become readily apparent.[38]

The placement and hasty removal of the statue of Confucius perhaps best illustrates Confucius's currently controversial position in contemporary China.[39] Post-1949 Chinese history achieves its most authoritative form in the physical space of Tiananmen Square, a tightly controlled political space of great symbolic importance.[40] The monuments in the square—the Mao Zedong Memorial Hall, the Great Hall of the People, the National Museum of China, a gigantic obelisk dedicated to the martyrs of the Chinese Revolution, and, of course, the famous portrait of the Great Helmsman himself above the Gate of Heavenly Peace—recount and celebrate a tale emblazoned in the name of a hall in the national museum: "The Triumph of the Revolution and the Establishment of Socialism." The decision that Confucius, a figure so lambasted during the period of high socialism, warranted recognition in this hallowed political space unmistakably reflected a conscious effort to reformulate the contemporary narrative of the nation-state. That the statue's life in the square was so truncated concomitantly reflects a fragmented state internally at odds with itself, its agents engaged in ongoing contests over questions of definition and value. It also reflects that the "Confucius" of the CIs, and the traditional culture promoted therein, may be more subject to question by policy targets, makers, and implementers than is typically assumed.

These domestic Chinese controversies over Confucius are certainly not raised in the CI classrooms themselves, and in fact the sage is a far less prominent component of the institutes' curriculum and programming than their name would suggest. Although Confucian philosophy has much of value to say about education, governance, and social harmony, in practice the CIs have very little to do with Confucius. While the walls of the classrooms I visited were frequently adorned with images of Confucius, the quotations above their whiteboards were ironically just as frequently from twentieth-century chairman Mao Zedong as they were from the sixth-century BCE sage. Similarly, the Chinese culture that students encountered in classroom lessons, texts, and activities was more often in the generic form of Beijing opera masks, food, and red lanterns than of Confucian philosophical thought.

When Confucius did come up in the classroom or on Hanban-sponsored study tours, the references most typically pointed to his potential global value as a guide to social health or idealized him as a model of China's cultural values. One classroom video that I viewed alongside students, for example, discussed how this "great wise man" had been born into poverty and advocated tolerance for others. And when discussing such Chinese cultural traditions as reverence and care for the elderly and valuing education, CI teachers would occasionally attribute these practices to China's Confucian history and value structure. On study tours to China, a statue of Confucius greeted us at the entrance to the school where we stayed in Beijing, and the introductory lecture addressed the importance of social order, good government, and filial piety in Confucian thought. When I asked one of the teachers about Confucius's relevance to the CI mission, she answered, "I am glad you asked that question. As you know, the main purpose of establishing the Confucius Institute is not doing research or offering courses on Confucius or his philosophy. But we name the institution after this guy because we are proud of him as a great educator and philosopher in China's history. We believe he will have an impact on the development of human society." Thus, despite the relative absence of Confucius in the CI classroom, this teacher's response underscores an underlying assumption of soft power efforts—that they will help non-Chinese understand that because China's Confucian tradition stresses harmony, diversity, and social order, the nation's current rise to power will be a peaceful and globally responsible process marked by the same practices and values. By also offering Confucius as a model for global harmony, CIs deploy Confucius not only to address perceptions of China as a threat but also to position China as a global leader.

One might also arguably conclude that the general absence of discussions about Confucius in the CI classrooms stemmed at least in part from a lack of knowledge on the part of the teachers. According to those I interviewed, little of their Confucius Institute teacher training involved the study of or strategies for teaching about Confucius. According to one teacher, outside of some "lectures on Chinese philosophy, Confucianism, Buddhism, and Taoism, there was not much that was related." Another could recall only a single reference to Confucius on the exams teachers are required to take prior to being selected as CI instructors: a true-or-false question that asked, "Confucius had many exceptional ideas about education, such as: Man follows earth, earth follows heaven, heaven follows the Way, the Way follows nature." The correct answer, she informed me, was false, not because Confucius did not have exceptional ideas about education, but because this particular adage does not originate in Confucian writings. In contrast, most of the required exams were about pedagogy or what one Confucius Institute teacher described as "psychological" tests to see if the teacher candidates were prepared to withstand the hardships of being far from home, family, and friends.

Whether intentional on Hanban's part or not, this limited instruction in Confucius's life and philosophy also made it less likely that controversies over Confucian thought itself and over the state-sponsored promotion of Confucius that might reveal rifts in government unity and the government's relations with its citizens would find their way into CI classrooms, thus concealing the paradox of the government's promotion of "Confucian" values and its unwillingness to implement them. Although the textual and visual representations in lessons about Confucius presented by teachers in the classrooms or by tour guides or lecturers during the Chinese Bridge summer program in China were highly scripted, the few occasions I observed where those speakers went off script and inserted their own interpretations exposed gaps between the government's promotion of Confucian values and its willingness to implement them. A visit to Beijing's Confucius Temple, for example, provoked a cynical response about China's educational system from our tour guide. While the official temple chaperone lauded Confucius for his commitment to education, our CI guide explained that Confucian temples are visited mainly by high school students and their parents praying to Confucius for a good score on the national college entrance exam. "Everything in China," the guide offered somewhat morosely, is "determined by that score," hinting not at harmony but at an educational system that favors the urban elite over their rural counterparts, and the rich over the poor, and that is a feared source of tremendous stress and discontent among students of all walks of life.[41] Likewise, a lecturer in Beijing, explaining the importance of the Confucian concept of harmony to good governance, segued into a brief aside about the Chinese government's unwillingness to allow free speech, hinting that this so-called harmony was achieved only through repression. These examples suggest that Confucius may be a more useful symbol for soft power purposes when the meaning of his contributions to Chinese and world culture can be so circumscribed. Surely, there are also aspects of Confucian philosophy, such as its hierarchical gender relations and stress on harmony over a more dialectical approach to change, that many Westerners might find no more attractive than the strict communism of the Maoist era.

Whether naming the institutes for Confucius has had any impact at all on the efficacy of CIs as a form of soft power has been a matter of debate among scholars. While Sheng Ding and Robert Saunders (2006) argue that the numerical increase in CIs around the world reveals that the Chinese language programs have increased China's influence abroad, Ren Zhe reasons that CIs' ostensible focus on traditional culture—they are *Confucius* institutes after all—has little attraction for younger people, and as such they play only a limited role as a mechanism for augmenting China's soft power potential (Zhe 2010). By noting that language and culture programs called "Mao Institutes" would have lacked global appeal, the *Economist* seems to insinuate that the naming process was less a result of the applicability of Confucian values to contemporary life than a consequence of China's limited options for promoting itself (*Economist* 2015). Nonetheless, naming the institutes after Confucius clearly draws attention to the cultural elements of China and to its long and storied past, thus distracting attention from its role as a current world power, and promotes and spreads a culturally prestigious character intended to supplant Mao as China's best-known symbol of national politics.

Yet some have argued that none of this matters a great deal, claiming that the CIs' invocation of Confucius operates more like a brand than a philosophy (Starr 2009) or merely constitutes an "admission that communism lacks pulling power" (*Economist* 2009; see also Brady 2012). The *Economist* has referred to CIs as an "international franchise" (*Economist* 2006), and Hanban officials themselves acknowledge that they view the name of the language programs as a brand. According to Hanban vice chair Chen Jinyu, "With regard to the operation of Confucian Institutes, brand name means quality; brand name means returns. Those who enjoy more brand names will enjoy higher popularity, reputation, more social influence, and will therefore be able to generate more support from local communities" (quoted in Starr 2009, 69). While such discussions of branding conjure a more cynical market approach and have led some critics to dismiss CI cultural productions as either hackneyed marketing schemes or essentialized protestations of Chinese exceptionalism, this book argues that these evocations of traditional Chinese culture can productively be seen as an *attempt* to stake claims to value in a world dominated discursively by Western ideologies and practices and as a form of globalization that appeals to cultural ideologies valued across cultures and history.[42] To fully understand the cultural arrangements and intended political functions of the CI program, it posits, we must take seriously their implications for China's perceptions of its place in the world. The ethnographic examination of the CIs as a Chinese soft power endeavor to win the hearts and minds of global citizens in the following chapters moves into the actual space of policy engagement to uncover how the cultures of production and the cultures of consumption mutually construct and influence relations between nation-states and their contestations over globalization, modernity, and the global order.

CHAPTER 3

Coolness and Magic Bullets

Studying Chinese to Manage Risk
and Constitute a Self

The atmosphere in the brightly decorated classroom appeared fairly relaxed and seemingly little different from that in other US middle school classrooms. One student playfully slugged his neighbor, while another surreptitiously removed a cell phone from his pocket and transmitted a text. Tablemates discussed their upcoming weekend plans and compared test scores. The tenor of the conversations varied; some students were enthusiastic about their educational progress, while others appeared bored, such as the student I observed glancing at the clock and audibly sighing, "Ugh, we still have twenty-five minutes left." Some students engaged in stalling tactics when the teacher asked them to grab their whiteboards, sauntering slowly around the classroom, while others, in particular, two self-professed "nerds," studied quietly together.

But when the students in this Confucius Classroom began to engage with the curricular materials purposely, it became clear that the space offered a unique encounter. In the Confucius Institute classrooms I observed, the distinctive attributes of the Chinese language and the perceived foreignness of Chinese culture provided teaching opportunities and learning experiences different from those in other pedagogical spaces in the school. Forgetting the character for "to go" (*qu*), for instance, led to witticisms about "forgetting to chew," while the sound for "but" (*keshi*) provoked laughter when a student remarked that it resembled a sneeze. A vocabulary lesson on eating and the teacher's request for students to translate "corn juice" into Chinese led to a discussion of cultural foodways. Observing students' blank looks, the teacher asked, "You guys don't have corn juice?" leading a student next to me to elbow his neighbor and whisper, "Stupid Americans. They don't have corn juice." An introductory-level high school class offered a similar situation. Practicing her culinary lexicon, a student announced in Chinese, "I like cheesecake," prompting her classmate to respond in English, "They don't like cheese in China, cheese haters." Overhearing their exchange, the teacher quietly interjected, "Actually, cheese is okay." On another day, a review of numbers provoked a dialogue on China's demographics. "There are like thirteen billion people in China," one student remarked, leading another to respond, "No, not thirteen billion," then asking the teacher, "How many people live in China?" and adding sarcastically, "Do you know all of them?"

On the surface, these students' puns, commentaries, and questions seemed predominantly to draw explicit attention to linguistic and cultural differences between China and the United States. Yet, as I followed the students in this classroom and others over the course of five years, many of them from middle school through their senior year in high school, I began to realize how they also signaled shifts in students' understanding of the changing global order, for their grasp of these cultural and linguistic differences was put to use in the composition of unique forms of subjectivity that depended upon China's very presence in the classroom in the form of language and cultural studies. During these years, some students abandoned Chinese as a course of study, finding the time commitment too onerous or the texts "weird": "They anthropomorphized backpacks!" one student exclaimed to me. Others continued. The bored, watch-checking student in the above-mentioned class struggled with the language but completed four years of study, while the two "nerds" parlayed their five years of Chinese language study into admission into competitive colleges, where they hoped to apply their knowledge of Chinese to technical fields. For these students, Chinese emerged as a way of locating a present self within their various social and academic networks and constituting a future self in the face of the exigencies of competitive college admissions or an unpredictable job market.

This chapter begins *China in the World*'s foray into students' Chinese language experiences in the Confucius classroom by examining why students chose to study Chinese and how teachers attempted to create a favorable impression of the language and hence of China itself. While CIs may be what Rui Yang calls China's "most systematically planned soft power policy so far" (2010, 237), a phrase that implies a structured and orderly exercise with predictable results, this chapter demonstrates that US students experience their CI courses and materials in ways that are anything but methodical and one-dimensional. Their understandings of Chinese and China ultimately were shaped as much by US educational and cultural landscapes and ideals for modernity in which students strategized to craft a sense of self relative to their peers and in light of postgraduation options as by China's desire for global approval and its consequent soft power engagements. While later chapters analyze the ways in which China's soft power engagements reveal to its policy targets how the nation's experiences of modernity and globalization challenge those of the United States, this chapter investigates how these engagements play a role in allowing US students to approximate American ideals of modernity and globalization.

Establishing Confucius Institutes: Neoliberal Demands, Multicultural Desires

As with any ethnographic study, it is important that the data be understood within its particular sociohistorical context, in this case educational trends in the United States in the contemporary neoliberal moment, since the kinds of decisions and experiences happening in the classroom and shaping students' attitudes toward China parallel and reflect some of what we see in the broader realms of international relations, globalization, and educational trends in general. During the last several decades in the United States, educational institutions have been increasingly subjected to what Wayne Ross and Kevin Vinson call an "unrelenting market fundamentalism" (2013, 17). This has been triggered both by changes to ideological approaches to education and, more recently, by a recession that diminished local school coffers as financial support for public universities and school districts dropped precipitously, forcing some educational institutions to seek funding from private and corporate sources, or in the case under consideration here, from the treasuries of foreign governments.

The combination of these factors, in conjunction with a highly globalized economy, has encouraged both a public disinvestment in education and a growing focus on applied education (Shore and Davidson, 2014), as well as an increasing educational stress on the production of what Steven Camicia and Barry Franklin call "neoliberal cosmopolitanism," a new type of entrepreneurial citizen who "navigates an increasingly interconnected global community" (2011, 311). China has become a focal point for both of these trends, because foreign language teaching, such as Chinese, is one of the places where new forms of citizenship education are occurring (Zhu 2013) in which the ideal citizen is global and multicultural, and because the Chinese government has emerged as one of the new sources of financial support. Here we have a situation in which the CCP's desire for an improved global image and its financial capacity to fund massive soft power global campaigns collude and collide with the neoliberalization of education in the United States and the formation of new forms of global citizenship. Yet, as scholars have explored, these collusions also collide with various expectations about value, ideology, and citizenship in education that continue to compete with the marketization and professionalization of education. In light of this context, Christopher Hughes argues that the vehemence of the debates over CIs and the risks perceived in hosting the programs are fundamentally direct "consequences of the CIs fulfilling the mission with which they have been entrusted" (2014, 45) within the context of a growing tension in Europe and the United States between classical models of education and the more pragmatic neoliberal models described earlier (see also Simcox 2009). Thus while Hanban and its state sponsors see material and ideological benefits from the complicity of its soft power engagements with the increasing neoliberalization of Western educational models, the most vocal critics of the CI program see both practical and ideological difficulties and risks in these forms of engagement. In her examination of CIs at three public universities in the Midwest, for example, Amy Stambach shows how these collaborations with China have rendered higher education a "tradable commodity" (2014, 2) that harms the relatively poor and disenfranchised students whom public universities are philosophically intended to serve and benefit.[1]

Yet, while Hanban seeks to offer the CI program as a form of globalization and as a mechanism through which to improve China's global image, it is not only financial support that matters to the schools in the United States. US schools, seeking to enhance their cosmopolitan bona fides, also strive to promote a form of multiculturalism that will instill a sense of global citizenship among their students. Having a CI at one's school has the potential to provide students access to a cultural and political reality beyond their immediate realm of experience, to broaden their perspectives and help them to understand what it means to be a citizen of the world in addition to one's own nation. In that sense, CIs offer a prepaid and packaged curriculum and staffing that enhances the US host school's sense of itself as a model for the cosmopolitan global. Numerous American CI administrators explained to me over the years that the Chinese language programs, while, in their words, "not perfect," provided their students with access to another culture. "We think of the CIs as power hour interventions. It's really important for this kind of community," one administrator at a rural school district explained to me. "The local community is very impoverished. There are sixteen trailer parks that feed into the [local high] school. And we've got the white power thing going on outside of town. The students and their families don't have worldwide experiences. Chinese is so different, the culture is so different. These kids don't have access to any other of these kinds of experiences." Similarly, a school superintendent of an urban, high-poverty district that had established an expansive CC program clarified that he knew "there was an agenda on the part of the Chinese" but justified inviting CIs into the schools through his district's goals for "mutual peace and prosperity." Another American CI administrator responded tersely to my question about why a school might seek to host a CI with, "It's all just about global literacy." As these comments and many other similar ones I heard over the years elucidate, while the fundamental realities of fiscal imperative may drive US schools to seek partnerships with the Chinese state, an idealistic vision for student futures exists alongside the more instrumental rationales, helping students to understand and appreciate difference and how to be effective global citizens.

The Confucius Classroom: Why Study Chinese?

When I first visited the Confucious Classroom described at the start of this chapter, I noticed how its difference from typical US secondary classrooms was immediately marked by a large bronze-colored metal and wood plaque adjacent to the door announcing in Chinese and English that across the threshold was a Confucius Institute. Inside the classroom, a large PRC flag above the whiteboard drew attention to the calligraphy that framed its two sides, which read, "Study diligently and make daily progress" (*haohao xuexi tiantian xiangshang*). This popular Chinese admonition to students was not attributed to its actual source, which is Mao Zedong, and US students and visitors to this Confucius Classroom might well assume that it originated with Confucius himself, a historical figure frequently lauded for his focus on educational attainment. A large map of the provinces of the PRC, which included Taiwan, hung to the left of the calligraphy, and next to that such globally recognized symbols of Chinese culture as red lanterns, calligraphic scrolls, Chinese knots, and Beijing opera masks, prime examples of the traditional patriotic state culture discussed in chapter 2. This physical space thus faithfully reflected the intended public persona of Confucius Institutes through a combination of state-sanctioned geography and popular visual symbols of Chinese culture while making very little connection with Confucius himself, save in the CI name and a paint-by-number image of the sage on a classroom wall.[2]

Over the years of this research, the décor of the classroom changed in subtle but meaningful ways that, as we shall see, mirrored pedagogical changes that also took place at this particular Chinese language program. While none of the teachers spoke directly to these symbolic changes, they highlight how the Confucious Classroom space and its pedagogical practices were constantly evolving over the years. At this school and others I visited over the years, there was never a single CI soft power package inserted into the classroom but multiple packages and practices that responded to diverse sets of variables whose utilization depended on the changing context of their implementation. In this case, although the painted image of Confucius remained, by the time of my last research visit, an earlier stack of Mao's Little Red Books no longer rested on the bookshelves below. According to a senior who had completed five years in the program, "We thought it was a little weird in the first place. What were we supposed to do with them?" Similarly, Mao's slogan admonishing the students to study hard had been replaced by a banner whose Chinese characters read "We Love Chinese." The large map of China had also disappeared, and in its place were hung three posters labeled "Impressions of China," which included Tiananmen Square, a troupe of martial artists, and Chinese minorities in traditional clothing. Mao's disappearance from the classroom, alongside that of the map that had included Taiwan as a constituent part of the PRC, further depoliticized an already purposefully depoliticized space, removing symbolic objects of potential conflict in favor of a focus on denoting desire for China. This was reinforced by a new vertical scroll that appeared on one wall, its Chinese calligraphy announcing a "China Craze" (*zhongguofeng*), or "China Fever," suggesting an excitement over all things Chinese. When I asked one of the teachers about this scroll, she snickered and rolled her eyes but said nothing, perhaps aware that an erstwhile peripheral nation's declaring a self-aggrandizing global passion for itself might come across as somewhat odd and perhaps presumptuous.[3]

Do students have a "fever" for China, as the Hanban scroll suggests?[4] And might this potential fever translate into soft power for China? This section explores this ostensible craze for China through examining why students study Chinese. As it will show, the already heterogeneous process of soft power policy assemblage and implementation in CI classrooms is also strongly influenced by particular constructions of the self among students, for it reveals how language studies emerge as a method of acquiring status in relation to their peers, college admissions officers, and postgraduate employers rather than merely reflecting on China or suggesting a desire for it.

Over the course of my research, I came to view students' rationales for studying Chinese as falling into two broad, albeit interwoven, categories. The first of these categories is what I call the "cool" quotient of Chinese language acquisition. Although, as will be explored, soft power policy technologies, including texts, the built environment, and teachers, have attempted to render China and Chinese "cool," in their discussions of why they were interested in learning Chinese, students used "cool" specifically in terms of the construction of a self in which being "different" often signaled their own originality and value, rather than China's, and referenced long-term orientalist ideologies about Asian exoticism. The second I refer to as "Chinese as a 'magic bullet,'" through the Chinese language's perceived capacity for providing a reliable path into college admissions and career opportunities, a process that reflected long-standing practices of middle-class self-improvement strategies in the face of an increasingly disempowering risk society. While these motivations are not mutually exclusive, both will be shown to result from a complex and contingent amalgamation of CI intentions and locally embedded experience. Understanding why students study Chinese language and culture provides an example of how official policy is "peopled" (Nielsen 2011).[5] By this Gritt Nielsen suggests shedding the practice of construing policy targets as "mere effects of . . . a political rationality" in favor of focusing on how policy targets *and* practitioners are "multi-dimensional actors whose subjectivities are created in the intersections" of policy practices (2011, 69–70). This helps to explain in this case how the reception of China's soft power policy occurs in ways that both reinforce and challenge assumptions about policy implementation and appropriation.

The Cool Quotient and Constructing a Unique Self

The perception of Chinese language learning as "cool" reflects a variety of associations with China as an exotic, ancient culture, but also its ability to define the speaker as "different" and thus special. When I asked students about their reasons for studying Chinese, some specifically linked their rationales to China's cultural and historical contexts. These students were attracted to China's rich dynastic history, its archaeological discoveries, and the challenging nature of the language. In the current cultural context in which people have Chinese characters inked onto their bodies regardless of their ethnic background and kung fu movies draw audiences worldwide, China and Chinese have become desirable in several ways.[6] As Beth, a senior, explained, "I get to tell people, 'I take Chinese,' and that's cool. I've always loved watching *Crouching Tiger, Hidden Dragon,* and now when I watch it, I can understand more and more of it. Sometimes I will mutter things in Chinese under my breath when I'm watching it with friends and they will think it's really cool. They say 'nice' when I do that."

In this context, being cool is defined as possessing a difficult and unusual skill, making the cool quotient of Chinese due less to China or the Chinese language specifically as objects of attraction than to its impact on the identity of the student. In a conversation with Danielle and her classmate Kevin, Danielle noted, "I think it's cool to be able to say stuff in Chinese. I want to be able to walk around and say random things in Chinese." When Kevin corroborated her assessment, attesting to pleasure of "yelling random [Chinese] sentences at others," Danielle responded by crying, "You look like a panda!" at passersby in Chinese, to the amusement of both. While both Kevin and Danielle expressed an interest in the history and culture of China, the dominant emphasis of their conversation was on Chinese as a source of a unique self-identity. One might thus conceptualize coolness here in reference to a broader cosmopolitanism that "gets" the value of the multicultural and the value of difference relative to one's peers. Yet this is a form of multicultural difference in which one's self need not suffer through the disempowerment of being ethnically "different" but through the "ownership" of multiculturalism that accompanies grasping the language of the Other. The ability to translate an immensely popular film, in effect to possess a privileged comprehension of globalized popular culture, and to speak a second language not understood by most of one's peers, allows the Chinese speaker to claim a particular identity that is in command of the global through a new language of power.[7]

Chinese also allows for an augmented identity in relation to peers as a marker of potential future value. Danielle and Kevin proudly informed me over lunch one day that they were the only students in their Chinese class to regularly receive A grades. Learning Chinese "is a lot harder than I thought," explained Danielle. "I can get easy As in all my other classes, but I have to study hard to get an A in Chinese."[8] In these two students' narratives, knowing Chinese gave the speaker increased value in a competitive academic environment. Through success in the Chinese language class, students thus negotiated identities that were also shaped by the environment beyond the walls of the CI classroom, specifically a college-preparatory social environment, discussed further in this chapter, that reinforces the hierarchies that result from educational competition.[9]

As part of its CC program, Hanban sponsors summer travel-study excursions to China for English-speaking students, and those students' stories upon their return sometimes followed a similar narrative, in which their tales of adventure rather than the Chinese language were the object of desire.[10] One student who attended the summer program praised the "resort" in which they were housed and reported being well-fed and royally treated. "I love China. China is awesome," he exclaimed. Yet when I asked him what he had specifically loved, he did not mention cultural glories or cross-cultural friendships, but rather that "everyone wants to take pictures of you. When we went to the Shaolin Temple, all the people there wanted to take pictures with us." In this answer, the desired object is the Western/foreign self, reinforcing the very global hierarchies of power that these soft power engagements seek to modify. While this process epitomized the romanticization of an ethnicized Other, it was not because of the nature of the Other itself, but, as Schmidt notes of CI student experiences in Canada, because it enriches "us" (2013, 664). In this story, the Chinese who sought to memorialize the US students' visits in their photos were shunted back to the global periphery as naive locals being offered a glimpse of the Western world. In this case, China and Chinese emerge as "cool" not because of some ontological imperative but because the target of soft power itself becomes a source of power and status. This is an orientalism that manifests in desires for control, but not exclusively, over the "Oriental" object (Said 1978). Rather it is through the production of the Other as a form of exoticized multicultural difference—an appropriationist form of orientalism to be sure—but one that simultaneously manages this Other *and* seeks to provide an apparatus for managing the self in relation to a local social hierarchy of power. The soft power target thus emerges in part as the agent of modernity, not China as policy intends, in a relationship that defies fixed assumptions about an unmediated correspondence between the coolness of studying Chinese and China even if Chinese emerges as the mode through which the power of the self is fashioned and revealed.

Sometimes the students' path to studying Chinese had very little to do with the language or China itself. A number of students, for example, mentioned that the popularity of Japanese manga and anime in contemporary Western popular culture had inspired them to pursue Chinese. Julie, a sophomore who was committed to studying Chinese throughout high school, explained that she was "really into Japan, Japanese," and that because she was "really interested in Asia," Chinese seemed the "next best thing" because the school did not have a Japanese language program. Lindsey, a junior who was enrolling in a Chinese immersion program over the summer to be able to jump ahead a year in her language studies, explained that she was "a little interested in China, but only because of art. I'm into Asian art, particularly modern Asian art like manga and anime." For these students, it was Japanese influences such as manga that had occasioned their presence at the CC, and Chinese and China appealed to them as generic Asian entities rather than as specific connections to the Chinese nation-state and its cultural self. Indeed, one student who capitalized on her excellent Chinese skills through acceptance into an elite college bluntly told me, "Frankly, I'd rather be doing Japanese, I really like manga, video games, I think the Japanese script is beautiful, the video games. I'm doing Chinese because it's close to that." She also mentioned that she was unlikely to continue studying Chinese once she had matriculated at college.

The ways in which students deploy Chinese as a source of cosmopolitan coolness allow them to create what Pierre Bourdieu has called a sense of distinction (1984). Through using Chinese to set oneself apart in the classroom as a student of academic prowess in an "exotic" and notoriously difficult language, to exert a form of mastery over global popular cultural forms as a marker of one's modernity, Chinese becomes a form of cultural capital, a nonfinancial social asset that extends social mobility to the students. Yet at the same time, while the supposed coolness of Chinese reflects an array of beliefs about what students personally value, it also rests on a contemporary political setting in which China's history and politics, both recent and ancient, sometimes obfuscate what might be attractive to them. "I always loved Chinese characters," explained Kaitlyn, a junior in advanced Chinese. "I always wanted to write them, so I used to trace them whenever I would see them." At that point, however, she launched into a story that complicates this fascination: "I've been interested in China my whole life. The history is so interesting. This is a weird story [she laughs], but when I was in fourth grade . . . I saw a movie on China in class. It was on the Great Wall and the emperors, but it was all about how they tortured these people. . . . I really wanted to go to China. Why would I want that after seeing this film?"

Kaitlyn's narrative is interesting on several levels. At first glance, it reflects the attraction of a national language and its cultural artifacts that is envisioned by Chinese soft power policies. Yet the remainder of her narrative broaches a frequently raised question about the CCP's soft power attempts at impression management: is culture sufficient as a tool of soft power if its targets reject a nation's political values and practices? As Kaitlyn's comments reveal, China's "cool" is embedded within a wider political context that frames China not simply as a cultural entity but as a political force that has historically been viewed as antithetical to the West's interests and values. Thus, while this yearning for coolness, framed within the exoticization of both a vague Asianness and an essentialized Chineseness, plays into CI messages about China as a locus of desire (the China fever) and marker of a new modernity, "China," in all its symbolic manifestations in the CIs, remains at least tangentially attached to a concept of difference that is less about multiculturalism and the value of the modern self and more about difference as fear, Otherness, and oppositional encounters.

Thus, despite Hanban's attempt to use CIs as a gesture of soft power goodwill, they were not necessarily received as such, and this research also reveals that the changes in perceptions of the global order in favor of China challenge assumptions about the formation or transfer of power in diverse, complicated, and sometimes unexpected ways. One afternoon, when I asked a group of students what they thought about the Hanban program, they offered quite a different interpretation of the effect of CIs' soft power efforts than Hanban clearly intends. We were sitting outside on a picnic table next to a bright red pagoda that Hanban had built in honor of the establishment of the school's Confucius Classroom. While students worked on their end-of-semester Chinese culture projects and discussed the Chinese program with me, one gestured and reflected on the complicated nature of student perceptions of China. This student, Samantha, was an accomplished Chinese speaker with an admitted fascination for China, but the gifted pagoda for her was decidedly not all about benevolence and warm feelings. "The pagoda is a symbol of how the school is changing. The pagoda, it used to be this big octagon, where we all sat to eat, met for outdoor activities, it was replaced with this shiny pagoda, as if it's replacing American values sort of, replaced with a Chinese pagoda. Lots of kids aren't even involved in the Chinese thing. Most kids would rather have had it stay the same, but it can't."

Samantha's description of her schoolmates' responses to the pagoda mirrored wider public assessments of US relations with China that perceive engagement as a necessary evil by seeing this gift as threatening to American values and the school's independent community. Another student's comment that "the Chinese government gives us the books and the pagoda" and Samantha's observation that "there is this financial thing, the program is good for finances" expressed less a sense of gratitude and desire for China than one of pragmatism. In this context, Confucian Classroom soft power image management intentions emerged instead as a hard power mechanism of unwelcome influence and control.

The diverse rationales for studying Chinese and the diverse responses to the presence of China in the US classroom hint at the struggles that soft power policies face in their implementation as well as at the conflicted nature of China's growing global power. While choosing to study Chinese reflects concretely on a changing global order in which China has become in some ways "cool" and as such emerges as an exoticized source of cosmopolitanism and difference, it also reflects on an educational landscape that "needs" but continues to fear China. On the one hand, student desire for Chinese has in part vacated the Cold War ideologies of older generations that located China within a broad "axis of evil" category of communist nation-states. Yet on the other hand, there sometimes remains a sense that engagement with China is the collateral damage of changing global hierarchies, an engagement in which soft power targets derive power from China/Chinese but a power that may be tinged with hesitancy and trepidation about its source. Nonetheless, sometimes this is a form of power that has very little to do with China or even with Chinese, even as it is written, both literally and metaphorically, in the form of the ideographic Chinese character. As we will see in the following pages, it is not only the immediate realm of the classroom that provides incentive to engage with these diverse forms and sites of power, for students take Chinese not only to forge a unique self in the present but also to mitigate against future risks, choices that again reflect on how CIs provide a venue for the constitution and projection of value in a manner that complicates our understanding of how policy works and how power flows between nation-states, between nation-states and institutions, and between institutions and individual selves.

Magic Bullets and Managing Risk

In 2012, while in the middle of this research, I sat inside a packed auditorium at an elite university in the United States listening to the director of admissions discuss the college application process with an audience of anxious high school students and their fretful parents. He spoke at an institution where the admissions rate recently has hovered around 5 percent and the vast majority of applicants, even those with perfect grades and SAT scores, varsity athletic honors, and packed community service résumés, are denied admission. In addition to facing a highly competitive college admissions process, college graduates at that point were confronting a nationwide recession and a postgraduation economic market in which nearly 50 percent of recent US college graduates were either unemployed or working in positions that did not require a college degree, resulting, according to a *New York Times* reporter, in "the chemistry major tending bar. The classics major answering phones. The Italian studies major sweeping aisles at Wal-Mart" (Rampell 2011). Those who did find jobs were earning salaries 10 percent lower than the salaries of those who had graduated during the previous three years and found themselves saddled with an average student loan debt of $20,000. Many of the questions from the audience concerned how an applicant might stand out from the crowd, for admission to elite universities was perceived as providing more secure access to gainful postgraduation employment. However, the admissions director's response did little to placate the concerned parents and high school students. "There is no magic bullet for admission," he insisted. "It's not as if studying Chinese is going to automatically gain you a place."

Despite the admissions director's advice, the economic context in which CI parents and students believed that student acquisition of Chinese language skills might serve as a magic bullet featured prominently in their narratives as the students navigated the waters of high school schedules and activities, striving to accumulate qualifications and credentials that might ensure their marketability to colleges and future employers. Thus, while the cool quotient of Chinese as a vehicle for the development of a cosmopolitan, multicultural self was often mentioned in students' explanations of why they were studying Chinese, their most common justification was a more utilitarian one: the hope that, contrary to the admissions director's disavowal, Chinese would help put them over the top in the competitive environment into which they would graduate.[11] One after another, students expressed their belief that Chinese had the ability to transport its learners into colleges and universities perhaps otherwise beyond their reach and from there into successful, high-earning careers. Here, orientalist ideologies parallel contemporary job-hunting practices that mandate the "branding" of the self through the construction of what Ilana Gershon calls a "corporate personhood" (2014) that equates marketability with immanent employability.[12] In this view, student enrollment in CIs is perceived to provide an exclusive skill set and body of knowledge that not only rendered them "cool" but also enhanced their chances of success in a competitive global future.

Many of the students appeared confident that Chinese would provide an advantage in the college application process. Lindsey, for instance, explained that Chinese "looks good on a résumé, it still has a reputation that no one knows it, so it's still really cool. Colleges will notice it, when you get good grades in Chinese, *that* they notice." Administrators, teachers, parents, and board members I talked with corroborated this perception, frequently commenting that certain students had gained acceptance into elite colleges not necessarily because of their overall exceptional academic performance alone but because of their Chinese studies. As one American CC administrator explained to me, "The way we sell the program to the parents is to tell them that it's really good for getting into college. It's a hard language, and parents need to know that there is a return on their investment. They are utilitarian about this. They see a few of our students with Chinese doing really well, getting into Ivy Leagues, getting scholarships to study in Beijing. . . . The kids also see these successes and see that Chinese might help them to similarly succeed."[13]

And although most of these students were a minimum of four to seven years from commencing their postcollege career endeavors, many of them projected a similar utility upon Chinese language skills as they envisioned the kinds of jobs they might be able to obtain. According to Ashley, a second-year Chinese high school student, "Having Chinese is really useful. It's so important to be allied with China these days because they are such a world power. I want to go into international business, so I'm taking German, Spanish, and Chinese. I want to work for Apple. I heard that Apple will take anyone who speaks Chinese." A similar sentiment was expressed by Kaitlyn, who also cited the Apple example: "I know that companies like Apple want people who speak Chinese. It will get me into doors. The pool of people who speak Chinese is smaller, they look and see a 4.0 and that the person speaks Chinese. That's unique. I can nail any job I want with that. You really need something to separate you from the others."[14] This understanding of Chinese and its opportunistic possibilities reflects Gershon's analysis of the job market for US-based undergraduate students who strive to assemble a neoliberal self as a "business" through the gathering of a set of "skills, assets, and alliances that must be continually maintained and enhanced" (2014, 288).[15] Chinese emerges in this case as the practical equivalent of proficiency in data analysis software or spreadsheets; it "brands" the corporate owner of the asset as in possession of the ability to manage the self correctly in light of the flexible demands of the modern workplace, a process that provides an "equitable distribution of risk and responsibility" (Gershon 2014, 288) for employer and employee alike.

In this model, and similar to the use of Chinese as a marker of cool, Chinese/China is attractive not necessarily in and of itself but as a source of power for the Chinese language speaker. Another student reported that "one of my dad's friends was talking about joining the navy, doing intel, and how it would be really useful to speak Chinese. It would be important for the future. I'm interested in programming and computer science. Anything I do along those lines will be dealing with Chinese computer products, apps, programming, et cetera." In this student's view, as she explained, "China is the head of the economic world," and thus "everything you do with technology, engineering, environment, is related to China's massive economy. Even though people there speak English, I felt it would be beneficial to learn some Chinese."[16] A graduating senior framed the utility of learning Chinese in terms of power: "I see Chinese as a new language of power. But we don't really talk about China at all in the classroom. Truly, students just don't have that much interest in China. We are interested in the language." According to that student, "I don't think about going to a Confucius Institute, I think about going to Chinese class. It has become normalized. The language is important for what it does for the students."

While these conversations are framed around the benefits accrued to students through the study of Chinese, they come with an implicit admission of a global order that differs dramatically from the one in which their parents' generation came of age. China was now a source of power here, not only because it funded the CC program, but also because its massive economic growth had rendered ignoring it a potentially dangerous proposition. In a conversation with Diane and Peter, each of whom has a child who studied Chinese, they both stressed what they saw as the practicality of Chinese for their sons and daughters and offered uniformly positive evaluations of the CC language program. In their telling, the benefits of the program accrued not to the CCP's soft power initiatives but to their children and the school. Peter and Diane both mentioned that the CC program had suffered "growing pains" with the inexperienced teachers and mediocre teaching material but felt that these had been minor inconveniences in light of the overall benefits learning Chinese provided. "Say what you will about the Chinese government," Peter argued, "they are major players in the world. My kids need to be aware of this and to be able to work with them. . . . It's a tremendous advantage for our students to have access to Chinese language. If we ignore that they [China] are a huge player, we do that at our own peril." Based on his family's experience, Peter concluded, the CC program is "good for the school, good for the mission of the school, and good for its economics. Our mission is high academics, to be college prep. . . . Having this program fits in with this mission." Diane agreed with Peter's assessment, adding that the CC also benefited the school by allowing it to compete for sought-after students and subsequently providing those students with a competitive edge. "There is an international component to the school, all are vying for the same positions at college. Our students are competing against the world's students," and the program "pushes students' minds to work in different ways that are good for the students." Importantly, these parents' interpretation of CIs recognized the potential threat of China's massive and rapid growth but disassociated CIs from that threat. To the contrary, Diane and Peter perceived CIs as providing an opportunity for American students to neutralize that threat, as a mechanism for besting China at its own power politics. In this context, the Chinese government's attempts to wield soft power actually enhanced the soft power of the United States by supporting the school's mission to emerge as a leader in global education. In the process, we also see how mastery of Chinese reflects a changing order of power within the United States as well, in which power is transmuted to the students as future actors through their ability to broker professional and personal attributes into future privileged positions as global interlocutors and translators of meaning and practice. This recognizes China's value in that country's ability to enhance the privilege of this new generation, but also the value of the new US generation itself and its grasp of new forms of knowledge as power that place them strategically in the new world order. There is a good deal of manufacture of power occurring through the CIs, but one must consider not only the source, but also to whom the power accrues through the implementation of policy.

For the students and their parents, this utilitarian use and promotion of Chinese accords neatly with the rarely questioned emphasis on individual self-development in the United States (Anagnost 2013), where the reasons that a student might engage in a seemingly endless pursuit of after-school sports, community service activities, and club memberships are generally taken for granted but also mirror a domestic flux in sources of power that both re-creates and results from the vagaries of power at the global level. As others have noted, this pursuit of self-development among youth around the world has created what Jennifer Cole and Deborah Durham (2008) term new cultural geographies that embody both globalizing practices and local contexts. These constant pursuits of self-development constitute a form of modernity that Ulrich Beck defines as a risk society, in which threats to one's well-being are seen as external to the individual and the market is discursively organized and understood as offering the solution to increased perceptions of danger (Beck 1992). According to Anthony Giddens, "Risk society" is "a shorthand term for modern society or industrial civilization . . . [that] is vastly more dynamic than any previous type of social order . . . which unlike any preceding culture lives in the future rather than the past" (Giddens 1998, 94). For today's youth, that society is dominated by job insecurity and rapid shifts in employment patterns, and in the context of these risks, China exemplifies the future.

The potential for upward mobility is an essential part of the American ethos (if not reality), and yet today's students face a greater statistical probability of downward social movement than previous generations. They, their parents, and the schools view credentialing, test scores, grade point averages, and participation in a wide range of extracurricular activities as means of mitigating the uncertainty of success within a globalized future in which modernity mandates a "do-it-yourself biography" of accomplishment (Beck and Beck-Gernshein 2002, 3). Many US secondary school students are thus engaged in a continual struggle to negotiate the shifting possibilities for inclusion in the American dream, trying to decipher which kinds of knowledge are likely to minimize the risk of marginalization. Just as some US schools have chosen to hedge risk by inviting the Chinese government to augment their waning educational funding by hosting CIs, many US students have turned to learning Chinese as a way to mitigate their own risk of declining economic and social mobility within a modernity that renders their expectations of future progress insecure.[17]

The global popularity of a national language has long been equated with political and cultural dominance on the global stage (Rafael 2009), and Chinese Mandarin is the most widely spoken language in the world. By some estimates, nearly 20 percent of the world's population speaks

Mandarin as a first language (Noack and Gamio 2015). In comparison, only slightly more than 7 percent speak English as a native language even though it remains by far the most studied language of the world (1.5 billion English language learners versus 30 million Chinese language learners) (Noack and Gamio 2015) and persists as the dominant language of global politics and business. This dominance pertains less to any linguistic specificity than to the assumed animation of the English-speaking world that it theoretically represents. "Spreading Chinese," reports a high-level Chinese National People's Congress member, thus becomes "a task of strategic [national] significance" (cited in Gil 2009, 62).[18] The "power" that is manufactured through the CIs in the form of desire for Chinese language becomes metonymic of China's growing state power and the language's presumed "magical" ability to transform the lives of the students who come in contact with it. The battle for "branding" that occurs through Chinese language, either for the skills-accumulating, job-seeking, or college-admissions-seeking student or for the Confucius-promoting, language-exporting Chinese nation itself, hence reflects an aspirational global context. Students' ability to conquer Chinese for their own personal endeavors reflects an understanding of language that instrumentalizes Chinese to serve the ends of maintaining US global dominance while the growing fever for Chinese reflects, the CIs hope, a symbolic representation of a *re*imagined global order in which CIs position American children in ways that are meant to indicate the growing dominance of China. That both CI soft power policy endeavors and students "misrecognize" the complicated and divergent sources of power likewise perhaps suggests a global modernity experiencing enough challenge as to make pinpointing its source an increasingly contested process.

Through understanding why students study Chinese, we see the inherent conflicts and instability in soft power policy productions. We can see how practices and outcomes are a result not only of assemblages of policy-specific technologies and intentions but also how multidimensional actors, discursive formations, and material practices are external to policy itself. Students' decision to study Chinese, whether based on coolness or risk mitigation, is shaped by broader processes of and ideals for modernity and globalization. Although CI critics fear that by studying Chinese, students are helping the CCP reconfigure the global order to its advantage, the responses of the students I studied reveal that they are also abiding by a long-standing American social contract in which, according to Constance Flanagan, students "accept the rules of a neoliberal order as a given, tie their hopes to the happiness it promises, [and] believe that their commitment to education and hard work will pay off" (2008, 125–126). At the same time, in understanding Chinese as a source of their own power, they recognize a shifting global order, even though they may not recognize China as a source of value in and of itself.

Both as a result of and despite the CCP's soft power policy intentions, student narratives of self-development reveal unexpected and intricate forms of identity predicated upon their knowing Chinese. That students viewed Chinese as a "language of power" certainly suggests that their participation in CI programs reflects and enhances China's global reputation and power. Yet their sometimes-instrumental view of Chinese language acquisition and association of the culture with a generalized interest in Asian popular culture also argues against a zero-sum or one-directional configuration of global relations and soft power production. It also suggests an attraction dependent not only upon orientalist ideologies or China's attempted production of a positive Confucian national imagery but also upon the current socioeconomic and historical conditions of modernity in which they are coming of age that leave youth uncertain about the criteria for inclusion and success in a global future. While China may remain "different" and hence cool, and while its rise to power intimates the potential for a changing global order, student engagements with it, through their concomitant desire for Chinese and their reduction of China to a tool of their own power, may suggest an evolving perception of China away from the ideological nemesis that has to date predominated in US relationships with the Chinese nation-state.

Making Chinese/China Attractive: Teachers Leverage Risk and Desire

While the most fundamental aspect of soft power production in the CIs requires getting students into the classroom setting, that alone cannot guarantee the creation of a more positive image of China. Regardless of the rationale behind student engagement, once students are in the classroom, teachers and texts must engage student interest in the language, culture, and history to continue to make China cool or useful. Yet students arrive in the CI classroom with varying degrees of prior knowledge about China that can frustrate or enhance this process. Some admit to knowing very little about Chinese history and culture, while others come with pessimistic information and opinions they have gained from the media and their parents. One student, for instance, reported that she had an "especially negative impression of China before beginning Chinese language studies," which she thought was "maybe because of my parents." She had been particularly struck by a story told by her mother, who "visited China when it was first open" and "saw a person getting beaten up for talking to Americans." Another said that she, too, "always thought China was a group of really bad people, controlling the world economy, like what we hear on the news." With great hyperbole, she then added, "I actually thought we would get beaten in class."

A central goal of the Chinese government's soft power initiatives is to inspire others around the globe to comprehend China more positively than expressed in these views, to convince them to perceive China beyond the confines of the threat model that recognizes China as what those parents and students saw as "controlling the world economy" in an attempt to "take over the world." This section examines the ways in which CI instructors strove to help students "unlearn" their entrenched perspectives about China and struggled with the task of not only teaching a foreign language but normalizing the nation it enacts. As we will see, they frequently did so through strategies that referred, both explicitly and implicitly, to the students' own rationales for studying Chinese that sought to construct unique personal identities and manage future risks.

Chinese teachers had conversations similar to mine with students and parents about the utility of the Chinese language and incorporated these justifications for Chinese language studies into their classroom pedagogies. Yet they did so in a manner different from student and parent rationales for engagement. While teachers similarly stressed the benefit of Chinese to student futures, they did so through a strategy that had the additional effect of directly promoting China's soft power through offering Chinese as a global language similar to English, a language comprehended globally as the preeminent language of power. To offer one example, like students, teachers emphasized that students could put their Chinese studies on their college applications. But in addition, they spent significant amounts of time emphasizing the credentialing utility of the Hanban standardized testing regimen, which includes several Chinese language exams designed to measure proficiency. Teachers promoted two of these—the HSK (Hanyu Shuiping Kaoshi [Chinese Proficiency Test]) and the YCT (Youth Chinese Test)—in the classroom.[19] Around testing time in the spring, the Chinese teachers devoted fairly significant class time to explaining the exams' structure and content, provided study materials, and arranged meetings with students outside of class for individual tutoring.[20] They promoted the exams' utility using the same type of language that students employed to justify the study of Chinese itself. "It's useful," one teacher offered, while another explained, "It's a good thing to have. You can put it on your college application. It's just like the TOEFL" (Test of English as a Foreign Language). When a student asked whether the HSK or the US Advanced Placement (AP) test was more important to take, the teacher replied, "The AP is only for those who are applying to college. HSK has high levels. It can help you to study elsewhere, even in China. This is how you prove yourself, so it's never too early to get used to taking the test."

This promotion of the HSK and YCT exams fits neatly into the current educational regime in the United States, which is increasingly driven by what Terry Woronov terms "numeric capital," in which test scores "play an essential role in the model of human capital accumulation" and "young people increasingly *are* their test scores" (2016, 13). By equating the utility of the Chinese exams with that of the TOEFL, a globally recognized English language exam that reinforces English's status as the dominant global language, the teachers also presented Chinese as similarly important to belonging in the international community and validated China itself as a source of globalization. To take the test was arguably thus to recognize that Chinese is indeed a "language of power," as the above-cited student proclaimed. If your language abilities are credentialed through the exam, a teacher explained, "you can even study in China," the emphasis on "even" normalizing China as an object of global desire just as the millions of TOEFL takers indicate their desire to study in the United States.

Another example of teachers tying classroom lessons to student aspirations to make the language relevant to student strategies for addressing risk became particularly visible toward the end of each spring semester as students prepared to take AP exams, including those in Chinese. While few of the students had reached the level of Chinese that would guarantee success on the AP exam, their desire to have Advanced Placement classes on their transcripts reflected an aspiration for the credentialing they perceived to be crucial to their future endeavors. Hence, class discussions about AP exams generated interest even among students in the early years of Chinese language studies. In addition to obviously perking up whenever the topic of AP Chinese arose, students continually directed questions to me about Chinese AP college credit.

Teachers often used the possibility of AP credit to overcome the sense of irrelevance the materials sometimes engendered in the classroom and thus justify Hanban curriculum. For example, referring to the historical and cultural materials included as part of the course, one advanced Chinese teacher told her class that "these things are always on the AP test": "China has a very long history. Spring festival is very important. You eat moon cakes on moon festival day. You will always have stuff [on the AP exam] on tea, food, festivals, painting, and calligraphy. There will be something on the Great Wall. You need to know it's from the Qin dynasty." At that point, a student chimed in, "I know that lots of people died building the Great Wall," and the teacher responded, "Yes, lots of people died. Just say as much as you know on the test," thus relying upon hopes for AP credentialing to elide a negative impression of China. The next day she continued this discussion by noting, "You will need to know some of the emperors," and proceeded with a quick history lesson that featured a song about the emperors intended to help students remember them in chronological order. Whereas lessons about emperors in the Chinese language classroom typically generated more eye rolling than appreciation among students, contextualizing this knowledge within the framework of an AP exam as a measure of achievement allowed the teacher to equate the value of Chinese culture and language with the value of their European nation equivalents. At the same time, it presented Chinese as a tool for the betterment of the middle-class self, rather than as what Sheng Ding and Robert Saunders have called a "tool in the arsenal" of China's soft power efforts to expand its influence and authority (2006, 19), a far more negative assessment of Chinese language acquisition.

Yet justifying these materials by their relevance to AP tests and middle-class credentialing could only go so far in attracting students, most of whom had Chinese language skills far below AP levels, and over the course of this research, I watched CI teachers come to rely less and less on Hanban-supplied historical and cultural curricular materials.[21] One of the teachers, for example, explained to me that she had run out of ways to make these materials interesting to students and related that her current classroom strategy was to focus almost solely on language acquisition and reduce the lessons on Chinese culture.[22] "Hanban emphasized the culture part too much [to keep the students interested]," she had concluded; "I learned how to do this [the cultural activities, i.e., paper cutting and calligraphy] in such exacting kinds of ways, but the students don't need that." The result, according to a student who had been in the CC program for the full course of my research, was that the pedagogical methods in the Chinese classroom had come to more closely resemble those used in the other language classes offered at the school, a direction of which he clearly approved. "Our teachers are from China. This gives us insight into the place. But really we are just here to learn the language. It's not a politics class. Maybe I'll read some of that stuff this summer. It would be interesting to know some of that stuff, but really it's just like any other foreign language class to us." Such changes to classroom structure not only rendered the pedagogical material increasingly relevant to student rationales for studying Chinese, but also normalized the teaching of the language, funded by a communist state whose ideologies and practices are often perceived to be antagonistic to those of the host nation, and rendered the Chinese classroom experience less different from that of any other foreign language.

In comparison to European languages, which share a script with English, however, Chinese can be a notoriously difficult language for US learners to grasp. As a nonphonetically based language, it requires a significant amount of memorization to acquire even basic literacy in Chinese, and speaking, reading, and writing can be experienced as separate tasks to master; one can read Chinese fluently without being able to speak and speak without being able to read a word. Even for native Chinese speakers, maintaining functional literacy in the language requires continued effort, particularly in an era in which writing Chinese characters with pen on paper is increasingly being replaced by inputting phonetic sounds on computer keyboards (Li 2017). As in other CIs globally, dropout rates in the Chinese classes I witnessed were markedly higher than those among students taking other languages at the same schools.[23]

To stem the tide of students fleeing the perceived rigors and the rote memorization required of Chinese language learning, the CC teachers worked hard, as one principal explained to me, to "make it easy and fun."[24] He described these attempts to me as a matter of job security: "The Confucius Institute teachers are under pressure. If they don't keep up enrollment, they lose their jobs, so they go easy on the students." Yet these efforts were also part of an attempt to generate a positive image of the nation through communicating the magnetism of its language. Hanban encouraged this strategy, and according to the teachers, their pre-posting instruction had strongly emphasized the need to diminish students' perceptions of the difficulty of the language and to augment their perceptions of Chinese studies as fun. Toward the end of one semester, teacher Wang Liqin, for example, engaged two of her lower-level Chinese classes in an art activity in which she asked students to paint a T-shirt about China. The results were frequently humorous and sometimes quite artistic, with pandas, tigers, and kung fu figures often taking center stage. Several declared "I ❤ China," one drew upon the ubiquitous US dairy industry campaign and essentialized representations of Chinese culinary culture to ask "Got Rice?," while another alluded to the eternally popular *Star Wars* series with "May the China Be with You." Looking at the activity from one perspective, their illustrative choices reflected CI soft power efforts to define China as its culture and language rather than its politics. As Danielle explained, "What I learn about China in class . . . is that China is so old and well-rounded. The arts are so developed, China has such a long history." From another perspective, the activity was just a matter of having fun. As one middle school student gushed to me, "I love everything about China, the culture, language, and people. I enjoyed everything about this class."

While such activities may make the classroom experience fun, reducing the amount of memorization necessary to learn the language is difficult and so teachers responded over the years by making it easier to obtain better grades. Examples are numerous but test-taking practices were particularly revelatory. During one high school Chinese class, the instructor informed the students that the following day they would be having a quiz on the day's lesson. On the day of the quiz, she gave them class time to review the lesson, and when they had questions during the test, she provided clues to the answers that were specific enough to make mistakes nearly impossible. Another teacher informed students that their quiz results would be recorded in the grade book only if they performed well on the following exam. Similarly, many teachers allowed their students to make up missed homework and retake quizzes. "If you aren't satisfied with your grade, you can change it," one informed her students.[25]

While making Chinese language classes less injurious to student grade point averages was one strategy for maintaining classroom enrollments, another involved classroom discipline. One high school CC teacher admitted, "I've never given detention or referrals to students. I want them to like me." Another similarly noted, "Discipline is hard. You can't be too strict because you want to keep them interested, keep them in the classroom. They have a choice of languages."[26] While keeping students happy (and hopefully keeping them in the classroom), this permissiveness in the classroom led to student behaviors that most US teachers would not have tolerated, and I frequently witnessed overt texting on cell phones, sleeping, chatting among friends, and rudeness to the teachers, among others. Although this classroom atmosphere may have produced a greater willingness among students to continue their Chinese studies, it also had the effect, as one teacher allowed, "of making us look weak." One teacher who had taught in CCs for several years placed the blame for this situation clearly on Hanban. "Hanban told us not to control the students too much, not to be harsh on the students. They told us that US kids have such strong personalities. So we didn't manage our classrooms well. We played games, too many games, and students didn't learn anything and it became a sign of weakness. . . . Hanban didn't give us enough guidance. We needed more training about management. They told us just to entertain the students."[27]

Part of teachers' strategies for entertaining students reflected student narratives of uniqueness and difference within which they produced the self as having value through learning Chinese. The standard Hanban curriculum lent itself to this process through its focus on Chinese history and traditional cultural practices that were inherently different from quotidian student experiences but whose mastery reflected a student possession of a multicultural global form of citizenship. During the week before the T-shirt activity in teacher Wang's class, for example, students watched a Hanban-produced video on the Tang dynasty (618–907 CE) that described imperial life, focusing particularly on its sartorial splendors. Describing clothing as "one of the earliest aesthetic forms," the narration explained that the specific clothing people were allowed to wear during that era "showed your place" and encouraged "people to obey the laws and . . . keep order. Clothes were symbols of place and power; the higher the status, the more color you could wear." The video also noted that the Tang dynasty was very "open to foreign countries" and stressed the level of economic and cultural development of the era. When I asked students about their impressions after viewing the video, wondering if they comprehended Hanban's recognizable message about the cultural practices of historical China that rendered it so advanced relative to the rest of the world, students had little to say beyond lots of giggling about the video's insistence that the "sexy" and sometimes "see-through" Tang dynasty clothing revealed the "openness" of the historical era.

China as defined by Tang dynasty grandeur, and by other popular symbols like pandas and kung fu, is clearly a limited depiction of the nation, reflecting what Geremie Barmé calls a "History Channel–friendly" vision of China (2008). Yet even though such activities are merely supplemental to the approved pedagogical materials, they and the symbolic representations they generate provide insight into CI pedagogical strategies to normalize the study of a nation that arguably carries more negative baggage in the minds of US students than many others. As a pedagogical strategy, this focus has several possible outcomes. On the one hand, presenting ancient China as highly advanced for its time and having a continuous five-thousand-year "glorious" history might suggest to students that the nation's present is and future will be equally splendid. On the other hand, it also made it possible for teachers to avoid discussions of contemporary politics that in the United States are often framed around China as a global problem.[28] Yet while these materials allowed teachers to sidestep some of the more controversial aspects of China's rise to power, including its political repression and environmental devastation, they also frustrated efforts to normalize China because they simultaneously rendered aspects of contemporary China as static and unmodern in contrast to a West perceived as constantly innovating and evolving, thus confronting the fundamental paradox of trying to convince the world of China's modernity while highlighting its glorious past. While in some ways "different" can be an attraction, as discussed earlier, because it renders Chinese language learners unique, "different" can also epitomize "lesser" in the sense of not reaching expectations for (assumed) "standard" global practices of more developed and politically progressive nations.

One language lesson on visiting the doctor, for instance, included a feature on the wonders of traditional Chinese medicine that prompted students' curiosity about what they called the "weird" ingredients used by the regimen's practitioners. Interrupting the teacher's lecture, one student declared, "I heard that people used powdered seahorse ash as an ancient Chinese medicine. I really want to know about that." Although the teacher ignored the question, students continued to whisper among themselves about the comment for several minutes afterwards: "Ooohhh, that's gross" and "Poor seahorse," I heard from the back of the classroom. In response, the teacher attempted to contextualize and validate traditional Chinese medical practices through a discussion of acupuncture in terms of its contemporary value rather than as a mere historical oddity.[29] "You know acupuncture?" she inquired. "It's hard to say if it's old or new. It's constantly evolving, changing. You can't really call it either just old or modern." In this classroom context, "different" transformed from exotic and interesting to an orientalist perspective on cultural practices that were "gross" and perceived as cruel to animals, thus also potentializing the construction of China as inferior on the global hierarchy of nation-states.[30]

The teachers in these classrooms thus faced a conundrum. By following Hanban's instructions to make it fun, the Chinese language program's reputation had suffered, in this case not because of fears of propaganda in the classroom or because History Channel accounts of China failed to neutralize perceptions of threat, but because of seeming instructor incompetence and lack of rigor. The lack of discipline in the classroom and focus on fun rather than language, exacerbated by the rapid expansion of the number of teachers—and consequent dearth of experienced ones—had the potential effect of reproducing notions of China as neither globalized enough to function effectively in the "outside" world nor attractive enough in its own right to prompt desire. At the same time, making it easy meant that students often failed to pass the AP exam, thus frustrating their efforts to use Chinese as a middle-class credentialing mechanism in the face of future risk, again reproducing China as the problem. And while focusing on difference as a mechanism of attraction may emerge as a marker of value for students, it may also emerge as a marker of stagnation and regression for the Chinese nation-state.

Conclusion: Abstractions and Appropriations

The narrative of suspicion that governs a majority of conversations about CIs in the US public sphere includes assumptions about the effects of soft power engagements as manifest in the Chinese language programs. Specifically, this narrative suggests that in their attempts to create a favorable impression of the nation, the CIs are promoting a false picture of China that ignores the human rights violations, political repression, environmental degradation, and unfair economic practices, among others, and creates an image that significantly conflicts with dominant depictions of China in the United States. That in itself would not be inherently problematic—after all, most nations seek to promote positive images of themselves—except that it also includes an assumption that student exposure to these images is likely to change their impressions of China, leading to an augmentation in China's power at the expense of a broader global well-being defined among others, in terms of human rights, environmental protection, regional security, and trade deficits. This is an assumption, as discussed and quoted in chapter 2, that Nielsen has labeled the rationality-technology-subjectivity problem of policy analysis that assesses policy subjects as "mere effects of . . . political rationality" (2011, 69).

This is not baseless speculation. As my research has found, students do sometimes change their ideas of China after being exposed to the Chinese language education offered by CIs. During a conversation with two seniors who had taken Chinese for four years, one told me that her opinion of China had become more favorable. Her friend corroborated this assessment and attributed that change directly to the CI program. "Yes, my ideas of China have changed over the years. Huge changes. Before I had these same stereotypes as others, from TV, where the characters are caricatures. But this changes when you visit China" through the CI Chinese Bridge summer program. "The general idea I had before was just of difference. And when you see difference you assume bad, uneducated. But by visiting you realize that we are all just humans."

Yet, as this chapter has explored, to take seriously moving beyond analyzing policy as a mere effect of political rationalities that would confirm suspicions of CIs as bastions of false propaganda leading susceptible young minds astray entails attending to policy "appropriation" (Nielsen 2011, 72) in addition to policy implementation. This means paying attention to why students might see Chinese as "just humans" at the same time as they maintain the stereotypes, caricatures, and fears of a rising China threat. This involves attending to the social and cultural contexts in which policy is enacted and the responses they elicit, both intended and unintended, rather than solely to the political contexts in which policy is conceptualized— therefore conceptualizing soft power not just as an instrument but also as a catalyst and practice.

While students may seek out Chinese language learning experiences, what they find appealing may or may not be a function of China itself but of the particular context in which today's students face tomorrow's socioeconomic realities. Why CI students study Chinese thus may provide insight less into China itself and/or the CCP's foreign policy goals than into how situated policy targets *and* strategists tactically deploy the language to negotiate positions of authority in their local networks of belonging. As we have seen in this chapter, while China may be "cool," this construct may be utilized more as a reflection of the self, relative to one's peers, and what the language rather than the nation confers upon that unique self. "Cool" thus functions in part through a persistent orientalist ideology that reinforces extant expectations for cultural value concomitant with protestations about the perceived value of Chinese difference. At the same time, this form of value cannot be dissociated from a broader socioeconomic context in which the assemblage of the middle-class self is engaged in amassing the necessary "skills" and "assets," such as they are defined by the demands of flexible labor in the face of a risk society that renders those skills and assets increasingly ephemeral. It is within this context that policy strategists—China's teachers, policy writers, political figures—strive to situate China and Chinese as the source of value, drawing directly upon student tactics for constructing the self, but locating power differently in aspirations for a reimagined global order. As such, as the introduction of this book argues about the debates over CIs, these approaches to the production of value say as much about the United States' and China's ideological preconceptions of the changing global order, and the Chinese language's role within it, as they do about the empirical nature of the Confucius Institute programs themselves.

CHAPTER 4

Conjuring Commensurability and Particularity
Reconfiguring Local and Global

We gathered, twenty-six high school students and three chaperones, at a US airport, sporting matching T-shirts that advertised our group as members of the Chinese Bridge summer program sponsored by Hanban. We were set to join more than six hundred US high school students on a seventeen-day study tour of China, starting in Beijing and then, in smaller groups of eighty to one hundred, heading to various provinces for an additional two weeks of language and culture instruction before returning to Beijing for more touring and an elaborate farewell ceremony. Each year, Hanban sponsors five to six hundred US students on a visit to China. While the students on our tour paid for their airfare and a small administrative fee, some of which was used to partially reimburse the travel fees of the chaperones, once they were in China, Hanban covered all expenses, including domestic travel, housing, meals, Chinese language classes, tourist excursions, and cultural performances. Members of our group came from a variety of local schools with Confucius Institutes and had studied Chinese for at least one year prior to our departure. Several had grown up in Chinese-speaking households in the United States and were functionally fluent in the language.[1]

After clearing US airport security with minimal difficulty, our Chinese Bridge group boarded a plane bound for Beijing. A layover in Tokyo offered one gleeful cluster of students an opportunity to avail themselves of "local" culture in the form of a Japanese McDonald's, while others gathered around the chaperones in the boarding area and chatted about what to expect when we finally reached Chinese soil. Questions about bathroom facilities dominated the conversation. "Will we be able to shower every day?" one of the students asked, and students groaned when a chaperone informed them that, yes, indeed, they would encounter many squat toilets and reminded them that "you are going there partially for the experience, too."

It was well after midnight when we arrived at our final destination, a boarding school on the outskirts of Beijing where a massive marble statue of Confucius saluted our entrance to the campus. While students were shuffled off to bed, chaperones were ushered down a dimly lit, cavernous hallway decorated on one side with a mural of China's cultural glories (including the Potala Palace in Tibet and the terra-cotta warriors) superimposed with images of a rocket, a bullet train, and the vibrantly red 2010 Shanghai Expo China Pavilion. The text on the mural, in English and Chinese, read "Beautiful China," providing a gloss for the meaning of these juxtaposed images. Upon reaching a large conference room, we were welcomed to Beijing by an official from Hanban who further elaborated on the mural's combination of the traditional and the modern. Although "the Great Wall is a famous symbol," she took care to tell us, "now Beijing is a successful and modern city. It successfully held the Olympics." Interpreting our presence as configuring desire, she added, "I'm so glad you find Chinese culture so amazing."

As a mechanism of soft power efforts to operationalize culture, the Chinese Bridge program hosts American high school students for a visit to China in the hope of creating a generation of citizens in foreign countries who hold favorable opinions about China and the Chinese state, thereby, as Nye explains, "getting others to want the outcomes that you want" (2004, 5) through co-optation rather than coercion. This chapter explores the paradoxes of modernity and authenticity that emerged as the Chinese Bridge program sought to create soft power through offering China not only as a source of globalization through the presence of nearly sixteen hundred CIs around the world, but also as a model of the global through reconfiguring local tradition as necessary for a new kind of global modernity, as the mural on the wall and the introductory speech suggested. We might think of these efforts as an attempt at the hybridity of what Latour (1993) calls the paradox of the modern, in which the modern has always existed in hybrid form. While Latour theorizes this in terms of rigid dichotomies of nature/culture, we might consider how China here invokes tradition in such a way as to conceptualize it as a source of the modern that contests both representations of China as ontologically backward and the West as ontologically contemporary and theorizations of globalization that see modernity and tradition as antithetical and distinctive projections. As this chapter shows, soft power engagements such as CIs reflect not only how nations assess both their assets and their locations in global hierarchies of power but also the complex ways that meaning is actualized by diverse constituencies and representations rather than by policy alone. Thus, although the Chinese Bridge program provides a valuable example of the CCP's attempt to redefine China's place in the world by positioning the nation as an agentive subject rather than an object of cultural and economic flows, it also demonstrates the paradoxes of authenticity when the international targets of those policies misinterpret or reject the program's reconfiguration of China's changing place in the world because of their own ideas of what constitutes the authenticity of local and global.[2] At the same time, this chapter explores the possibility that there are different target audiences for soft power efforts and that these paradoxes are "read" differently by distinct audiences. From policy's perspective, such paradoxes are read as "misinterpretations" by the global audience but are countered by a domestic audience whose "appropriate" reading of soft power engagements—China as an emergent embodiment of modernity and the global—encourages national unity and stability, conditions that are central to China's global goals of projecting itself as a peaceful superpower and to its domestic goals of continued development.

Evoking International Desire for China

From the very beginning, China's CI program has troubled the assumed processes of globalization, an example of an erstwhile peripheral target of globalization now engaging in the process as a source rather than a recipient. Historically, dominant Western representations of globalization have configured the center or the "metropole," broadly understood as Europe and the United States, as the cradle of globalization and the model of what is considered the cosmopolitan and modern global. The "periphery" then is theorized as the parochial local as well as the recipient of globalization. The global, in contrast, represents the commonsensical "norm," the unmarked universal that is an "obvious" object of desire (the West), while the local is marked as particular to a place—the counterpart of the global—quaint perhaps, but not an apparent source of universal value and practice.

The juxtaposition of the global (bullet trains and Olympic games) and the local (terra-cotta warriors and Tibetan palaces) in the CI official's introduction and the boarding school's mural reflected two mechanisms employed by CIs to challenge these assumptions and establish China as a model for the global. I term the first of these strategies "witnessing the modern," through which summer program students were provided with numerous experiences that allowed them to "witness" the expected tangible results of China's fast-track modernization and its rightful place on the global stage, phenomena that evoked what Tsing (2000a) calls the "charisma" of the global. The second strategy I term the "embodied performance of tradition," in which students were invited to experience China as a model for a singular kind of global through encounters with traditional Chinese culture, what Schmidt labels a "politics of affect," through which students are meant to demonstrate a desire for China through "mimetic cultural performance" (2013, 661). As we shall see, the first of these strategies replicates dominant concepts of the global—China as a place of avant-garde architecture, high technology, and luxury consumption—while the second presents China as a new model for globalization precisely because it has resisted globalization's homogeneity by maintaining its traditions.[3]

Witnessing the Modern

After two days in Beijing, the students and chaperones in the summer program were dispatched in smaller groups to various provincial cities, where they were hosted by a variety of universities that had formal affiliations with CIs in the United States. Our cohort was joined by two other groups of American students for a total of fifty students and five chaperones. We were posted to a large city in eastern China where we studied at a small inner-city branch of the university and were housed at a hotel on the outskirts of town, a thirty-minute bus ride away. Our host university had also built an immense new campus in the suburbs, and on our first day after leaving Beijing we were treated to a tour of the grounds and the campus' new library, a stunning, multistoried granite building replete with floor-to-ceiling stacks of books and the latest in computer technology. The university had yet to open fully for operations, and as we meandered through the otherwise silent hallways, one of the CI teachers asked a student why she was not taking pictures of the library. "They took off all the plastic on the computers for you," she remarked, seeming to suggest that the students failed to comprehend the importance of the occasion. The students, who were no strangers to architectural grandeur and familiar with more bustling libraries, were not entirely clear about the rationale for our visit until I explained that the school was excited to show us their new campus, which was a marked material improvement from the old and somewhat decrepit buildings the university had occupied before. Although our hosts had anticipated that the students would be eager to share pictures of this architectural and technological splendor with friends and family at home, the students were not interested in replicating experiences with which they were already familiar, as their apathy and shuttered cameras suggested.[4]

Over the next two weeks, our excursions to such sites as museums, an airplane assembly factory, and extravagant shopping malls confirmed our hosts' commitment to our witnessing the modern, taking routes to our destinations that revealed to us newly developed thoroughfares, luxury automobile dealerships, "villa" housing, modernist skyscrapers, and lush golf courses, all internationally recognizable as contemporary manifestations of global arrival. The sites we visited and witnessed through the bus windows reflected common expectations about what constitutes a global built environment, and scholars have noted how emerging nations, as Aihwa Ong explains, "exercise their power by assembling glass and steel towers to project particular visions of the world" (2011, 1) that resemble the skylines of "global cities" such as New York and London. Ong also notes how Asian cities have emerged in the twenty-first century as "fertile sites" for architectural experiments that "reinvent what urban norms can count as 'global'" (2011, 2). In twenty-first-century China, billions have been spent hiring the world's most high-profile architects and constructing a skyline that, as noted architect Rem Koolhaas explains, now "rises in the East" (cited in Ong 2011, 2), drawing attention away from New York and London as the foremost sites of architectural innovation and symbols of globalization. These CI tour group excursions reconfirmed the conceptual terra firma of the built environment, offering students an opportunity to witness the monumentalization of space. These particular tours were revelations not of "we can do it differently" but of "we can do modern, and do it as well," pedagogical experiences that substantiated an accepted form of globalization through a built environment that, while not unique or reinvented as a form of difference, was recognizable globally as a contemporary manifestation of presumed globalization.

Another such CI projection of China's ability to embody the global was through introducing students to the city's "Italian-style street"—a former Italian concession in an old Western treaty port with Italian-style buildings that had been restored and turned into a pedestrian mall. The introduction began with a film shown in the CI classroom that described the area, which we were to visit shortly, as "a dramatic experience with humanity and commerce, an emotional clash between tradition and modernity, a fantastic journey to search for exoticness and Chinese style." With Italian opera playing in the soundtrack, the film's sepia-toned on-screen images moved fluidly from ancient Italy to ancient China before ending in a burst of color showing China's own version of an Italian town, a scene of well-heeled travelers, late-model cars, and rows of equal-sized Chinese and Italian flags flying side by side that suggested the equivalence of the two nations. Subsequent images featured advanced development and urban renovation, and voice-overs touted the neighborhood as the "largest place of Italian culture in Asia" and as an urban space of "unending prosperity." Employing a language of syncretism, the lecture that followed the film explained that this neighborhood was an example of "Chinese lifestyle European architecture" and a "typical blend of Chinese and Western culture" that exhibited how "China is able to blend different cultures so successfully." During our visit to the Italian town, we witnessed tourists being taken for rides in horse-drawn carriages by drivers wearing American-style cowboy hats and Chinese brides and grooms having their pictures taken wearing Western wedding attire. Dining on pizza and sipping Starbucks lattes despite the heat, the students experienced China as a globalized space of consumption meant to showcase the level of luxury achieved by China's economic boom and the country's ability to globalize in syncretic and imaginative fashion. Ong notes how oftentimes these manifestations of globalization are assumed to "create a global space that effaces national identity," thwart "national sovereignty," and subject local spaces to the "logic of placeless capital" (Ong 2011, 205). Yet, what we see in this case is not merely a reduction of the nation to the logic of global capital, but more what Ong calls a "play of exception," in which it is global capital that is the tool for national sovereignty, marking the nation as the manifestation of the global for the sake of local (China's) political power.

Riding back to our hotel, one of the CI officials sitting next to me reiterated the intended purpose of such tours, exclaiming, "This is a really worthwhile program; it changes students' ideas about China. They realize that China is much more modern than they thought." And indeed, students frequently expressed a new awareness. "I'm surprised at how modern China is," one told me. "I hadn't expected that." Similarly, another stated, "I thought China was going to be big and crowded," then added, with a tone of surprise, "but it's modern." CI teachers I talked with in the United States were accustomed to such reactions and over the years had recounted to me the sometimes anachronistic images students and parents brought into the CI classroom. "A parent asked me if we had two-story buildings," one teacher told me, while another reported having been asked if her parents would arrange her marriage and if women still bound their feet. Although "they know about the Olympics," this teacher continued, "I think we need to show them the real China, modern China, that it's like the United States, the modern cities. They are surprised by this." Yet the summer program students often appended a caveat to their appreciation of China's modernity, such as one who noted, "But then when you're sitting on the bus and the guide is pointing out all this modern stuff, you look on the other side and you instantly see all this real poverty. The two are right next to each other." In these narratives, somehow "real poverty" at home in the United States had less symbolic power. While modern and antiquated were visibly contiguous in both China and the United States, modern rarely emerged for China as the predominant signifier, while poverty never emerged as an essentialized indicator of the West. And rather than the luxury car dealership, what the students chose to memorialize in their photographs was the urban Walmart, the American purveyor of inexpensive products made in China, thus configuring China as a supplier of consumption for global others rather than a model of the global, the object, not the subject, of globalization.

Koichi Iwabuchi argues that the cultural effect of globalization often has little to do with the cultural nature of the products themselves when they originate outside the global North (Iwabuchi 2002). For example, while Sony products depend upon a Japanese culture of labor and innovation, those products do not contain what Iwabuchi calls an "odor" of Japanese culture; their global consumption projects a domestic consumer's status rather than a desire for the source nation or an example of "Japanization." In contrast, when a citizen from the global periphery consumes a product that originates in the West, the process is theorized as evoking a desire for its place of origin. For example, when Chinese consume McDonald's and Kentucky Fried Chicken, it is understood as a process of Westernization that leaves intact the assumed directionality of globalization and location of the global as well as their implied hierarchies of value.[5] Thus Hanban's claims about fulfilling the world's desire, "We just do something all people like" (Paradise 2009, 658), are meant to suggest a shift of aspirational objects in which China is responding to a global desire less for "odorless" consumer exports—iPhones and fake handbags—than for Chinese culture and therefore, ostensibly, for China itself. However, through their readings of this globalized landscape, the students confirmed what Sally Engle Merry describes as a recalcitrant perception of the "local" that stands "for a lack of mobility, wealth, education, and cosmopolitanism" and a global that "encompasses the ability to move across borders, to adopt universal moral frameworks, and to share in the affluence, education, and cosmopolitan awareness of elites from other parts of the world" (2006b, 39).

(Mis)Reading the Modern

After several days of such experiences, on a bus ride back to our hotel, students asked me why, if they were there to study Chinese and learn about China, we were spending long days visiting museums and airplane assembly factories and driving by car dealerships and skyscrapers. Less than a week into our seventeen-day excursion, the planned and clearly didactic activities were already beginning to wear on students' nerves. "My mom tricked me into coming here," one student moaned, expressing his frustration with a tour that was clearly not meeting his expectations. Attempts by Confucius Institutes to establish appreciation for China by providing evidence that would allow students to categorize China as the unmarked global rather than the particular, traditional local were not read as identification with their norms for the global but rather as betrayal and coercion. "It feels like jail, bus jail, school jail, no opportunities to just wander around," another student moaned, slumping into a lounge chair in the hotel lobby and pulling out his cell phone to check his texts from home.

The sites that our Chinese hosts had intended to model the irreducibly global—the dramatic architecture and world-class museums—were instead being experienced by students as forms of censorship and control that reinforced common Western perceptions of China's authoritarian political life. Rather than reading along with a narrative of spectacle that offered visions of Chinese global commensurability, they had come to view these experiences with disbelief and distrust. As we chatted one day, one of the girls said, "If I had known it was going to be all this museum stuff, I wouldn't have come. . . . It's all image control. . . . I would like to know what China is *really* like, not the PR trip we've been on." These students equated the "real" China they were being shown with image control, not with evidence of modernity.

While the historical eras and global hierarchies of power are different, China's efforts to fashion a particular image through cultural exchange reflect Soviet-US/European cultural exchanges in the period between the two world wars, in which the treatment of European and

American visitors to the Soviet Union speaks volumes to how the Soviet Union understood itself as a global power (David-Fox 2011). Drawing upon the concept of the Potemkin village, originally staged to deceive Catherine the Great into thinking Russia more developed than it was, Michael David-Fox explores how the Soviet Union guided foreigners through a "cultural show" (2011, 98) that staged political lessons for visitors from the capitalist West designed to counter assumptions about Russian backwardness and institute an image of Russia as the path forward for global development. This era led directly into a cultural Cold War period that David Caute characterizes as follows: "Never before had empires felt so compelling a need to prove their virtue, to demonstrate their spiritual superiority, to claim the high ground of 'progress,' to win public support and admiration by gaining ascendancy in each and every event of what might be styled the Cultural Olympics" (cited in David-Fox 2011, 321). Yet while the original Potemkin villages were temporary structures, designed purposefully to deceive, there was nothing either provisional or intentionally misleading about the monumental built environment featured on the CI tours that caused the skepticism. It was not so much the object but the pedagogy that proved frustrating for the students.

In case the students should miss the intended meaning of these expeditions, the guides and teachers continually engaged in a process I began to think of as the "perpetual presence of the adverb": China had "skillfully" integrated, "rapidly" modernized, "successfully" globalized, they informed us. Teachers and guides also frequently attempted to shape the students' learning by making sure they recognized that the intended objects of attention, in the words of one teacher, were "specific to Chinese culture and can teach us about China." Clearly, our guides believed that China needed to be taught, not merely experienced. This belief—or at least this hope—was expressed by our host university's vice dean of international affairs shortly before we returned to Beijing: "You must feel so proud of what you did in this short ten days. You've learned so many new things and had so many new experiences. It all must have impressed you and left a big impression. You can now see what Chinese culture is like. . . . You can now see what China is really like. It's better to see than to hear."[6]

Confucius Institute guides, who were themselves often impressed by and proud of how rapidly China had come to embody these markers of the global, were perplexed by the students' responses and questioned me about why the students failed to come to similar conclusions. Interpreting the students' dissatisfaction as a result of their not yet being "used to" China, the response of the guides and teachers, like that of any good host, was to try to provide students with what teachers assumed they were accustomed to in their everyday lives.[7] One day, for example, we pulled into a deserted parking lot at lunchtime and waited in confusion for fifteen minutes before employees from a local McDonald's climbed aboard with boxes full of Big Macs, French fries, and sodas. But as we chewed on our burgers and sipped our sodas in the parking lot, the student sitting next to me, rather than appreciating these efforts, complained, "I didn't come to China to eat McDonald's; I came to China to eat Chinese food," his earlier dash to the Tokyo airport McDonald's clearly forgotten. During our visit, I often noticed similar forms of hospitality, particularly at mealtimes, when alongside Chinese food, students were offered French fries and milk. When I questioned one of our guides about the ubiquitous French fries and the trip to McDonald's, she replied that they wanted to make the students feel comfortable and "at home." While making the students feel at home was a marker of gracious hospitality, it also demonstrated that China, too, had McDonald's and milk and other recognized forms of global consumption. But out of context, students often found these reminders of home unwelcome, both because they were seeking experiences that were the opposite of home and because these attempts were often perceived as inadequate. The French fries, the students complained, were usually cold, and the milk was always warm, suggesting to the students that despite China's efforts to achieve global commensurability by showcasing its modernization, the nation remained, in Homi Bhabha's words, "almost the same, *but not quite*" (1984, 127).[8] Although China might have gotten monumental architecture and luxury goods right, the same could not be said about the consumption of fast food and dairy products. Hospitality, Andrew Shryock contends (2012, S20), can be seen as a "test of sovereignty," and the students' refusal to submit to the CI guides' assemblage of meaning in these interactions injected doubt about China's ability to be the protective host and to model the global.[9]

However, the more our hosts provided material examples of China's modernity that were meant to stress China's rightful position on the global stage, the more their efforts were met with skepticism from the students, setting off what Robert Albro calls "boundary-patrolling" discourses that reify cultural difference and confirm negative stereotypes rather than promote diplomacy (Albro 2015). Indeed, as we exited a museum after having listened to detailed information on the building's spectacular architecture and world-class status, and on China's history of persecution at the hands of foreign imperialists, two students pulled me aside and asked why the museum tour guide "seems to leave out stuff and make it always seem like they [the Chinese] are the good guys."[10] "It's all so controlled," another grumbled. The CI program's categories and opportunities for witnessing the modern had produced "zones of boredom and unreadability" (Tsing 2005,172). Confucius Institute attempts to relocate the locus of the global, to construct a global marker of appreciation for China through powerful and even charismatic evidentiary moments of categorization and validation, were not read by students as identification but rather as betrayal and coercion.

Embodying Tradition

The existence of these zones of boredom reveal how Hanban's efforts to produce soft power sometimes failed to resonate with American students. While Hanban strove to contour an image of the Chinese nation as universally modern, student responses suggest that rather than commonality, commensurability, and evidence of China's status as a global power, they sought particularity and what they perceived to be Chinese authenticity. The Chinese Bridge program attempted to fulfill that desire and advance its soft power objectives with a second strategy of presenting China not only as a worthy member of the global community but also as a superior model of globalization that, by maintaining a vibrant traditional "local" culture rather than succumbing to Western cultural imperialism, rejected the widespread perception that globalization initiates the cultural homogenization of the world.

The form of local particularity emphasized throughout CI programming and curriculum around the world highlights a China defined not only by its global modernization but also by its long cultural tradition of the patriotic cultural sort explained in chapter 2. As Schmidt has argued, Hanban's presentation of Chinese tradition suggests an attempt to "replace affective economies of fear" regarding China's place in the world with "affective economies of a beneficial and good PRC" by making Chinese culture fun (2014, 357). I also suggest that this turn to tradition entails an attempt to restructure relations of global and local. As Jean Comaroff and John Comaroff have highlighted, " 'Locality' is not everywhere, nor for every purpose, the same thing; sometimes it is a family, sometimes a town, a nation, sometimes a flow or a field, sometimes a continent or even the world; often it lies at the point of articulation among two or more of these things" (1999, 294). It is this point of articulation that is important here, for the CIs thus not only posed China as challenging what "counts" for the local and the global; they also suggested a reconceptualization of the relationship between the local and the global through invoking both the unmarked "universal" global and the local particular as ontologically present. China, through the CIs, thus deployed its assumed parochial Other to make claims to power, remapping the United States as the "frontier zone" (Tsing 2005) of possibilities at the same time as it selectively deployed and reframed its own local to produce a vision of globality that trained the eye toward China as a model for what counts for global precisely because of the continued presence of the local.

The first stop on the Chinese Bridge program's tour of Beijing was a trip to Hanban headquarters, an interactive and educational space that offered a glimpse of how that local tradition would be rendered and experienced over the next two weeks. In the "Exploratorium" section, an instructional space that resembled US children's museums by offering opportunities for hands-on manipulation of artifacts and computerized lessons on history, students could don Beijing opera costumes, manipulate beads on a massive abacus, make paper and print a book, and view ink-brush paintings, all either common symbols of traditional Chinese culture or recognized examples of historically advanced technological accomplishments. Students could also take computer quizzes asking such questions as "Which of the following is in Beijing: the Terra Cotta Warriors or the Temple of Heaven?"—an ostensible geography question that also called attention to globally recognized historic and cultural splendors of China. In a nearby room, students engaged in more applied activities, moving between tables staffed by arts and crafts experts demonstrating how to paint Beijing opera masks, tie Chinese knots, and cut paper into intricate forms, and offering samples for interested students to take home.[11]

The lessons on cultural tradition continued later that afternoon and into the evening. Our visit to Hanban headquarters was followed by stops at a Confucian temple and a Tibetan Buddhist temple, which the tour guide framed as examples of China's ethnic harmony, cultural focus on education, and religious freedom (the last of these "as long as it doesn't get too political," he cynically explained). During our evening lecture, titled "Getting to Know China," the speaker referenced these afternoon activities and explained that Confucianism is key to understanding Chinese thought, emphasizing its philosophical focus on social order, good government, harmony, education, and filial piety (joking "That's why we have tiger moms"). Much of his lecture provided background information intended to set the stage for the presentation of cultural traditions that would dominate our activities for the remainder of our visit, including discussions of yin-yang symbols, calligraphy, Chinese food, the Chinese zodiac, and the color red.

What was omitted from this lecture became inadvertently visible when the speaker ended his presentation with a question-and-answer session. One student, speaking in Chinese, seemed to equate Chairman Mao with the absolute rulers of China's imperial past by asking why the speaker had excluded Mao from his hurried list of Chinese historical dynasties. His face clouding over, the speaker brusquely responded that the last dynasty had ended in 1911, well before Mao came to power, and that Mao was not an emperor. The student, looking confused, asked her question again in English, which revealed that she had actually meant to ask why cats (a word that in Chinese has the same sound as Mao) had not been included in the list of zodiac signs. What had been perceived as a challenge to the lecturer's apparent repression of contentious figures in Chinese history was in fact merely a reference to a cultural product (the Chinese lunar calendar) that is standard pedagogical fare in CI classrooms and was invoked frequently during the rest of our journey.[12]

After leaving Beijing, on most days the students gathered for several hours of Chinese instruction in the morning and after lunch for lectures on traditional culture and historic sites, including such topics as tile-roofed architecture, Confucianism, and the terra-cotta warriors. Following the lectures, local experts would demonstrate China's art and craft traditions and then set students free to try their hands at cutting "double happiness" symbols from red paper, painting Beijing opera masks, and tying Chinese knots. These activities not only replicated almost exactly those at Hanban headquarters but were staple activities in CIs' pedagogical method of combining language learning and cultural appreciation activities, and thus the students had "performed" China this way many times before in their Confucius Classrooms.[13]

As I watched the students perform China through these activities over the span of our visit, it increasingly became clear that the practices intended to promote soft power had actually backfired in several ways. While this may have been a result of cultural differences in expectations—with American students perhaps less tolerant of repetition and uniformity than their hosts expected—their effectiveness also appeared limited by Hanban's strategy of defining authenticity as "Culture with a capital *C*," demonstrated by these projects' failure to produce the intended admiration and appreciation. "Do we really have to do this?" one student moaned as an instructor pulled out piles of red paper and boxes of scissors to explain traditional Chinese paper-cutting techniques, complaining that "I've done this so many times." To spur interest, one of the chaperones suggested having a competition for the best paper cut, but it seemed to have little effect, as evidenced by a row of boys in the back napping with their heads on the tables. And on opera-mask-painting day, students engaged not only in eye rolling and nap taking, but also, to the displeasure of the teachers, took considerable poetic license with their projects, several of which more closely resembled characters from *Planet of the Apes* and *Batman* than standard Chinese opera characters. As one student said to me toward the end of our seventeen-day tour, stressing the last word, "I want to come back on a college overseas trip, but not on a Confucius Institute trip. I want more culture, not all this *Culture.*"

Instead, students were eager to experience culture with an anthropological lowercase *c*, a different kind of particularity than was offered by the CI program. The contrast between the normalized "global" Chinese culture presented by the Chinese Bridge program and the exoticized local Chinese culture desired by the students demonstrates the gaps that can occur between soft power policy intentions and their actual effects. The students' grumbling was not about China itself but about the didacticism and pedestrian art projects through which it was being experienced.[14] The frames of reference through which Hanban attempted to advance China as characterizing the global remained illegible to the students, highlighting the paradoxical notions of authenticity that the various actors brought to the setting. Precisely because China has not consistently preserved past traditions within the modern, Hanban could only resort to paper cutting and terra-cotta warriors as emblematic of "tradition." And yet, the authentic local offered by the CIs through these traditional practices had become so common and normalized— so global—that they no longer constituted a form of essentialized difference or at least the exoticized difference sought by students, as we will see in the following pages.

While the final week of our visit continued this pattern of language instruction, visits to historical sites and cultural monuments, meals with host families, and traditional arts and crafts projects, the afternoons were now dominated by hours of practice for a grand finale performance that would be presented in Beijing on the last evening of our stay. Local instructors had choreographed traditional and modern dance routines and selected students to perform, dressing them in traditional Chinese minority and Han costumes accessorized with feathered fans and elaborate headdresses. I grinned as I watched one Chinese American student, outfitted in a leopard-print costume, leap across the floor and proclaim himself the "Asian Macklemore," a reference to the Seattle-based American rapper, and grimaced as I overheard the following exchange between two students: "What do we win if we're the best group?" "Nothing, they make you stay in China longer."

During the final performance in Beijing, students from all over the United States came together to perform their routines. One group breakdanced to Taiwanese pop idol Jay Chou's hit sensation "Qinghuaci" (Blue and White Porcelain), a melodramatic love song that evokes traditional Chinese art forms, while another performed a tightly choreographed paean to filial piety that included prostrations before an immense image of Confucius and was set to a Chinese song about respecting one's parents and elders. Still others mimicked the elaborate kung fu moves of Shaolin monks set to music. In the finale, all the performers joined onstage to sing and dance to "Beijing Welcomes You," a theme song of the 2008 Beijing Olympics.

These kinds of cultural performances are standard fare in China, similar most notably to the popular *Chinese New Year Gala,* an extravagant dance and musical variety show regularly viewed by more than 90 percent of the population (Liu Kang 2012, 928). Comparable state-sponsored "minority" performances featuring dancers and musicians in ethnic dress performing "traditional" routines are also common, an attempt to demonstrate China's ethnic heterogeneity and multiculturalism.[15] But the students themselves tended eventually to see these performances as what Dean MacCannell has termed "staged authenticity" (1976, 91), a phrase that implies the opposite of authenticity. Well before our arrival back in Beijing, many of the students in our group had wearied of Hanban's attempts at inducing students to embody tradition; paper cutting, painting opera masks, and dressing up in traditional and minority costumes were not the form of authenticity they expected or desired to encounter during their visit, where they had hoped to learn about what they understood to be "the real China," not Hanban's sanitized version.

Ironically, the soft power objectives of the Chinese Bridge program were often more effectively met by moments in which the more blatant attempts to win hearts and minds were trumped by the unplanned and unintended. The unscheduled and unguided evening activities of the students illuminate some of the disparate assumptions and objectives of the China tour held by students and Hanban officials and teachers. The highly scripted days of the program often ended with students, tired and frustrated, wandering around the hotel hallways in search of experiences that seemed less derivative and universal. Because our hotel was located in a newly emerging area of town that afforded little in the way of entertainment and commerce, I frequently found myself the leader of unscripted nighttime excursions to an adjacent outdoor night market. Chinese night markets are typically informal and dynamic open-air spaces that come to life after sunset. This particular market was tucked into a corner of an intersection of two main thoroughfares and consisted of temporary stalls set up largely by migrants to the region or laid-off local laborers to market their various foodstuffs.

Most of the food at the market was quite unfamiliar to Americans, including baby octopus skewers, deep-fried grubs on a stick, "stinky tofu," and spicy mutton. Yet, upon our arrival at the market, the students would race from stall to stall, asking questions about the cuisine, pantomiming animatedly when their rudimentary Chinese proved insufficient or enlisting my help with translation, and purchasing various food items, the more unrecognizable the better. Using their cell phone cameras, which were constantly out, they captured images of the sellers, the fare, and fellow students. "This is the real China," one exclaimed as she stuffed a pungent bite of stinky tofu into her mouth. After our first visit, other students pleaded with me to accompany them to the market upon hearing that this was where one could find what they understood to be a genuine version of China. These market excursions provided students with an opportunity to experience what they perceived as a form of Chinese authenticity, in which snacking on unidentified creatures roasted on a stick delineated the "real." To students, the value of these encounters rested upon a margin of essentialized difference that could not be overcome by the host university's endeavors to improve the image of China by providing them with the global familiar or the prepackaged traditional. Student constructions of authenticity were based on consumption of the forbidden, the off-plan, the exotic unknown. Yet, what they placed value on was not the object of consumption itself, which was typically proclaimed "gross" by those who consumed it, but the *act* of consumption.[16] Here the students performed China for each other and for the recipients of their Instagrams and Snapchats back home, mugging grimaces after ingesting deep-fried silkworm or smirking with octopus legs protruding awkwardly from the corners of their mouths. Here the exotic indigestible was the object of a desire not to satisfy hunger, but for adventure and difference that reinforced, one could argue, their own sense of cosmopolitanism and globality.[17]

Other visits to various retail outlets illustrated the distinctions between what students and guides considered culture that spoke positively for China. When our guides took us to upscale shopping malls whose luxury rivaled anything in the United States, students would wander around in desultory fashion and complain about the excursion. They appeared to come alive, though, on shopping trips to the informal markets that sold imitation Western products and inexpensive Chinese handicrafts. Indeed, some of the most animated discussions of the trip consisted of "battle stories" about bargaining with merchants for fake Beats headphones and Converse knock-offs. As a student I interviewed in the United States explained, visiting the "fake brands market" was "really cool": when her group went to the market, "they [the merchants] tried to rip us off, of course," which she found to be "the funnest part of the trip." Seeming to reinforce the hierarchies of difference and power the program was intended to refute, the "fun" for this and other students lay in conquering the local by refusing to pay the higher prices targeted for global tourists, demanding that the market salesperson surrender to student demands to lower the price of the counterfeit goods. Rather than situate China as a model of the modern global, thus, these excursions offered a space for the relatively affluent to enact their self-conceptions as knowing, cosmopolitan travelers not willing to be duped in a market whose flexible pricing was based on one's skin tone or, for the phenotypically Asian students, one's Chinese language abilities.

While students in general complained about the cold French fries, warm milk, lack of hot water, and somewhat neglected living conditions, they were forgiving of what they perceived to be the authentic China—symbolized here in exotic foodstuffs and bargaining for merchandise. Even if the food was "gross" and goods were overpriced imitations, they were imagined as involving experiences of the real China. That student assessments of local authenticity reflected not only the object (exotic food or branded products) but the form of its delivery (night markets or upscale shopping centers) was perhaps most visible when the CI offered this same "authentic" culture but in a different format—alien foodstuffs at an expensive restaurant. By the end of our stay outside Beijing, the teachers and guides had become aware of student complaints and responded by trying to add activities to the standard Hanban package in order to counteract students' seeming weariness with the familiar.[18] One of these special activities was a guided boat tour of the city's river that meandered through the downtown region, an experience that one of our guides suggested would allow us to witness the "spectacular sights and impressive development of the city," while another was an elaborate and costly lunch at a local restaurant that was renowned for its preparation of a local delicacy called *goubuli*.[19] During the lunch, the *goubuli* buns were accompanied by an endless stream of intricate delicacies that were greeted with vocal approbation by the Chinese guests and skepticism by the students, who found the food unfamiliar in texture and taste and ate very little, to the dismay of their hosts, who had spent a good deal of money on the adventure and gone to great lengths to procure last-minute tables at this popular upscale restaurant. Although the dishes at the banquet were no more "exotic" than those the students consumed so gleefully at the night market, they remained largely untouched and students complained to me that they were being "forced" to attend another boring public relations production. As Mei Zhan reports of a similar incident when soccer star David Beckham toured China and refused to consume the "exotic" dishes of a celebratory banquet in his honor, for the students, this food, in this context, was coded as the "imaginary of a traditional, exotic Chinese culture out of sync with a cosmopolitan world" (2005, 33). In contrast, the teachers and guides who accompanied us were aghast at the waste that sat before them and on the return bus revealed that they had not eaten because their university could not afford the extra expense of feeding everyone. As we got off the bus and the teachers ran into the cafeteria to see if any food remained from lunch, it was clear that the lunch had reproduced differences that confirmed rather than challenged global hierarchies of power.

Even when the CI offered particularity through opportunities to perform and consume the local, the activities failed to bridge the gap in expectations of the students, who resisted CI offerings of culture as tainted by an attempt to render them malleable soft power targets. These perceptions seemed confirmed when, at the end of our stay in China, students were required to compose final essays describing their experiences and many of them wrote about the excitement over their night market encounters for what they considered to be authentic China. One, for example, wrote as follows: "One night my friend and I got invited to visit the night market and we really wanted to go. Once we got there, I instantly loved it. Even though there were so many exotic foods and smells, I was out of the hotel and just enjoyed being out and experiencing in person instead of from a bus window. That night I felt adventurous and I managed to try a larva and octopus! It was really interesting and fun. . . . Overall I really enjoy walking on the streets day or night and just feel immersed into the culture because that it is why I wanted to come to China."

However, when students turned in their essays, CI teachers quickly instructed them to remove references to their night market adventures and instead highlight Hanban-sanctioned activities that reflected the official intentions and values of the Chinese Bridge program. When one of the teachers explained to me that the students "need to mention the extra things that Hanban has done for them," such as "the special lunch and the boat ride," and I passed on this request to the students, they moaned, "But the night market was my favorite." But by then, students had gotten the message that Hanban meant to communicate China as an exemplary peaceful and first world nation, not a land of bizarre indigestibles. Along with their required essays, they were asked to hand in a copy of their favorite picture of their time in China, and I overheard two debating which one to choose. One asked the other, "Which official picture are you going to send?"—by "official" clearly referring to a picture that would portray China "appropriately" in the eyes of the CIs. Acerbically, her friend responded, "They want the photo to show the way they want you to see it, and then you need to say thank you." The tourist boat trip, opera masks, and traditional foodstuffs in an upmarket restaurant intended to improve China's image had simply fed into student skepticism and perceptions of propaganda and, by this time, a desire for home.

Russell Cobb notes how the word "authenticity" is only "a few linguistic paces removed from the word 'authoritarian'" (2014, 1), and the paradox of authenticity could hardly be less palpable in these student CI experiences. While students were unable to articulate what, for them, constituted the authentic real of China, they presumed that anything prepackaged by Hanban, precisely because it was prepared, could not count for an authentic China/local that might be understood as an alternative form of modernity. Although students identified their own subject positions as grounded in and attributed to a universal global, China reemerged in these excursions as the parochial local that rendered their own resolute globality possible. In this construction, students embodied the global and China the local, and the CI program, rather than successfully producing a vision of China as an alternative global through invoking authentic tradition, offered the opportunity to produce the students as the "adepts" (Orta 2013, 697) who managed the global. As for students in the MBA study tours in Mexico studied by Andrew Orta, these excursions in China were "value added" projects that boosted CI students' worth as global citizens (Orta 2013, 697) rather than that of the Chinese nation, precisely because of their ability to recognize and manage the authentic local.

Evoking Domestic Desire for China

The paradoxes of modernity and authenticity seemingly inherent in the CI program did not necessarily mean the China tours were entirely unsuccessful in terms of their goals of soft power production, both because there were always a few students who truly enjoyed their experiences and, as is discussed in this section, because there is more than one type of spectator whose opinion and support are at stake. As student experiences of this tour frequently revealed, the more Hanban's instrumentalization of culture became apparent—the less "authentic" and more "authoritarian" it was perceived—the more it fed into students' worst perceptions about China's structures of governance and control. However, translating culture into national comprehensive power on the global stage requires more than the acquiescence of a global audience; soft power is not reducible to the realm of international diplomacy. As scholars of soft power have observed in general, power in the global arena also necessitates domestic approval of processes and practices that structure China's place in the world (Barr 2012; Cai 2010) and as Ingrid d'Hooghe (2014) has observed in particular, Chinese officials recognize that soft power and public diplomacy also serve an important domestic function.[20] Framing the CIs solely as a tool of global persuasion misses an important point about the language programs as a form of *domestic* soft power in which China tells a story to its own citizens about globalization in order, as Shanghai's Tongji University scholar Cai Jianguo explains of another soft power project, to provide "my nation" and "Chinese people" with the opportunity to "learn from the [2010 Shanghai] Expo through embracing the latest achievements of human civilization" (Cai 2010). Considering soft power from a domestic perspective also allows us to grapple with the rise of China in a more complex fashion than common discourses of a global Chinese threat might suggest.

Before I ventured to China on the Chinese Bridge program, a principal at a high school with a CC reassured me that in his experience, although "there's a blatant propaganda element to all of this trip" that would "include a lot of cheesy photo opportunities . . . the photos are as intrusive as it gets, no one's trying to indoctrinate anyone. These photos end up on the desks of politicians, who can say, 'See what we do.'" What this comment about photos ending up on official desktops suggests is that soft power efforts are intended not only to provide global audiences with information but also to respond to domestic concerns about authority, representation, and CI program expense.[21] While, for instance, Italian Town might seem to a global audience just another unauthorized reproduction of global products akin to the fake designer handbags that proliferate at informal markets in China, to a domestic audience it might indicate the authenticity of the nation's global-ization and encourage the nation's citizens to "feel confident in their home-land and [promote] a sense of belonging" (Barr 2012, 82). Chinese scholars have argued that soft power must assume a holistic approach and be developed both internationally and domestically through "making China's culture . . . attractive to both a Chinese and an international audience (Glaser and Murphy 2009, 20). The soft power of spectacle, in other words, depends as much on the specific audience as it does on the performance itself.[22]

Scholars have argued that being "global" means to be perceived as the site of universal desire and value "that needs no justification" (Handler 2013, 186; see also Ho 2009 and Orta 2013). A central facet of reconcep-tualizing what counts as local and global—as China is trying to do—thus involves the production and materialization of desire, something that is at the heart of soft power efforts. And on our first day in Beijing, we were given several hints of the mechanisms through which soft power produc-tions were also a domestic mode of engagement that sought to show a local audience the world's desire for China's globalization. It was also clear that attempts to illustrate desire for China were not entirely directed toward a global audience. The hour-long bus ride from our dorm to Hanban head-quarters on our first day in Beijing took us past suburban housing develop-ments with such names as Beijing Riviera and Palm Beach, reproductions of a more commonly assumed flow of desire from East to West. Upon our arrival, however, desire that was represented as flowing instead from West to East was on immediate and evident display. In the first room of our headquarters tour, glass cases arranged in a maze-like formation led viewers through a display on the history and current state of the CI program. One of the first displays began with a quote from Wang Yongli, current deputy director of Hanban: "China, like an economic giant, suddenly appears in front of the world and everybody is shocked. They want to know the history and the home of this giant." The global encounter in that case was embodied by a young Chinese teacher, Yu Liu, assigned to the CI at the London School of Economics, where she tutored "high profile business professionals from London's bustling economic sector in Chinese for business dealings." This display's illustration of the world "working together" presented CIs not as an attempt by China to push its programs onto an unwilling global population but as a response to a demand for Chinese for the purpose of increasing the economic productivity of Europe.[23] The direction of this desire was later reinforced by a display that quoted a statement by the director of an American CI at a major US university that the US government itself was "pushing for students to learn Chinese."[24] As an affirmation of Hanban's success in fulfilling that American desire, a nearby poster declared that 82 percent of surveyed Confucius Institute students liked the program, 76 percent believed that learning Chinese would help them in the future, and 75 percent were interested in visiting China. While this display could easily be interpreted as an attempt to convince the American students and chaperones of the direction of desire—we were, after all, the invited guests—in practice it was the Chinese teachers and guides who composed the main audience. Students assiduously avoided the display cases in favor of the more interactive sections of the building, while the CI teachers and guides with whom I toured the building remarked consistently with both surprise and pride at the spread of the CIs around the world and at how much China had accomplished in such a short time.[25]

This first day at headquarters provided us with a second hint of the mechanisms through which soft power productions were also a domestic mode of engagement in the form of a fifteen-foot banner that identified us as part of the Chinese Bridge program and accompanied us for the duration of our stay in China. The welcome speech that day was followed by the first of many photo sessions of the students with CI administrators and chaperones in which those in front were kneeling and holding the banner. For all seventeen days, we were rarely without a professional photographer documenting our experience in China, the banner unfurled and our visit memorialized at museums, airplane factories, Beijing opera performances, airports, and restaurants and through the images and videos that were reproduced in local media and on the Hanban Web page that evening or the following day.

On our visit to the airplane factory, for instance, our guides positioned us in front of the massive corporate sign outside the entrance gate holding the banner as the official photographer took numerous pictures, simultaneously documenting our American presence and China's accomplishments in the field of aviation. The next day, one of the young tour guides ran up to me after breakfast and asked excitedly if I had seen the local news that evening, which had featured a story about our presence in the city and visit to the factory that included our picture with the banner. Rather than address an overseas audience, this story offered Chinese citizens the opportunity to behold foreigners appreciating China's global modernity under the tutelage and beneficence of the CI program. Hanban's efforts to demonstrate China as an object of desire by inviting six hundred American students to consume its globalization also provided evidence to its domestic population, which might read the very presence of the students as desire for China.

Yet, as I had suspected from earlier conversations with American CI administrators and as became increasingly evident throughout our time in China, the CI photographers' photos and videos were not randomly composed but highlighted a particular type of foreigner desiring China's global modernity and consequently challenging what counts for the global and assumed object of desire. Although half of the students in our group were phenotypically Asian, the photographers typically focused their lenses on our Caucasian members.[26] This intention could be observed even on our first-day visit to Hanban headquarters, where the opening exhibit of the world's CIs consisted almost exclusively of photographs of European and US CIs. This was augmented by a continuously looping video of the previous year's Hanban-sponsored international Chinese Bridge language competition, which featured only the Caucasian and a few African youth exhibiting their Chinese language skills in performances and "expressing warmly their love of China."[27]

This process of particularizing the ethnically appropriate target of soft power policy begins even before the students arrive in China. One of the American CI administrators on the Chinese Bridge trip that summer explained to me that when the program first began, Hanban had been explicit about which ethnic groups were eligible for the program, and another administrator reported that she once had to advocate specifically for the inclusion of a couple of Chinese American students, arguing that, because these particular students spoke better Chinese, they could assist the non–Chinese language speakers. Yet another related a story about the trouble several years ago their group had including a Chinese American student who had been adopted from China. Yet over time, the programs became increasingly unable to fill their available slots with non–ethnically Asian students, and by the year of my visit half of our group consisted of children of immigrants from China, Chinese children adopted by Caucasian parents, and other Chinese Americans. Nonetheless, the final video montage of our group's activities revealed this preference for the white witness, as nearly all the close-ups were of non-Asian students. Similarly, the two students who were chosen to introduce the final celebratory performance in Beijing, which was performed in front of a line-up of dignitaries from central headquarters, appeared to be the two blondest, most classically "foreign" girls of the six hundred students invited to China. One who was observably not selected for her prowess in the language, ended her introductory address exclaiming in Chinese, "I love you, I love China."

This emphasis on the white foreigner desiring China projects a particular claim about China's global position, one that upends extant racial hierarchies that undergird global hierarchies of power. Although the Chinese American students in our group were largely invisible in the visual record of the program, they themselves largely rejected the "brother" and "sister" appellations they were subjected to in public markets or in the assumption, by teachers and guides, that they felt some sort of "natural" affinity for China. Their responses to the program instead reinforced their own structural "whiteness" as members of a middle class who failed to engage with the CIs' offerings that were intended to produce appreciation. Playing on this identity, one of the Chinese American students, when called upon in class to write a paragraph in Chinese, jokingly responded in an indignant voice, "What do you think I look like, Chinese?"

Despite this structural whiteness of the Asian American students, Hanban photographers repeatedly overlooked those students who presented less obvious "difference" from the local norm, less seeming need for education about China, and less symbolic power as a CI soft power policy target.[28] In the displays at headquarters, the promotional videos, and the closing ceremony, it was the white foreigner, the assumed universal norm, who was revealed as appreciating the Chinese other. This marks a reversal of common assumptions of desire that challenges the directionality of globalization and the assumption that global means whiteness. Yet as I sat in the closing ceremony pondering the photography and the performance, the obvious delight of the first two rows of the audience, which were filled with visiting dignitaries from Hanban and other governmental offices, and the massive Chinese couplet that framed the stage on both sides quoting the last line of an esoteric Tang dynasty poem by Shi Jianwu—"Conviction allows one to cope with changes in the world"—it was also evident that the white foreigner was not the only potential target of Hanban's representational efforts. It was unlikely that the students and US chaperones around me could either read or comprehend the couplet's message that the global order was indeed changing and that China was offering a new model for managing that change. Its message addressed not only China's power in the international realm but its national cohesion and cultural significance in the domestic context,[29] offering visions of national greatness in the interest of state power to a local audience.[30] Soft power production in this case is as much in the interest of enhancing domestic governance and civic pride as it is about global competitiveness.[31]

This pleasure among Chinese officials and guests in seeing the students perform Chinese culture so successfully, despite the students' often negative responses to the cultural activities of the Chinese Bridge tour, to a certain extent reflects, perhaps counterintuitively, a measure of success for the CIs in their ability to have globalized China. While student expectations for authentic cultural difference were not met by the paper cutting and opera masks, these practices and images had become so common and normalized that they no longer constituted some form of essentialized difference. Students had mastered paper cutting and knot tying, they could already sing along to Jay Chou, and they were familiar with the basic tenets of Confucian philosophy that stressed the importance of family ties and education. Thus rather than analyze Hanban's efforts merely as hackneyed attempts to create desire, we can also see how these invocations of tradition are central to China's claims of political legitimacy domestically (Hubbert 2017) and, in the context of the CIs, constitute a key method of soft power strategy for a nation that sees its cultural heritage as a "huge reservoir of great and positive assets" (Guo 2008, 28). Watching students confirm this was clearly a joyful experience for the domestic audience.

Conclusion: An Economy of Appearances

This chapter has explored one of Hanban's most popular programs, the annual Chinese Bridge travel-study excursion to China for high school students studying Chinese at CIs in the United States. The program marks an effort to contest conceptions of the global as a fixed space located in the West and to offer traditional culture as a site for the production and expression of alternative ways of being global. The summer program was not suggesting the universal promotion of Confucius or opera masks—the content itself is somewhat irrelevant—but arguing that a nation may be "global" through the production of the resolutely and authentically "local." Yet the fundamental problem for China's attempts to establish soft power through this reconfiguration returns directly to the product itself and the fraught nature of "culture" as a form of power. For it was clear in the Chinese Bridge program that not all culture is equal and official strategies for the promotion of soft power through Chinese culture collided with student expectations for what constituted the "real" cultured China. While Hanban sought to remap the United States as China's frontier zone of possibilities, the students were more likely to see China as their own untamed Wild West, to be conquered as a marker of their own cosmopolitanism, not China's. Summer programming worked to redefine globalization and position China as a subject rather than an object of cultural and economic flows, and as an initiator of what it means to be global, yet the objects of its soft power efforts often failed to recognize it as such; the officially authentic local sometimes emerged as "jail," reinforcing perceptions of censorship and political control. And bizarre indigestibles, perceived as the truly authentic, constructed value, but not for China. Similar to how Chinese medicine operates as "bridge" between cultures (Zhan 2009), the "bridge" of the Chinese Bridge program is not easily spanned, for "East and West, China and America . . . are not fixed and easily identifiable nodes within circuits of globalization but rather are shifting and uneven spatiotemporal imaginaries produced and refigured through particular translocal encounters" (Zhan 2009, 179).

Yet, it is not merely a "gap" between policy and practice that is at work here, nor a necessary result of a set of practices that produce policy only "in the sense that actors . . . devote their energies to maintaining coherent representations regardless of events" (Mosse 2005, 2). As this chapter has explored, the CI production of power for China occurred sometimes through the nonscripted, ad hoc, off-policy experiences of China, rather than the planned excursions and characterizations, and sometimes had little relationship with policy itself. Rather, these frictions emerge through the inherent paradoxes in the forms of global modernity and authenticity promoted through the CIs and anticipated and experienced by the students, manifest in this case in the illustrations and expectations of global and local on the part of both policy makers and policy targets.

To invoke, in a modified manner, Anna Tsing's idea of an economy of appearances—what she defines as the dramatization of dreams that attracts investors (2000b, 118)—here the CI economy of appearances depends upon the simultaneous production of geographic and dramatic performances, the self-conscious making of a spectacle to aid in the gathering of power (Tsing 2000b, 118). Tsing's discussion of the economy of appearances renders evident how analyses of the global frequently juxtapose both its physical presence and its spectacular conception to an imagined, parochial Other, understood as the "local." Here, the geographic production of globalization arrives in the form of the Chinese presence of nearly sixteen hundred CIs around the world, evidence, Hanban's displays suggest, of the world's desire. And when CI critics equate the growth of CIs with a necessary diminution of US power, it is presence that is fetishized as performance, marking a successful economy of appearances in which the "self-conscious making of a spectacle" (Tsing 2005, 57) emerges as a form of presumed state power. Yet global presence remains insufficient as a foundation for embodying the global, and China must also dramatize, through the actions of those who are meant to "desire" China, a coherent narrative and practice of globalization to render geographic presence an efficacious source of power. Hanban expects the students to appreciate the glories of China's ancient past *and* revel in its astonishing modernity and yet fails to grasp the paradoxes in trying to present both simultaneously as markers of an authentic globalization. The oxymoronic goals of convincing a foreign audience of China's modernity by stressing its glorious past represent an attempt at rewriting the implicit rules of the source and directionality of globalization and its constitution but appear to have in this case reinforced the juxtaposition between the spectacular conception of physical global presence and its imagined, parochial Other. Victims of Hanban's own "success" at globalizing the CI programs, the authentic ancient, now standard fare around the world, emerged in its origins as a metaphorical cousin of authoritarian politics.

Indeed, after most of the Chinese Bridge's scheduled programs were completed and the only thing left was the farewell ceremony and a bus ride to the airport, students were instructed to complete an exit survey that included, among many others, two questions that asked, "Do you intend to further your study in China?" and "If not, do you plan to learn Chinese in the future?" Interestingly, many of the students answered the first question in the negative and the second in the positive, not intending to study Chinese within China in the future, but continuing to learn the language. While the tour may have frequently rendered the object "China" problematic,

"Chinese" may persist as an object of desire. In that case, language remains intact as an intended soft power attraction and route to the global, but sometimes only when divorced from the broader intended object of desire—China—itself. Considering how practices produce policy also allows us to expand our conception of soft power's audience and hence of soft power policy effect since "proper" delineations and engagements constitute different communities in relation to different goals and encounters, and policy "success" may also be defined by the reactions of the domestic audience as well as the foreign global. Thus, through attending to both policy strategy and engagements in practice, we can see more clearly not only how China is working to challenge expectations for the global, but also how soft power policy effect is more than the sum of its intentional parts.

CHAPTER 5

Imagining the State
Constitutions and Conceptions of
Government and Governance

In a 2010 episode entitled "Socialism Studies," Jon Stewart's *The Daily Show* skewered an incident regarding a Southern California school district's decision to establish a Confucius Institute. Opening with Stewart's striking his finger on his desk and declaring, "Our schools are in crisis," one that "threatens to destroy everything we hold dear," the segment then shifted to footage of a school district board meeting in the California suburb of Hacienda Heights, where a local resident protests that "if it comes from communist China, it is tainted with communism. You can't lie to us. We should not be teaching our children about Mandarin language and Chinese culture. . . . That's brainwashing." To get to the bottom of this controversy, *Daily Show* correspondent Aasif Mandvi visited a Confucious Classroom, where he finds, in the predictably ironic vein of the show, what he calls an "army of tiny Maoists who had to be stopped."

A year later, the *China Daily*, the Chinese government's principal English-language newspaper, purchased a two-page color advertisement in the *New York Times* that disputed this image of CIs. In contrast to the *Daily Show*'s comic image of the Chinese state as propagandistic, authoritarian, and ideologically dangerous, the *China Daily*'s representation, structured as a series of three articles about the CIs but purchased as advertising space, depicted the PRC government as benignly curious and globally sensitive, "sowing the seeds of better understanding and better communication with the world" (Peters and Zhang 2011, A8). The state here was embodied by the youthful, "bright-eyed" teachers who are striving to "learn about the students' interests, character and cognitive development levels" and eagerly "sharing their language and their culture and building the foundations for better understanding," not politically motivated Maoists out to recruit converts to communism.

This chapter begins where these two radically different perspectives on the nature of the Chinese state leave off by offering an ethnographic examination of the PRC government as constituted in and by a CI classroom in the United States. In the same way, as discussed in chapter 1, that anthropology approaches the study of power differently from the disciplines of international relations and political science, here it analyzes the state by subjecting it to cultural critique. Anthropologists have long approached the state as an ambivalent object of study, wary of its ambiguous nature and of how one actually quantifies it.[1] Anthropological studies often refer to "the state" in scare quotes to avoid promoting an image of the state as a monolithic, reified entity, and turn instead to the problematic of culture, scrutinizing how states come into existence as assemblages of cultural practices and value-laden formations.[2] Yet rather than avoid the study of state institutions and practices, anthropologists, as Michel-Rolph Trouillot notes, are ideally "suited to study the state from below through ethnographies that centre on the subjects produced by the state effects and processes" (2001, 133). This chapter aims not only to invert the study of the state, as Trouillot suggests, but to study it through scrutinizing not only the "below" of the state, in this case the policy targets, but also the agents of the state—the CI teachers—and their complex, contingent, and sometimes contradictory relation to it.

To that end, this chapter offers an anthropology of the imagined state as produced within the context of a Confucious Classroom to examine how students and parents in the United States experience the Chinese state through their everyday encounters with its policies, stagecraft, and representatives. Examining CIs at the ground level of their implementation, it investigates how those targets of the CCP's soft power policies *imagined* the Chinese state, not to suggest that there is anything "unreal" or "false" about the state but to avoid privileging a particular government bureaucracy as an archetypal instantiation of "the state" and to reveal how the "idea" or the "reality" of the state is forged through everyday encounters with government agents and representations.[3] To examine this idea/imagination of the state, this chapter asks the following questions: How do representatives of the Chinese state, such as teachers and texts, devise an idea of the state in the Confucious Classroom? How do US parents and students actually identify, negotiate, and conceive the Chinese state in response to their everyday encounters with its CC representatives? How are these responses embedded in local structures of knowledge that particularly and normatively define global citizenship? This chapter begins by analyzing one of the most important tropes through which the Chinese state was understood in the CIs—communism—and then offers a discussion of the pedagogical materials and practices through which soft power policy targets apprehended the Chinese state. It ends with an analysis of the role that teachers played in formulating the Chinese state in a manner less antithetical to US ideals of modernity as they concern issues of government and governance. Ultimately, this foray into the Confucious Classroom reveals the disarticulated and conflicted nature of the imagined state—in effect disaggregating the state—and offers new insights into the relationships among state policy, state policy making, and state policy targets and into the very assumptions about modernity that undergird contemporary notions of the state.

Cold War Politics in the Confucius Classroom: Understanding Communism

Confucius Institutes arrive at their host campuses facing a variety of expectations and assumptions, not only about the language programs but also about the government that funds them. On the one hand, soft power policy projects are inherently political. They are conceived to accrue power for the state and the CIs are understood fundamentally and rightly as politically motivated institutions. And because the programs are from China, and that carries with it broadly articulated assumptions about political value and practices, the expectations are especially politically laden. On the other hand, despite the ostensible end of the Cold War, China continues to be seen by many Americans as ideologically opposed to the United States. As the incident in Hacienda Heights skewered by the *Daily Show* and as my research observations suggest, communism, which is widely viewed as a rejection of modernity's most fundamental precepts (Arnason 2000), remains a powerful indicator of meaning in the United States. Illustrating this succinctly, one middle school student blurted out in a Confucious Classroom I observed, "Oh, they're all communist. I don't like the communists." As my research observations reveal, the trope of communism often functioned to frame the programs politically regardless of the curricular content of the Chinese language courses themselves or the teachers' identifiable political ideologies and practices.

As the aforementioned *Daily Show* episode suggests, communism has emerged as a key trope for understanding the CIs. Although satirical, the show chronicled an actual incident that signposted how China's arrival in the form of a language exchange program in a California town was perceived as "tainting" local schools with communism.[4] The parent opposition to the program, featured in the *Daily Show* segment, was joined by the former Hacienda Heights school district superintendent, who declaimed, "I am not against the teaching of foreign languages, but this is a propaganda machine from the People's Republic of China that has no place anywhere in the United States. . . . Our kids need to be taught Americanism" (quoted in Ni 2010). At the real board meeting selectively featured on the *Daily Show*, participants accused the school board members who had approved the CC of being "corrupted by the Chinese communist government"; one speaker alleged that "everything coming out of that regime is a lie. . . . If we deteriorate into a morass by the Chinese propaganda machine through the Confucius Classroom . . . , then the country is finished."[5] A particularly strident member of the audience, a former marine dressed in full uniform decorated with military medals, directly berated a school board member who had grown up in the United States but had an ethnically Chinese surname and phenotypically Asian features, declaring, "Us marines have more right to be here than you. We fought for this country to keep communism out and you're inviting them here. Shame on you."

Before I arrived at my main research site for my first extended stay, the administration had sent letters home with the Chinese language students introducing my research project and asking for parent volunteers willing to discuss the culture and language programs with me. Below I highlight two groups of these parent interviews. In the group interviews I held with parents during that and all consequent visits, I began by explaining that the purpose of my research was to provide an anthropological perspective on a subject that had been previously considered primarily through the framework of international relations, with little understanding of actual classroom practices and experiences. In the first of these interviews, even before I finished introducing myself, Rachel, the parent of a sophomore in the CC program, very pointedly asked whether the "Chinese communist government" was funding and directing my investigation. Despite my assurances to her that my research funds were supplied by the US university where I was employed, her suspicions seemed to color the remainder of the discussion that day. Rachel's question was soon followed by one from her husband,

Karl, as to whether I knew how the CC Chinese instructors were chosen: "Was being a Communist Party member necessary?" Again, before I could respond, Renee, the mother of a senior, replied, "Of course they're Communist Party members. Party members have connections. . . . To really move ahead [in China] you have to have connections, to bribe people." At this, Karl and Rachel jumped back into the discussion:

> *Karl:* I know the Confucius Institutes are trying to portray a very positive image. Our daughter's impression of China, what has bothered me, is that she thinks communism is a viable form of government.
> *Rachel:* Well, it is. It works in China.
> *Karl:* It's not.
> *Rachel:* We've discussed the negative aspects of China, the human rights violations, the authoritarianism, the repression.
> *Karl:* She thinks communism is okay [but] it's not. We have different values. It's our values versus their values, like the redistribution of wealth. They do that there. It's not okay; she thinks it's okay, I don't.

In contrast, when I discussed these suspicions about the links between Chinese teachers and Communist Party politics in the other group, Diane and Peter, unrelated parents of children who had studied Chinese at the CC program, were dismissive of the concerns raised by Karl and Rachel.

> *Peter:* Why would we be suspicious?
> *Diane:* It's not like [the teachers] are putting red propaganda slips in the kids' backpacks. They don't talk about politics in the classroom.
> *Peter:* If they are here to spread communism, it isn't working. I'm just not hearing, "Oh, that Mao, he wasn't really so bad," or "Those millions they killed, really it was just thousands." I'm not hearing that.

One of the schools in Diane's and Peter's district had a boarding program for international students that included many from China, one of whom had lived with Diane's family for a period of time and several of whom had joined the soccer team that Peter coached. These parents' perceptions of the potential harm posed by CIs had clearly been diminished by these exchanges. Unlike Rachel and Karl, who worried that students in the CI classroom might warm to communist political ideologies antithetical to dominant US ideals, Peter and Diane posed CIs as potentially dangerous to China, not to US students:

> *Peter:* Our students are very glad they are American. They are intrigued by China and feel fortunate that we have these exchange students.
>
> *Diane:* I don't think they laugh a lot in China. We bring levity to the Chinese students' lives. I talk a lot with my boarder about happiness.
>
> *Peter:* The worry should be on the part of the Chinese government. China risks more with these exchanges than we do. They should be more worried. We don't need to fear them. Their students see another land, they actually laugh. . . . I've never heard a single [US] student say a single positive thing about communism.

Even as the two sets of parents understood the potential danger of the CI program differently, the framework through which they understood the value and significance of the programs was in fact quite similar, thereby highlighting the importance of local ideologies and practices beyond the goals of official soft power policy endeavors. Whereas Karl and Rachel maintained fears that Hanban's goals of creating a favorable image of China included proselytizing communist political ideologies they perceived as antithetical to their values and against US interests, throughout our conversation, Peter and Diane reiterated their impression that the actual CI practices intended to make China more attractive to US citizens had not only proven ineffective but were in fact almost deleterious to the CCP mission. For them, the "China threat" posed by CIs was rendered unlikely by what they perceived as the fundamental natures and relative values of capitalism and communism.

In these and other conversations, communism emerged as an important lens through which many of the parents comprehended the Chinese state. As they understood and used it, communism was a historically embedded, overdetermined term that evoked a range of events, practices, and values that included Vietnam, atheism, breadlines, and permissive abortion policies. Although the CCP had dispatched CI teachers and Hanban materials to the United States to dispel images of the Chinese nation as a

threat to global well-being, my discussions with parents and students indi-
cated that both were received as proxy for a state that had already been
locally defined by this history and through the association of communism
with human rights violations, authoritarianism, repression, and despondency
among its citizens. Even when communism was not seen as a direct threat,
the trope was important to how they understood the Chinese state and its
relations with domestic citizens, as in the case of an American teacher who
had accompanied students on one of the Hanban Chinese Bridge summer
programs to China who described it as "a propaganda trip" precisely
because "there wasn't any mention of the communism thing." Parents' impressions of the state were highly culturally constituted, not through access
to Chinese culture or explicit "evidence" from the CI classroom materials
or CI teacher behavior, but by US culture and the ideologies of democracy
that shaped their conceptions of the Chinese government's intentions and
practices. Roger, for instance, speculated that CI "teachers have to be
politically trustworthy to be chosen to come here," even though he recognized that the US probably "wouldn't send teachers who aren't politically
trustworthy, either."[6] Another parent, Julie, who was willing to give the
program the benefit of the doubt, also expressed similar suspicions: "Every
government has its heinous and positive things. It seems to me a positive
thing to be teaching the world about your language and culture, but I also
see China as a colonialist and repressive communist nation that has entirely
ruined a culture. I can hold these two views at the same time. We can send
out Peace Corps volunteers and have Guantanamo at the same time. The
US has done heinous political things as well."

As Julie's and Roger's comments make clear, even when parents were
willing to concede that China's governmental practices may in some instances mirror those of the United States and that in certain contexts they
make sense, parents tended to view the communist government, the source
of CI teachers and texts, with suspicion. These perceptions of a communist
state thus permitted parents to mobilize democratic ideology uncritically as
an ethical alternative even when their own countries had done "heinous
political things as well." Such mobilizations, as Akhil Gupta notes in a
different context, reinforce conceptual and discursive barriers that obstruct
what are in fact more capricious "modalities and techniques" (Gupta 2012,
42) of governance, obscuring that power may function more similarly
within different state systems than previously assumed. While Timothy
Mitchell (1991) argues that the agency of states depends on the production

of conceptual boundaries between state and society, here I would argue it depends on the cultural production of conceptual frameworks of essentialized differences between modes of state governance; in this case between ideas of communism and democracy, in which communism is considered to lack value because of its perceived distance from "democracy," even as its practices might sometimes mirror those of its Chinese political Other.

China has long been historically subject to racist exclusionary practices and it is easy to speculate about how long-embedded anxieties about race may become mapped onto essentialized representations of political practice. Critics of the CI program are rightfully concerned that their negative appraisals of the language programs might be glossed as anti-Chinese sentiment and have been consistent about making the distinction. Some claim that their concerns are not meant to be fundamentally anti-PRC, or anti-communist, or anti-"the people," while others claim distaste for communism, but not distaste for "the Chinese." Congressman Smith at the House of Representatives hearings discussed in chapter 1, for example, noted multiple times his enthusiasm for the Chinese people but disassociated them from the Chinese state: "You know, we all want to get closer to the Chinese people, but when this [the CIs] is all about a dictatorship that is adversarial in the extreme towards its own people, woe to us if we are enabling that dictatorship through this means" (US Congress 2014, 47). This is not, such caveats insist, about "judging China," but about judging the human rights effects of various political systems, academic freedom, and educational integrity. Yet, we might also see how in these caveats, as Eric Hayot explains in a different context, that "the announcement that China is not on trial is an announcement that China is on trial . . . a trial in which the most damning evidence is damning precisely because the text excludes it" (2009, 71). To assess and analyze may not be to judge, but it is implicitly to compare, and while judging may not be the intent, it is often a rhetorical effect that not only reflects China's place in the world but also creates it.

My point is not to argue that these caveats are purposefully disingenuous but to reemphasize that the ways in which the CIs are experienced reflect as much upon historical American ideological preconceptions and discomfort with the changing global order as they do upon the language programs themselves. And we can see this in the changing nature of these experiences over the course of my research. While the production of essential difference was particularly true in the early years of this research, by the end of my five years conducting research at CIs, I found more parents who either contextualized the programs relative to US political practices, as Roger and Julie did, or were far less suspicious after having been exposed to the course content and realized the apolitical nature of CI pedagogy. American school administrators noted a similar trend among the local community. One school principal explained that when he was first setting up the program, "There were these conspiracy theorists out there . . . who saw the Confucius Institutes as the way to bring down the United States, as if somehow China has figured out that [our city] is a strategic center and the Chinese are coming in to take over." Five years later, a response was just as likely one principal's comment that "in some ways, China still remains a mystery to people. But in general, it's all become more normal. Few really care much any longer. Suspicion has become apathy. I no longer get the questions about Chinese teachers being spies or secret service kind of people."[7]

This concept of normal is central to this transition. The period of time in which this research occurred encompassed a great recession in the United States that, as discussed in chapter 1, was often attributed during American campaign seasons in part to China, but ended with a relative economic renewal, albeit one in which political hopefuls continued to blame China for a host of evils ranging from job loss to the perpetuation of the "hoax" of climate change. One could logically speculate in that context that relative economic vitality had lessened some of the more rampant concerns of a China threat in favor of a more comprehensive perspective on global well-being that might render communism, too, a less powerful trope for analysis. Yet while parents talked less about the evils of communism over the years, their focus continued to rest concretely upon what studying Chinese could offer to their children in ways that in effect rendered China and its system of governance somewhat irrelevant to the betterment of the US student self, except through its role of financial support for the language programs. This role, while sometimes begrudgingly respected for its long-term perspective (teaching today's students in the interest of future global relations), was rarely if ever read as philanthropic or generous at heart. As we saw in chapter 3's discussion of student rationales for studying Chinese and teacher strategies that hinged upon these desires, the teaching of Chinese in their schools had become more normal than the perceived "abnormality" of the communist government that funded it, nation and its system of governance thus unmoored from national language as a source of value.

The CC students who were centered in these concerns mentioned communism far less frequently during our conversations than their parents, and primarily did so in terms of their classroom experiences rather than in terms of their long-standing political perspectives, as one would expect of youth whose political experiences remained limited. Their understandings of communism, which were less ideologically and historically specific than those of their parents, had been augmented by information provided by their teachers, particularly discussions about teachers' experiences at home in China. When students mentioned communism during our conversations, they most commonly associated it with repression: "They can't do Facebook"; "They can't talk about certain topics"; "Their lives are completely censored"; "YouTube is banned, it's like North Korea."[8] Much of this perception was based on their own freedom of sociality—the ability to use social media—or the lens of their parents' historical experiences during the Cold War. Yet despite their often negative impressions, the students were curious about communism and recounted multiple incidents in the classroom in which they had asked their CC teachers what it actually meant in practice in China.[9] Rachel and Karl's daughter Kathleen, for instance, reported that when a student asked their teacher about what it was like living in a communist country, the teacher had "spent fifteen minutes explaining it, that communism in China isn't much like the communism that Americans have a perception of. That it's not pure communism. The government intervenes, but not like people here think." As our conversation continued, Kathleen described how during this and other discussions with their teachers, students wanted both to learn what communism was like and to convince the teacher that it was "not a good system of governance. The teacher told us that she couldn't explain it to us if we were so dead set against it, if we just assumed it had to be negative. She explained it as the government wanting to take care of everyone. To do that, individuals have to make sacrifices, but it's good for the whole." Admitting that "I know that my impression was a little negative at first," Kathleen acknowledged that "these classes have had a little effect on me": "I had always learned that everything about China was negative, that they had no freedom, but I understand it more now. Communism looks good on paper, but isn't implemented well. . . . I didn't know enough about China before to gauge how my impression has changed . . . , but it's pretty positive now."

Taken at face value, Kathleen's comments would seem to validate critics' fears about the potential effect of CI propaganda and image management. Clearly Kathleen and other students with whom I spoke had come to view China in a more positive light as a result of the language programs. But in many ways, as discussed in greater length in the following pages, this more favorable impression was often based less on the positive image of Chinese political ideology that the CIs attempt to project, for example, that communism was either desirable or viable, than on perceptions that China was becoming more like the United States in its practices and values and increasingly less of an Other, in effect denoting a growth of rapport based not upon appreciation for difference but on affinity.[10]

Political Absence and Political Presence: Texts and Teaching Practices

Given the negative impressions of communism that framed many US parents' and students' understandings of CIs, Hanban's effort to manage China's image had the potential to be a bit of a Sisyphean task. As discussed in chapter 1 of this book, a central operating premise of CI policy makers is that the gap between China's hard and soft power is primarily a function of foreigners' not understanding the "real" China rather than one of material and/or ideological concerns within China itself as the China-threat theory would suggest. Accordingly, as insinuated by the student comments given previously, the CI teachers' discussions of communism were spent not denying its existence but softening the perception of China as governed by a repressive state apparatus. Hanban-published or approved textbooks and other pedagogical materials were a central mechanism for countering student and parent concerns about the Chinese state. Yet, as we will see in the following pages, Hanban's strategy for modifying encounters with the imagined state to more affirmative ends was not through constituting a different "real" of the state but through avoiding it altogether, absenting the state from the nation-state in a manner that often had the countereffect of reaffirming it as a repressive mechanism of power.

One of the introductory textbooks adopted by several of the teachers I observed, *Chinese Paradise,* typifies Hanban's teaching materials. Its introduction sets the tone of the text:

> Do you know there is a country called China far away in the East? China is not only an ancient country but also a modern one, where live pandas and golden monkeys. In China there are 56 nationalities living in harmony. And there are also many scenic spots and historical sites, such as the Great Wall and the Terra Cotta Warriors and Horses. Besides, the famous fairy tale of the Handsome Monkey King, Sun Wukong, was created in

China. If you want to know more about China, please come and join us to learn Chinese, an ancient and beautiful language (Liu et al. 2005).[11]

Like most foreign language texts, the first two years of the Chinese Paradise series contain language lessons on general and seemingly nonpolitical topics including kinship, food, occupations, and the natural environment. The first-year text features photographs of historical monuments such as the Great Wall and the Tibetan Potala Palace that reinforce the "China" of the introductory paragraph: a Disneyland of exotic animals, kung fu, and historical architecture. The second-year *Chinese Paradise* text includes additional images of avant-garde architecture, upscale shopping malls in Beijing, and majestic Buddhist temples, illustrating a cosmopolitan China with a highly developed, consumer-oriented economy as well as a strong cultural tradition. Taken together, the images presented in these texts suggest that the Chinese culture presented in the early texts, which reproduced the patriotic culture of the Chinese Bridge summer program, is the cause of the nation's modernization and progress shown in the later texts. These images thereby strive to counteract the widely shared Western view that China's modernization is a product of political repression and massive environmental degradation. By contemplating China through its historical and cultural glories, avant-garde architecture, and endearing zoo animals rather than through its political system, which is perceived as antithetical to US ideologies and interests, these curricular materials are intended to serve the CCP's soft power policy goals by facilitating perceptions that the nation's increasing international engagement is neither antagonistic to the Western status quo nor repressively authoritarian despite its lack of democratic processes.

None of the language texts used by the CC teachers explicitly mention the Chinese state, government, or politics.[12] China's CCP politics do appear throughout the texts in more subtle ways; however, learners would need to have a fairly comprehensive knowledge of Chinese history to appreciate them. One of the vocabulary terms in a lesson on occupations, for example, is *nongmin,* which dictionaries and scholarly materials typically translate as *peasant.* The term *nongmin* has concrete and important political connotations within China, having served as an important political category during Mao's regime, in which it signaled a category of social belonging that was lauded by the Chinese state as the vanguard of revolution. Now, however, peasants are more commonly perceived as a drag on China's attainment of modernity. The Hanban textbook, however, translates *nongmin* as "farmer," an ideologically neutral term that resonates more with global agricultural workers than with communist revolution. One day, as students were struggling to translate "the tea is too strong," the teacher explained that the character for strong or concentrated is *nong*, which sounds the same as the *nong* in *nongmin* but is a different character. This coincidence led one student to send his classmates into peals of laughter when he declared, "That's how I'm going to remember it, the tea is too farmer," their laughter demonstrating that this politically loaded concept carried no meaning for students who lacked the context through which to grasp its more political implications. Although this exemplifies a moment in which CCP-originated political concepts are communicated in official texts aimed at children, the students so targeted had no historical knowledge through which to engage them as such. For these students, this was just another vocabulary lesson, one with more potential for comic relief than ideological indoctrination.

Although government officials and curriculum developers view the CI programs and materials as an important part of the CCP's soft power attempts to reframe perceptions of China as a threat to global welfare, my research findings make clear that these policy objectives do not always equate with policy effects. Because the Chinese state is routinely portrayed in the US public sphere as politically repressive, the purposefully apolitical stance of its pedagogical materials and classroom practices sometimes actually functioned to work against Hanban's efforts by appearing to be a concrete example of repression. In our conversations, students and parents regularly commented upon the dearth of explicit politics in the texts and classroom discussions, which they ironically understood as politically motivated rather than pedagogically imperative. The "classes have always felt politically closed," one student told me. "There's a big elephant in the room, just a limited amount of safe things to discuss. . . . The more they try to hide stuff, the more it seems as if there must be something to hide." Samantha, a senior, similarly noted that "in our textbooks we have some units, discussion on China—the cultural aspects, festivals—[but] nothing on modern history or the government." Particularly telling was a discussion I had with two sophomores who compared the much-publicized 1989 Tiananmen crackdown on public dissent to the censorship they perceived to be taking place in the classroom:

> *Carly:* When Tiananmen Square comes up in class, we all look at
> each other. The teachers talk about it as this beautiful square, a

nice place to visit. But it's like, "Wait, hold on, we're missing
some context."

Lindsey: If you ever get into these issues in the class, it gets steered
away. "Wait, there's no Tiananmen Square. Let's talk about
fluffy bunnies."

Tiananmen Square holds a particularly prominent place in Western
discussions of Chinese censorship and political repression. A 2006 *New York
Times* article on Internet censorship in China, for example, included side-
by-side images titled "What Chinese Searchers See" when they perform an
image search for "Tiananmen Square" on Google's China-based Web site,
Google.cn, and "What American Searchers See" when they do the same
search on its US-based Web site, Google.com (Kahn 2006).[13] The differences are striking. Whereas the Google.cn results feature the architectural
wonders of the square, smiling tourists, and a soldier raising the national
flag, Google.com results offer row upon row of images of "Tank Man," the
iconic photo of a lone protester blocking the forward progress of a line of
tanks shortly after the 1989 massacre of Chinese citizens around the square.[14]
This invocation of the 1989 event surfaced in multiple classroom observations and conversations with students and typified widespread student
perceptions of the Chinese state in general. Andrew, a senior, summoned its
symbolic power when discussing his Hanban-sponsored tour of China: "I
went to Tiananmen Square. I was so interested in going there, in the history
of Tiananmen. I asked the tour guide about 1989, [but] he just ignored me,"
which Andrew interpreted as a purposeful refusal to discuss the issue.
Although these students were not alive in 1989, the Tiananmen incident
remained a key symbol of the presumed power and oppression of the
Chinese state among them and in the West more generally.

For CI teachers, however, most of whom were attending elementary
school in 1989, Tiananmen holds different connotations than those that
dominate US apprehensions.[15] A common response when I asked teachers
about students' and parents' perceptions of China as defined by its political
ideologies was succinctly expressed by a second-year instructor, Liqin: "The
political issue, it's not the whole reality. It's not real life for people. Politics
isn't our whole life." Teachers' comments to me made clear that they understood that CIs were sometimes seen as propaganda machines, designed to sell
US children on the soft side of a perceived authoritarian, oppressive, communist regime. Indeed, one teacher reported to me that when she first arrived

on campus, a parent asked her directly if she intended to spread communism, to which she responded, "Can you even tell me what communism is? Because I can't." Nonetheless, students and their parents did not perceive the teachers' apolitical presentations in the classroom as a reflection of their broader understanding of or optimism about Chinese culture or economic development but as the epitome of politics itself, leading the targets of this soft power initiative to interpret political absence as authoritarian presence, thus reinforcing perceptions of a repressive Chinese governmental apparatus.

In fairness, as students themselves pointed out to me, elementary French and Spanish language textbooks used in US schools are not expected to dwell on contentious aspects of those countries' national histories. As one student explained, because "our teachers are from China, this gives us insight into the place, but really we are just here to learn the language—it's not a politics class." Nonetheless, the lack of political content within the Chinese classroom was often cited as "evidence" of Chinese censorship, propaganda, and compulsory politics. In contrast, several students and parents commended an American teacher who taught a Chinese history course for what they saw as his "objectivity" and willingness to "tell the truth" about China because he spent considerable class time covering China's troubled past.[16] Referring to this history course, Andrew said that it "taught me so much, it taught me a lot about Tiananmen Square," his wording seemingly equating knowledge of Tiananmen Square to a comprehensive knowledge of China as if the repression symbolized the substance of the nation. By attributing the absence of politics to politics itself, the students demonstrated Trouillot's (2001) claim that the effects of government institutions and practices are never exclusively a result of their institutional efforts.

All of the CI teachers I interviewed, however, recognized that Hanban's attempts to depoliticize the classroom had this paradoxical effect and so had developed various teaching strategies to address the issue. One of these was the use of comparisons between China and the United States to normalize China by rendering it similar to the students' experience. Responding to a prerecorded listening exercise that included a story about a young man buying red clothes for his girlfriend, for instance, one teacher quipped, "Too much red. It sounds like a Lady Gaga outfit."[17] Another day's discussion, during an off-subject tangent about stereotypes, similarly occasioned a sympathetic response from the teacher that established middle-class equivalence. When a student made a comment about "white girls" in the United States, who "wear yoga pants, drink Starbucks constantly, and always have their iPhones out," the teacher responded: "Oh, that's just like Chinese girls. Always on the phone, taking selfies, drinking Starbucks, posting pictures of themselves online." These examples illustrate what Amy Stambach calls "domain shifts" (2014, 57–59), in which teachers and students reinterpret information to make sense of it within the context of their own experiences, allowing CI teachers and their students to see these agents simultaneously as of and not of the state and their actions in the classroom as generated through these student-teacher interactions rather than solely as a form of soft power propaganda.

Another example of this technique of creating equivalence, one used by all the teachers I observed, was presenting visual images of Chinese schools to demonstrate that student life was similar around the world. While conversations about expensive coffee drinks and athletic gear elicited supportive understanding from the students, the comparison with educational practices tended to backfire, as US students often interpreted these images and documentaries on student life in China as indicative of Chinese oppression. To Tyler, a middle school student, the students in the videos appeared to suffer from a "tyrannical government" under which they "have no life, they just sit all proper, not talking, they can't talk in class unless the teacher talks to them." US students' expectations that education should be "fun" led them to view classroom discipline as a marker of the CCP's repressive authoritarianism rather than as a familiar or culturally specific instructional technique. In my discussions with students about these videos, only one mentioned Chinese student life in a positive light: "Wow, their schools. They work really hard, how do they do it? They are really smart. I hope our Chinese class learns from this." In later years, teachers became more discerning about how certain curricular materials intended to indicate global commonality simply reinforced students' preconceptions of essentialized difference and as a result began to exclude them from their teaching repertoire. "It's kind of scary to them," one teacher said of her students' responses to videos about educational practices in China: " 'Did you really go through this?' they asked me. 'How can Chinese students survive this?' They can't match this video with what they know about me." This teacher faced a perhaps unavoidable conundrum. While the pedagogical materials were meant to insinuate equivalence, the CI model of value structured through traditional culture was predicated on the production of exotic difference. Yet exotic difference, as discussed earlier in the book, was more often read as a form of value for the student who managed to preserve it in the domain of self-production rather than national value. Or difference had become so "familiar" as to have no ability to enhance the self and hence was of little significance to the construction of that self.

A second strategy teachers adopted to decrease students' and parents' perceptions of political control in their classrooms that reinforced assumptions about Chinese state repression in general was to ignore some of Hanban's teaching guidelines. Zhen, who had been teaching Chinese to foreigners both in the United States and in China for more than a decade, insisted to me that Hanban instructs teachers to "do whatever you want" in the classroom. When I pointed out that by "do whatever," Hanban meant with official Hanban materials, Zhen responded with a withering critique of the official texts and announced that she had dispensed with them and adopted the Boston-published Chinese textbooks also used by Chinese language professors at my own university. Zhen also frequently ignored "suggestions" about ancillary materials sent by Hanban, such as a video of the celebrations of the sixtieth anniversary of the PRC's founding, which features goose-stepping soldiers and massive displays of weaponry and was viewed in the United States as a "symbol of [the] country's rapidly expanding might" (NBC News 2009). Zhen admitted that the video was unlikely to have its intended effect upon her students:

> For example, the sixtieth anniversary. In China, I thought it was great, but I realized that here they might not think so, so I didn't use it. I thought it might remind people of North Korea. . . . It seemed like it was back thirty years. We were proud of all the stuff, but also a little worried about going back. We won't [go back], of course; we argue so much about politics these days in China.

In rejecting Hanban's curricular materials such as this video, Zhen recognized that what might chart national pride in one context could be seen as military threat in another, as a reflection of totalitarian possibility rather than of what she viewed as a modernized and reformed political system, demonstrating that the interests and identity of the government and of its local representatives are neither necessarily identical nor aligned in purpose.

Yiwen, another CC teacher, was similarly critical of the official teaching materials and like Zhen had almost entirely dispensed with their use in her classroom, a process that has the possible effect in perception of decoupling the Chinese language from China and the CI Chinese teachers from the Chinese state. "The pictures are stupid," Yiwen asserted as she handed me an offending text. "They are silly and distracting to students. It's like a children's book, and the questions that are asked are not questions that real people would ask." Yiwen attributed this problem both to "professors who write the books who don't know much about teaching in an actual class-room" and to CCP interference: "The problem with the Confucius Insti-tutes in general is that you can't separate the language programs from the government because the government interferes so much. If the government wants to make these programs better, they need to separate government and language. Most of the people in the program are just teachers. They don't know anything about politics." At this point we began to discuss some of the controversies over the CIs that were caused by government interference, including a recent incident (discussed at greater length in chapter 6) in which Xu Lin, chief executive of the Confucius Institutes, ordered pages torn out of the European Association for Chinese Studies conference program that advertised a Taiwanese foundation as a sponsor. "The government leaves us speechless sometimes, at the stupidity," Yiwen retorted in exasperation. She was well aware that such interference was ultimately detrimental to Hanban policy goals. "I see the Spanish program from Spain and I think of it as a language program, not a government program. One American teacher asked me if the Confucius Institutes were set up so that China could take over the United States. I responded that there were Confucius Institutes all over the world: 'Do you see China taking over the whole world? Just because people speak English everywhere, it's a global language, do you see Britain taking over the whole world? Is this a concern?' . . . China needs to let the politics go."

In an example of what Gupta calls the "pluricenteredness" of the state (2012, 62) and what Hoag calls "being within but not necessarily of the state" (2010, 20), the teachers, despite sharing a normative belief in the value of CI intentions with Hanban officials and curriculum designers, regularly contested official guidelines. In contrast to arguments that the state's agency, here understood as the effectiveness of policy, depends on policy targets' perception of unity among agents of the state (Mitchell 1991), I observed the opposite: the perceived unity of the state diminished that effectiveness when the state was imagined as a coherent, censorial body of governance. Yet at the same time, while the pluricentered nature of the imagined state posed methodological dilemmas for studying its constitution, these conflicts and divergences in the CI classroom also revealed how "the state" as an imagined, reified entity dissolves upon "close inspection" (Harvey 2005,126). When students and parents assessed teachers as embodying the state, they tended to assume the state as a model of tyranny. When teachers critiqued and diverged from its policies, students and parents began to envision a nascent Chinese political modernity, which has the potential effect, somewhat ironically, of improving the chances that the soft power goals of Hanban and the PRC government might actually be achieved.

Affable States and Everyday Lives

Over dinner one evening with CC teachers Meirong and Liqin, both of whom had been teaching in the United States for two years, Liqin, her frustration palpable, addressed what she saw as local perceptions of China. "It's all this negative stuff about China," she explained with a heavy sigh. Her students, she reported, "know about the one-child policy, they get these ideas from their parents. They think that if you have a second child, the government will kill the baby." Meirong, too, noted that "there are misunderstandings. It's unfair. They think the policy is inhumane, but then they turn around and complain that there are too many people in China and that the Chinese people are out to seize everything." While I sympathized with her frustration about the barrage of critiques she encountered about her home country, I laughed out loud when Liqin recounted another of these hyperbolic suspicions of Chinese state repression: "I had an American teacher ask me—he was going to China that summer—if he would get stalked and followed and spied on. I told him, 'You're not that important.'"

These types of negative perceptions of China and the Chinese state were precisely what has led China to deploy teachers like Meirong and Liqin as the public embodiment of the state and the CCP that funded the CI program. While texts and pedagogical strategies were important elements in this image management, the human contact with and experiences of the CI teachers themselves were essential to the soft power efforts of the CI programs. Liqin stressed to me that one of her main goals in the United States was to employ her own experiences to illustrate that politics was not the defining factor of her daily life, to "teach students about the real China" and thus allow them to "make their own conclusions": "I show them about Chinese students' lives, about the modern cities. They are surprised by this. . . . I show them that we are a different generation. We are pretty open about things, more open to talk about stuff. . . . There really isn't any need for limits. My point is that I just tell them the truth, that it's normal to hear different opinions. . . . That's a really good part of the job for me, to share that."[18]

Based on my observations and conversations, it was these personal relations with the CC teachers more than anything else that decreased students' and parents' negative perceptions about the Chinese state by allowing them to envision a humane social order in China that complied with their ideas about individual agency, uniqueness, and universality.[19] As one parent put it, "Teachers tell stories about their own lives, their experiences, that's what the students remember. It's really these cultural influences that are the more influential." Students' comments to me affirmed that the teachers' stories about contemporary everyday life in China, living in modern apartment complexes, dining in international chain restaurants, and wearing popular Western brands of clothing generated soft power more effectively in the CI classroom than official curriculum materials or apolitical classroom discussions. Teachers recognized that this personalization helped humanize them in the eyes of their students, even when their examples revealed cultural differences with a typical American way of life. As one teacher recounted, "One of the fun parts is that through meeting me and learning Chinese, they also look at America in a different way. My [non-English-speaking] mom came in, and the students got to 'interview' her. One of the questions was 'Do you like pizza?' My mom said, 'No,' and they all thought this was wild. They start to begin to understand that not everyone thinks or does things like they do. It opens their minds to new ideas."[20] The Chinese language learners I spoke with responded positively to the teachers' personalizing efforts and, as a result of the more intimate contact that the students had with CC teachers, began to see China less as the epitome of an authoritarian state.

Samantha, a senior quoted earlier, explicitly described how this process had worked for her: "I've asked [the teacher] a lot about China, she's very open . . . and I know her really well now. . . . It's kind of fun to ask about the [controversial] stuff sometimes. . . . She's thoughtful about her answers. . . . I've gotten to know her, not just as a stereotype of a person from China." Whereas the CIs' attempts to rid the classroom of explicit politics often resulted in perceptions of censorship and of the state as an agent of political subjugation, Samantha's comments reveal that this "openness" on the part of the teachers led students and parents to see them as candid and introspective individuals rather than subordinated representatives of a socialist state.

Yet the teachers were also aware that, as embodiments of the state, their relationship to its ideologies and institutions risked damaging the growing perceptions of common humanity they had forged with students. This was particularly true in terms of the teachers' participation in Communist Party politics. Some teachers were CCP members and some were not; nonetheless, they knew that at least some parents perceived their presence in the United States as dependent on their membership and thereby viewed them as unfree transmitters of communist ideology. Meirong confessed a fear to me that if her party membership became public, people "won't believe what I say, that I'm just saying government stuff. But I could quit the party right now and I would say the same thing. It's not the party telling me what to say. It's like they can't believe I am a party member and I love shopping." One of the American teachers at Liqin and Meirong's school recounted a conversation in which several CC teachers similarly explained to her that while Americans see CCP membership as something extraordinary, Chinese see it differently. "Oh my goodness," the CC teacher exclaimed, "being a CCP member is like having a Costco card!"

Although the teachers' insistence that their ideas and conversations were not products of state control or censorship might be dismissed as simply parroting the official Chinese line, they intended their comments to reflect that the quotidian experience of state interference in their personal lives had been relatively less than that experienced by previous generations and less than was assumed by outside observers who were the targets of soft power policy. Politics was not, they were effectively arguing, the determining factor of meaning in their lives. But in either case, these relationships' potential to produce new interpretations of the Chinese state and China was demonstrated by a narrative offered by Claire, a sophomore student, one day over lunch. "I thought China was really third world and communist," she explained; "I had a really bad idea of what China was. Now I know it's not like that." When I asked what she meant by being "really communist," she responded, "I'd heard stories, that they killed the girls, tortured them. This was really wrong. I heard that people had to abide by the government, if they talked back, they went to prison. That was wrong, too. It's not like a democracy, but it's not crazy tyrannical rule." When I asked what had led her to change her opinion, she specifically pinpointed her teacher's personalizing her instruction: "She talks about it a lot, she talks about her everyday life. I thought citizens were inspired by fear . . . but the Chinese . . . are just normal, they don't worry about dying. It's not like she goes to the store and waits in line and there is nothing there. She goes shopping just like we do, she does the same things."[21]

That teachers proffered this freedom to consume ("she goes shopping just like we do") as part of the "real China" and that students accepted it as evidence of political reforms and growing modernization reflects a shared acceptance of US discourses of modernity and value in which freedom of choice is reflected through consumption. Through this example, which I heard frequently over the years, students' notions of modernity became a way to locate China within a normative framework of global citizenship. As students became better acquainted with the teachers, the value they placed on individual agency and uniqueness led them to view the Chinese state more favorably by perceiving it as freeing its citizens to act independently of its will.[22] According to these student conversations, if teachers are able to "shop just like we do" rather than wait in breadlines for basic goods and can talk freely about politics rather than just parrot CCP propaganda, as is discussed at length in chapter 6, the Chinese state can be understood as no longer exerting its "crazy tyrannical rule" over its citizens. For these students, this had the effect of elevating China into the world of the "particularly universal" rather than the "universally particular" (Eng et al. 2012, 5), in which "universal" indicates a very culturally specific notion of "proper" state-society relations that free citizens to consume and in particular indicates assumptions about Chinese state repression of its citizens.

Conversely, CI teachers mobilized shopping in the United States to demonstrate their global buying power and the nation's consumerist, global modernity in relation to the West and as an improvement upon it. In a change from a recent past in which US travelers to China returned home to regale their friends with tales of cheaply tailored suits and inexpensive knock-off Nikes (Schmindle 2010), these Chinese teachers spoke with glee about how designer goods were significantly less expensive in the United States and how they entertained requests from friends and family in China to act as purchasing agents. Indeed, a continuing conversational thread in a series of Skype interviews I had with Changying, a future CI teacher who was living in Beijing at the time, was her intended purchase of the latest iPhone, which was substantially cheaper in the United States than in China. These relocations of "the bargain" had the paradoxical effect, implicitly at least, of inverting the hierarchies of power in which cheap consumption marks a lower stage of development. They also implicitly signaled alternative images of global place that are foretold through consumption practices as they reinforced the shoppers as agentive subjects free to make individual choices.

In the CI setting, to use the shopping example, the teachers' ability to make complex consumer choices had become shorthand for many Westerners' expectations about the potential for democratic governance in China. As I have explored elsewhere, this popular conflation of market privatization and democratic politics holds that as China develops economically (i.e., increases its private market mechanisms), it will also advance ethically (i.e., become a more democratic society) (Hubbert 2014b). In this paradigm, shopping thus symbolizes the replacement of state determinism with individual choice. But even as shopping led students to see the teachers as "real" rather than as state-sanctioned automatons, more like a Western "us" than a Chinese Other, it also affirmed the success of the Chinese state's development model and advanced its soft power projections around the world through buttressing a consumerist development model that scholars have argued "purchases" the quelling of dissent.[23] Thus, it may be more helpful to consider teachers' personalized improvisations not as inherently or necessarily dismissive of Hanban's pedagogical instructions or as a form of resistance, but as forms of mētis, of "contextualized local knowledge and practice" (Li 2005, 384) that may have been beyond the scope of official policy but upheld the bureaucratic schemes of the state all the same. That is, the less "state-like" the teachers seemed, the more their everyday practices actually worked in the service of the state and implied both China and the state as increasingly affable entities.

Conclusion

While scholars have called for growing attention to the translocal nature of the state, this chapter offers parents' and students' perspectives to suggest a transnational approach, exploring how global constituencies experience and imagine the Chinese state. As the findings of my research in CI classrooms demonstrate, how the targets of this soft power project understood the Chinese state depended at least as much on that local audience's cultural practices and historical discourses as on Hanban's policy intentions, practices, and discourses that worked to both signify and structure China's place in the world. They also make clear that the disparate parts, in

this case the teachers and texts, often had different and sometimes conflicting agendas and policy practices despite their being constituent elements of
a broader institutional structure known as the state and finding common
value in the state's policy goals, making clear that states are "multilayered
[and] contradictory" institutions (Sharma and Gupta 2006, 6) and inherently
messy (Li 2005).

As this chapter shows, soft power attempts to influence the global
construction of legitimacy are ultimately, at least partially, dependent upon
local discourses and agendas that interact with global policy to create new
nodes of contact and new forms of imagination. The culturally situated exhibitions of the state that emerged from the interactions among students, course
materials, and teachers in CI classrooms demonstrate that as long as communism remained the central trope through which China was understood, the
perceived unity between state and society undermined the intended effect of
CI soft power policies. The findings of this study thus suggest that the power
of states to enact policy has as much to do with how the targets of that policy
experience and thus contemplate the state as it has to do with policy intention
or implementation. In this case, the policy targets' perceptions of an authoritarian Chinese state were influenced by classroom experiences of state censorship and the agency of Chinese citizens in ways that both reinforced and
challenged their images of communist governance.

The culturally situated representations of the state that emerge from
CI classroom interactions allow us to contextualize and problematize the
means through which Cold War rhetoric is recast and recirculated in the
contemporary, ostensible, post–Cold War historical moment, thus interro-
gating assumptions about China's "difference" as soft power policy targets
negotiate complex and disputed understandings of China, Chinese culture,
and Chinese politics. Trouillot (2001) urges anthropologists to examine
the effects of the state while Mitchell (1991) suggests concentrating on the
"state effect," defined not as the consequences of state policies but as the discursive practices that create the perception of a bifurcated state-society,
a central component of dominant Western assumptions about modernity
that frames responses to the CI state. When communism emerges as an
important trope through which to understand China, state and society are
understood as coterminous rather than separate entities and the "state effect"
is in fact diminished. The more the agents of the state appeared unified
with state intentions, the less CIs' soft power policies had their intended
effect.

Yet as Li (2005) has pointed out of resistance in a different context, to understand the teacher's pedagogical practices as resistance to the state or shopping as an oppositional discourse would fail to recognize that these actions remain embedded within and continue to advance the goals of a soft power policy intended to soften impressions of the political goals of the state. Studying the state, as Gupta argues, involves a certain amount of "misrecognition" (Gupta 2012, 53), for no singular branch embodies the state in its entirety, either structurally or philosophically, and despite discursive unity, state representatives often have different and sometimes conflicting agendas and practices. Although CI teachers may have shared Hanban's soft power policy intentions to create a different vision of the "real" China, their diverse engagements with official pedagogical guidelines allow us to problematize the perceptions and depictions of the Chinese state as a monolithic entity that feature prominently in global representations of Chinese difference and exception. When students no longer perceived representatives of the state as ineluctably unified with it, soft power was at its most effective and the state was perceived as more benevolent. In the case of these CIs, soft power cultural engagements functioned, even if unintentionally, to "hide" the mechanisms of soft power in a manner that could arguably augment the power of the Chinese state. Indeed, this lack of cohesion among the various manifestations of the state and between the intention and implementation of state policy—what we might call the "moral economy of disagreement"—may paradoxically strengthen the state by undermining perceptions of its uniformity and might.[24]

CHAPTER 6

Rethinking "Free" Speech
Debates over Academic Independence

From the time the first Confucius Institute was established in the United States in 2004, scholars, journalists, and independent citizens have voiced concerns about the possibility for freedom of speech within the language programs. The Chinese government's domestic suppression of free speech is well documented. Indeed, as President Xi Jinping has publicly declared, in China, higher education "must adhere to correct political orientation" (Phillips 2016) and all media "must be surnamed Party" and "love the Party, protect the Party and serve the Party" (quoted in Bandurski 2016), and by many accounts, this censorship has worsened since Xi assumed office. As part of the context in which CI watchers, students, and parents understand the language programs, in 2018 China ranked 176 out of 180 on the World Press Freedom Index for the fourth year in a row and was dead last on Freedom House's 2017 Freedom on the Net list for the third year in a row. These long-standing positions and practices have understandably generated apprehensions about the government's propensity to engage in similar practices beyond its national borders, concerns further exacerbated in the case of the CI language programs because one of their explicit goals is the creation of a highly favorable image of China that will further its economic and political goals and because there have been instances where Hanban has directly interfered with programming on campuses with CIs.[1]

In late 2013, a provocative and widely read article by University of Chicago anthropologist Marshall Sahlins in *The Nation* (Sahlins 2013) set off a firestorm of public controversy over these concerns about the programs in online forums, congressional hearings, local newspapers, and academic conferences.[2] Six months later, the American Association of University Professors (AAUP) went so far as to recommend that US host institutions either end their CI agreements with Hanban or renegotiate them to maintain control over the programs' administration and implementation (AAUP 2014).[3] As a result of these debates and recommendations, several high-profile educational institutions, including the University of Chicago, the Toronto School District, and Pennsylvania State University, decided to shutter their programs. As the debate raged and as I presented and published the findings of my research on the topic, I was contacted by a reporter from the *Chronicle of Higher Education* and several documentary filmmakers, including from NBC News, seeking interviews, and specifically asking for evidence of censorship and the repression of free speech in CI classrooms. I also began to find anecdotes from my research being cited as proof that CIs were a threat to academic freedom in the classroom by a variety of media outlets, from the *Chicago Tribune* to *Bloomberg News,* and in Sahlins's own highly visible efforts to close the Confucius Institute hosted by his campus.

Yet not everyone familiar with the programs or engaged in these debates shared those critics' fears about threats to freedom of speech in CI classrooms. Some scholars and school administrators, including several who contributed to the extensive *ChinaFile* debate over the Confucius Institutes, claimed that Hanban had never attempted to interfere in the programming at their schools and argued that, rather than pose a threat, the Chinese language programs had opened "new opportunities for faculty, students and the community to engage with diverse international points of view" (*ChinaFile* 2014 [Hanson]) and made Chinese instruction available to "legions of young Americans who would otherwise not have an opportunity to experience that language" (*ChinaFile* 2014 [Kapp]). Even as some schools discontinued their associations with Hanban, others established new CIs to launch Chinese language programs or to augment their current Chinese classes. As unsurprising as this may have been, I also started to find my research results, sometimes even the same anecdotes that were used to support the opposite position, offered as evidence of the benign nature of the language programs, at least in terms of their impact on freedom of speech in the classroom.[4]

This chapter explores the debates around freedom of speech—defined as a fundamental human right in the United Nations' Universal Declaration of Human Rights—as they pertain to the CIs.[5] From my years of research in China and with the CIs, I understand and sympathize with concerns about ideologically tainted knowledge production, and later in the chapter I offer specific examples of the different ways knowledge is produced in the Chinese language classroom that support both sides of the debate over freedom of speech. However, I offer these data not, as will be clear, to argue that some form of ethnographic "truth" arises from these materials but to shift the terms of the debate, in effect, to make an argument for rethinking the metric that is used to make sense of the normative implications of the concept of freedom of speech.[6]

As this chapter argues, the mixed readings and uses of my research actualize something more than a diversity of perspectives regarding China's soft power projects. Most fundamentally, they reflect the role that an ethnographic approach can play in discerning what is actually happening in the classroom setting, as opposed to analyses based on printed documents or in abstract speculations on the programs. Although commentators on both sides of the debate over censorship and freedom of speech in CIs often buttress their arguments with specific examples and anecdotes drawn from their experiences with CIs at their own institutions, a number of commentators have also acknowledged how little of the extant analysis has examined actual in situ pedagogical practices.[7] As some of those calling for more analysis of on-the-ground practices suspected and as this ethnographic examination makes clear, the classroom engagements within these language programs are considerably more complex than current discussions would suggest, offering both what Perry Link has called an "overly rosy" image of China (*ChinaFile* 2014) that ignores the destructive and repressive nature of the CCP's political and economic systems *and* a significant amount of criticism and debate. Yet, it is not mere complexity that is at stake here, for in embedding questions of freedom of speech within practice, this chapter also challenges a conception of freedom of speech that too often views only one kind of speech as free and regards CI personnel as mindless functionaries stripped of their own agency. These widely held assumptions about what counts for free speech and liberal subjectivity, the chapter will posit, can have the unfortunate effect of foreclosing more expansive understandings of freedom and political agency in the modern world.[8]

Unfree Speech

I began my research on the CI language programs in 2011 fully expecting to find numerous examples of ways in which they attempted to produce an idealized view of the Chinese nation through suppressing other perspectives. As a longtime scholar of China, I came to these expectations not only because of the debates over the programs but also from having engaged in years of research on China's massive soft power projects including the 2008 Summer Olympics and 2010 Shanghai Expo, which were occasioned at least in part by the CCP's desire to project a particular optimistic image of the nation to the global audience that unambiguously inhibits the repressive and alarming manifestations of China's rapid development and political subjugation. I was also deeply curious about how CI teachers would address or stifle discussion about sensitive political topics such as environmental destruction or human rights violations, most particularly about what are often called "the three Ts"—Tibet, Taiwan, and Tiananmen. And find such examples I did.

As eventually became apparent, these attempts to control the image of China presented in the programs fell into three broad categories: representations of history that resembled propaganda; the aggregation of positive imagery about the nation; and the avoidance of conversations on controversial topics. Among the more obvious examples of soft power image management in the classrooms I visited were the content of the CI-authorized textbooks and reference books.[9] CI history textbooks, for example, routinely ignored the Mao era and focused instead on the glories of the imperial past (such as China's invention of gunpowder and the compass) or on the nation's more recent successes (such as in athletics and space exploration). In its references to international conflicts, these books consistently presented China as a peaceful and stabilizing force rather than as an aggressor. One text, for instance, referred to the Korean War as the "War of US Aggression in Korea."[10] According to another, "In 1950, civil war broke out in Korea. The United States immediately sent troops to interfere in internal affairs . . . [and] manipulated the UN Security Council. . . . China insisted on a peaceful solution. . . . Upon request of the Democratic People's Republic of Korea, China made a decision to aid Korea, crushed the imperialist aggressive ambitions, and enhanced China's international prestige" (Overseas Chinese Affairs Office 2015, 253).[11] Although many international media commentators and private US citizens have viewed China's recent rise as an economic and military threat to global stability, the books and videos shown in the CI classrooms I observed presented demonstrations of that power, such as China's massive military parades, as evidence of modernization rather than military threat. Other historical textbooks and reference books I examined focused primarily on economic development, including lauding the Ming dynasty as an example of China's earlier cosmopolitan sophistication and posing the present era as its natural successor. One of these, for example, *Common Knowledge about Chinese History,* included chapters on Confucius, Sun Tzu's *Art of War,* the Silk Road, and early pioneering scientists, but also prefaced the text with a discussion of the rapid rise of China's status on the international stage and the "phenomenal" increase in Chinese-language learners around the world, hinting at a causal relationship between power and desire for cultural access.

By suggesting a linear path from a glorious past to a superpower present, such curricular materials mirrored official rhetorical strategies commonly exercised by the government in mainland China. One such strategy is a change in the language of a common public narrative from what was earlier termed China's national "rise" to its current "rejuvenation" and "peaceful development" (Mueller 2013; Zhang 2010), as also discussed in chapter 1.[12] This discursive tactic is intended to depict China's growth not as a rise from an abject or backward position but as a revitalization of a nation that had once occupied a vaunted place in global hierarchies of power, and therefore as a legitimate *return* to power rather than a conquest or usurpation of power that would threaten the global hierarchy of nation-states. Materials that presented China as a peaceful and diplomatic global player similarly reflected the increasing CCP promotion of such seemingly apolitical Confucian concepts as harmony (*hexie*) and civilization (*wenming*) to pose the Chinese government as more concerned with good governance and domestic tranquility than with global domination (Hubbert 2017; Mahoney 2008).

These strategies are thus consistent with the soft power mission of the CIs to project a less threatening image of China to the world. "When people know China better," a 2006 article in the *People's Daily* proclaimed within a discussion about the Confucius Institutes, "they will find out that harmony is an essential part of China's tradition, and a country that values harmony poses no threat to the world" (cited in Niquet 2014, 79). And it is this correspondence between CI classroom materials and the dominant political narratives within China that leads many critics of the CI programs to view those materials (and the programs in general) as propaganda machines intended to shape the ways in which students understand China and to counteract US media narratives of Chinese aggression, domination, and backwardness. Sahlins, for example, includes the description of the

Korean War quoted earlier in his much-cited pamphlet on the CIs under the heading, "Censorship in University Activities: Direct Chinese Political Influences" (2015, 34–35). Indeed, the discovery that CI materials described the Korean War as a war of US aggression caused a minor scandal in US schools, leading Hanban to remove a related animation from its Web page that, according to Hughes, "demonized the United States forces and portrayed the Chinese soldiers as heroes" (2014, 70), although the textbooks containing this narrative remained in CI classrooms.[13]

The second form of pedagogy that CI critics often categorize as stifling freedom of speech is the programs' presentation of highly positive images of China that disregard some of the more troubling aspects of its modernization. As discussed in chapter 5, CI language textbooks engaged heavily in these forms of image management. Introductory texts staged China as a pristine theme park of pandas, kung fu, and historical architecture, while more advanced texts offered images of avant-garde architecture, upscale shopping malls, and majestic Buddhist temples to compose an image of a cosmopolitan China with a highly developed, consumer-oriented economy and strong cultural traditions, illustrations Hanban must have assumed US students would admire. As described in chapter 4, these are also the kinds of images that are staples in the traditional Chinese craft activities that take place in nearly every CI classroom and on the Chinese Bridge summer program. Like CI history materials, the language learning materials made no mention of the political, environmental, or human rights issues that tend to dominate US reporting on China.

This selective presentation of China-positive images was reinforced by a third mode of image management that I observed during classroom activities, the avoidance of controversial topics and criticisms of China. According to the CI teachers whom I interviewed, their pre-posting orientation training in China had included explicit instruction on how to avoid or discourage politically charged conversations. As one high school CC teacher told me, "In reality, I had not just one, or two, or three, but all of the Hanban trainers tell me, 'It doesn't really matter how much language the student learns. What is most important is that you be a positive image for China. Let the neighbors, the community, the school see you and let them know how positive the Chinese are, give them positive pictures of China.'"

In practice, I observed teachers instructing students who wished to study Tibet-related topics to employ a cultural rather than political perspective, for instance, and discussing Tiananmen Square only as a tourist destination rather than as a site of governmental repression.[14] I also saw teachers unequivocally presenting Taiwan as just another province of China, and indeed Hanban's initial agreements with host institutions included a clause that schools must abide by the one-China policy that recognizes Taiwan as a province of the mainland, illuminating how certain PRC-approved political positions were an overt and documented precondition for CIs rather than a surreptitious pedagogical practice once they are established in a host school.[15] Despite the later elimination of that clause, in all the classrooms I visited the official one-China position was reinforced by the cartographic hegemony of maps on classroom walls that presented Taiwan and mainland China in the same color, indicating their common belonging to the PRC nation-state.[16] A CC teacher, who had years prior become a US citizen but was originally from Taiwan, told me that Hanban had required that she remove a small Taiwan flag she had displayed in her classroom beside the PRC flag. While many students knew very little about China's emergence as a superpower on the global stage other than in terms of its economic might, some who were more attuned to political issues surrounding China's rise to power would try to goad the CC teachers into addressing those controversies. One CC teacher, for example, recounted an incident in which "we were learning country names and one student mentioned 'Taiwan.' I was mad. I told him Taiwan was a province, and all the students rolled their eyes at each other and went 'oooohhh.'" Rather than respond directly, however, the teacher followed the instructions she had received from Hanban: "When we were doing our training, they told us if this stuff came up, just to calm down, to not talk about it in class too much."[17]

As discussed in chapter 5, in my conversations with students, they often viewed what they perceived as implicit and explicit repression of controversial topics and negative portrayals of China in their CI classrooms as confirmation of their own impressions about Chinese political repression more broadly. One high school student, for example, was well aware that what the teachers "throw at you in school" was "not entirely accurate": "They are trying to get in touch with the rest of the world, be seen as an equal, but there is a clear avoidance of controversial issues. When the teacher talked about Tiananmen, about how it is this beautiful square, I kept waiting for discussion about the protests. My parents were incredibly surprised that they didn't talk about the protests—how do you talk about

Tiananmen and not talk about the protests? When she was talking about Tiananmen, we asked her what else happened there, this set her off! She got all red and mad and said, 'We don't talk about that kind of stuff.' "[18]

Some parents of CC students were not only worried about the suppression of information about China by the presentation of only benign accounts of the nation, but also suspected the teachers and materials of having explicitly propagandistic purposes. One parent who told me that she had been skeptical about the content of her son's textbook joked that "the red cover might have been a bad color choice." She clearly viewed the color red as an emblem of communist political values that, despite the ostensible end of the Cold War, many Americans continued to view as anathema and potentially frightening, unaware that the potentially problematic textbook was actually an American text from a Boston-based publisher.[19] Similarly, as discussed earlier in chapter 5, another parent worried about the positive image of China being projected in his child's Confucious Classroom, which he suspected of being potentially dangerous communist propaganda: "We see the negative stuff in the news, but nothing negative comes up in the classroom. The teacher never says anything about Mao, Tibet. The PR is more subtle. They are trying to portray a very positive image and impression of China. What has bothered me is that [my daughter] now thinks communism is a viable form of government. . . . It's not."

Free Speech

Given the controversy over CIs and the often negative media portraits of China, I, like many of the students and parents I interviewed, began my investigation into the CIs ready to read censorship and image management intentions into even the most banal of textbook materials and teacher comments in the classroom. Over time, however, I began to wonder whether it was entirely accurate or fair to see these examples as unambiguous censorship or as incontrovertible proof that the Chinese CI teachers were either willfully complicit with or dupes of the authoritarian aims of the Chinese government. After all, I began to think, we would not expect US teachers in ESL classrooms to insert discussions of America's weaknesses and historical traumas into their language instruction, nor accuse them of performing as state puppets for not doing so.[20] I similarly started to doubt whether a CI teacher's positive presentation of China's current experience, of its contemporary architectural wonders, for example, must necessarily be construed as thoughtless propaganda, or whether a Chinese teacher's agreement with some aspect of state performance necessarily replicated a desire to "escape from freedom," to borrow Slavoj Žižek's phrase (2005, 119).[21]

Students raised the issue of different normative expectations for different nation-states to me more than once. During a conversation with two students, for example, one observed that the CI teachers "do focus on the good stuff, but at the same time every country does that," to which her schoolmate responded, "Yeah, when you're learning German, you're not learning about the Holocaust," both recognizing that the teaching of Chinese was sometimes being held to standards that are not applied to instruction in other languages. In addition to recognizing explicitly that contentious national histories were not the focus of instruction and intended learning in Chinese language classrooms, their comments implicitly acknowledged their awareness that critics expected unbalanced assessments of Chinese history because the programs were both perceived to be and are ideologically motivated. Similarly, in response to my arguably overly leading questions about possible free speech violations by CI teachers in the classroom, a high school senior I had interviewed several times over the years of my research responded caustically, "Well, we're missing the iron fist of Mao Zedong, just kidding. If you're looking for me to say that there is this propaganda going on in the classroom, well, it's not there."

As my research continued, such comments pushed me to question my perspective more closely. I eventually concluded that, in my readiness to find examples of censorship, repression, and propagandizing, I had been overlooking a good deal of what even CI critics would define as "free speech" by CI teachers and Hanban administrators, on study tours to China, and in conversations with me, students, parents, and one another outside of the classroom.[22] During my observations and interviews, for example, very few of the teachers stuck to an "official script" of soft power image management. While most of the teachers were excited about teaching their native language and sharing information about China and its modernization, they were also willing to discuss political controversies during our conversations and even openly expressed frustration with the political motivations of the program and the fears of a "China threat" that it engendered. During interviews and dinner conversations, many teachers were, in fact, quite disparaging of the CI program, frequently for what they perceived as a waste of financial and personnel resources that might be better spent improving China's own impoverished rural educational system.

A particularly common source of frustration among the CI teachers was the curricular materials provided by Hanban. Teachers complained about the "irrelevant" vocabulary included in the official textbooks and that it was sometimes "hard to find something appropriate" to the needs of US learners when "the texts focus on ancient China." As one university-level CI instructor told me disparagingly, within the context of a conversation about his perceptions of the ineffectiveness of the materials and the programs in general, "If this is how Hanban is going about telling the world how great China is, they are in big trouble." Many of the instructors and some entire programs that I visited responded to this problem by abandoning the official curriculum in favor of Chinese-language texts published by US-based institutions and YouTube videos, or creating their own materials. In one high school I visited over several years, the teachers had assigned the textbooks published by Hanban and Hanban China-based affiliate publishers during their first few years teaching in the United States but by the fourth year were using Chinese-language texts from a US publisher that were widely used in US high school and university Chinese courses. Thus, although Hanban supplied the official language texts and formal policies of engagement in CI classrooms, I observed the teachers and programs on the ground clearly taking more liberty with the curriculum and its enactments of China than most accounts and suspicions of the program would suggest.[23]

Discussion sessions and workshops at the several teacher training sessions I attended offered another space for CI teachers and administrators to engage in critiques of official curricular materials, practices, and expectations. These sessions were typically scheduled for weekends, when the teachers were not in the classroom, and were led by Hanban representatives with classroom experience teaching Chinese to foreigners and Chinese scholars with expertise in effective pedagogical practices for teaching foreign languages. Unlike the explicit instruction about avoiding contentious political discussions during the pre-posting training in China that CI teachers reported, the training sessions I attended in the United States were more concerned with etiquette lessons, problems encountered in the classroom, and even coping strategies for dealing with US parents and administrators who could not pronounce foreign names.[24] One session, for example, began with the moderator running through a litany of difficulties facing the CI program, including a shortage of sufficiently trained teachers, infighting among staff, inappropriate curricular materials, and methodological inconsistencies among instructors.[25] Despite their many complaints about their initial training and the program itself, CI teachers appreciated the applied rather than ideological advice they received in these US-based workshops. As one teacher told me,

> We get some instruction before we go, like they tell us how to deal with political questions in the classroom, they tell us not to talk too much about politics, religion, just to say that it's not a classroom discussion and let's talk after class. The people in Confucius Institutes, though, are the most flexible [*linghuo*], they are concerned that we do what is good for the classroom. Meetings in China are so boring. They don't talk about the real problems. But the Confucius Institute meetings [in the United States]—we do talk about the real problems. They ask us, what are the issues, the problems? And then they make real attempts to address them. What are the problems in teaching? In your lives?

After discussion of these "real problems" and practical questions about classroom practices, this particular session ended with an extended lesson on the importance of adhering to Western behavioral norms in and out of the classroom. This part of the session covered the importance of maintaining good oral hygiene, avoiding encounters with students or parents after consuming alcohol, and refraining from smoking, spitting on school grounds, using the middle finger to point, and nose picking. The effect of such instruction may very well have been to promote the soft power goals of the Chinese government through projecting China's representatives as "modern" citizens of an increasingly modern (Western) nation-state in the eyes of US citizens, in this case defined by standards of etiquette. However, this was not the kind of modernity, as is explored later in the chapter, that dominated what CI watchers considered to be central to their disquiet over the programs: the willingness and ability to be critical of the state.

At these training sessions and during interviews with me, teachers and Hanban administrators thus exercised at least some freedom to critique China and discuss the difficulties of achieving soft power goals in the Chinese language programs. Although critics of the programs might argue that these spaces of engagement were relatively safe for the teachers because they occurred on US soil or in private conversations in which I guaranteed them anonymity, I observed similar examples of CI teachers, guides, and administrators exercising free speech in China in public spaces generally understood outside of China as marked by censorship and repression. During the bus ride to Hanban headquarters on our first day in Beijing on the Chinese Bridge summer program, for instance, the tour guide referred openly to the demonstrations of 1989, the Dalai Lama, and the government's extensive politicization of religion, all topics that students, parents, and outside observers, both those on the tour and those back in the United States, frequently believed were too politically sensitive for public conversation in China. The guide also described in some detail the frustrations of living in the nation's capital, including its oppressive pollution, incessant traffic jams, and housing shortages, all results of the rapid transition to capitalism that Hanban textbooks presented as nothing short of a consumerist miracle. Throughout our seventeen-day journey in China, other representatives of the program also made statements critical of the nation and its official agents and referred to contentious state-society relations in a variety of settings. A notable example took place as early as the opening ceremony in Beijing. During a brief introduction to Confucian thought in a lecture titled "Getting to Know China," the lecturer explained that Confucius's notion of a "harmonious society" is currently used to refer to the government's attempts to bridge growing economic disparities so as to maintain social order and good government. To illustrate this point, he explained that the composite Chinese character for harmony consists of the individual characters for grain and mouth, meaning that "if you feed the people" (literally, provide grain to the mouth), "then you have harmony." After a brief pause, however, he added, "Only if you allow the people to talk," an aside that clearly alluded to the repressive tactics taken by the CCP to construct a hegemonic pro-government discourse. In the current Chinese vernacular, in fact, to "harmonize" has also come to mean to "censor."

Scholars over the years have come to argue that nations that reveal their "warts," as Kalathil phrases it (2011), tend to be perceived from the outside as having more liberal states.[26] Yet, one of the ironies of such examples of seemingly free speech is the manner in which students and chaperones on the tour often understood them as an aberration rather than as a regular feature of Chinese citizenship that might suggest a common modernity or as accruing soft power for China. Before our group left for China on the study tour, a number of parents, students, and other chaperones questioned me about what forms of censorship might be encountered on Chinese soil. US media accounts had made many aware of the extensive forms of censorship that plague China, including the blocking of Facebook,

YouTube, and Google, and several mentioned they understood that the 1989 Tiananmen Square massacre was a forbidden topic.[27] Therefore, many on the trip were surprised by the tour guide's mention of what they had presumed were taboo topics during our first day in Beijing.[28] Indeed, these titillating references to the perceived forbidden were the topic of more discussion at the chaperone table at dinner that evening than the two-thousand-year-old cultural sites we had visited.[29] Yet the targets of these soft power efforts saw the critical remarks of the guide and lecturer not as examples of freedom of speech exercised by China's unrestricted modern citizenry but as those individuals' momentary and potentially dangerous escape from a repressive state; the comments were only interesting insofar as they were interpreted as forbidden. In other words, the presence of free critique simply served to reconfirm the American visitors' perceptions of oppression.

Yet another irony of these examples of critical speech was that they were expressed by the very teachers and administrators feared by critics as potential vehicles for Chinese propaganda. Their critiques were often made through negative comparison with US practices; the Chinese teachers and administrators who implemented the soft power policy often viewed their own practices and experiences in the United States as evidence of China's relative shortcomings, rather than the positive images intended in the soft power rationale for the exchanges. Thus this attempt to impress foreigners with the glories of Chinese culture often appeared to have the unintended effect of making the educated Chinese instructors posted to the United States less content with their domestic conditions in China, in effect one might argue constituting a form of soft power for the United States. The perceived deficiencies of Chinese educational practices, for example, were a common topic among the teachers with whom I spoke. According to one teacher who admitted to making efforts to keep his children in US schools after his CI posting was complete, "The pressure on students in China is so great. Students are ranked from day one. There is so much homework. First graders are doing homework until ten at night. The kids are so unhappy and there are forty to sixty children per class. There is no creativity. No one challenges the teachers. No one is told to think about the meaning. You just memorize the poem but never think about the meaning of the poem." Similarly, several teachers, comparing life in China to conditions in their host cities, lamented their home country's growing income disparities, rapid urbanization, and environmental devastation. They attributed these national woes to government leaders "wanting to enrich themselves and be successful," their desire for "absolute power," and their "excessive need for face" reflected in soft power projects such as CIs, the 2008 Beijing Olympics, and the 2010 Shanghai Expo that "exhaust the people and drain the treasury."[30] Many found the United States a welcome refuge from such problems. "I don't see that the United States has that many big problems," one insisted, despite my protests to the contrary.

Authentic Free Speech, Agency, and Modernity

Although parents of children considering enrolling their children in CI programs and scholars attending my talks on the programs have sometimes pushed me to offer a definitive judgment about whether CIs are positive or negative for US students,[31] the ethnographic data I have collected do not offer a clear or simple answer to that question. Certainly this ethnographic examination uncovered numerous examples that would seem to support the arguments of those who consider CIs a danger to Western notions of free inquiry and Sahlins's claim that their intention is to facilitate "the global spread of academic and intellectual principles contrary to those upon which they are founded—human knowledge in the interest of human welfare" (2015, 62). Yet, at the same time, these same classrooms, teacher-student interactions, and study tours also manifest examples of what most of the debates over CIs would characterize as free speech: critiques of the nation and its state policies and practices, including those of the CI program itself.

This evidence arguably has as much to say about the premises on which those assessments are based as it does about the programs themselves. In addition to demonstrating that analyzing soft power policies primarily on the basis of their stated intentions and official documents does not accurately reflect what takes place in the space of the classroom itself, a closer analysis suggests that in our attempts to understand what is happening in the programs we have been asking incomplete questions. Rather than focusing on the narrow question of whether or not free speech exists in the spaces of the Chinese language programs, these data force us to address the question of what actually counts as free speech and its effect on our understanding of the agency and modernity of the subject being analyzed.

Although, as numerous scholars have explored, discourses regarding human rights such as freedom of speech have been framed as reflections of a universal moral order (e.g., Bornstein 2012; Zigon 2013), they also represent what Sally Engle Merry describes as "historically an artifact of Western cultural traditions" (1996, 67) and a result of a "Western liberal legalist construction" (1996, 68) that have been "raised to the status of global normativity" (1996, 67). On the global stage, as Merry and others have argued, this conception of human rights has also come to be used as a measure to define individuals and nations as civilized and modern.[32] At the heart of this assumed relationship between freedom of speech and modernity is a conceptualization of the citizen of a modern nation-state as a free-acting and free-knowing individual whose voice is recognized by the state as a legitimate actor and whose legal desires are not repressed or impinged upon by state power and mandates. The students and parents I met during my research recognized that the CIs' soft power efforts reflected an aspiration for modernity—what a student quoted earlier described as a desire to be seen as "equal" and to "get in touch" with the world. Yet their responses also suggested that they viewed being equally free and modern as the ability to discuss particular topics they presumed were opposed to Chinese national interests and to be openly critical of the Chinese government, in effect reproducing this dominant, Western understanding and projection of the constitution of modernity. These responses are perhaps why Sheng Ding calls human rights the "Achilles' heel" of China's soft power (2012).[33] As Žižek (2005) argues in a broader conceptual vein, human rights discourse has the potential to emerge as a new form of Western imperialism, naturalizing a politics of rights as an ostensibly nonideological instrument for personal autonomy. By invoking "free" as a characteristic that must always already be separate from the state, we may collude with the reproduction of a depoliticized and problematic separation of public and private spheres experience.

When teachers and lecturers reproached the Chinese government or were critical of China, students and parents understood them as enacting a nascent freedom of speech that marked them as modern. But when CI representatives praised China or supported state policy in ways that diverged from dystopian US assumptions about and depictions of their version of the "real" China, students and parents viewed this speech as propaganda mandated by the Chinese government. For example, when CI teachers claimed that Taiwan was a rightful province of the mainland or commended China for its rapid economic growth, students and parents usually interpreted their commentary as yet another example of the Chinese government's repression of freedom of speech. Similarly, when

Chinese teachers discussed Tibetan culture rather than Tibetan independence politics and taught the history of calligraphy rather than the history of Mao, students and their parents were quick to equate the absence of politics in the classroom with authoritarian presence, reinforcing their perceptions of a repressive Chinese governmental apparatus that stifles free speech and of pro-China speech as an absence of freedom.[34]

Ironically, the cultural and political norms for what constitutes free speech and freedom, or what Judith Butler calls the "emancipatory model of agency" (Butler 1997, 136), played a censorial role similar to that which parents and students imagined the Chinese state to play. This suggests a different kind of "unfreedom" that reproduces hierarchies of global power through conceptually limiting the composition of free speech and what it means to be a free subject, thus granting free agency only to those who define it. Whereas Western notions of modernity are based on the assumption that citizens have a choice to speak, the Chinese teachers in these examples were generally understood as free to choose only one form of speech.[35] Within this context, students and parents often comprehended CI teachers and guides as what Diane Nelson, in a different context, refers to as dupes "of the modern fact"—as agents lacking the political and cultural capital to speak freely (2009, 154), whom they assumed were either forced to reproduce an official line or unaware of the "real" state of affairs in China because of the repression of information.[36] In effect, when CI representatives presented favorable details about China and the favorable was defined as ineluctable propaganda, only information critical of the state could be construed as constituting true and free speech. The CI teachers I interviewed were quite aware that students and parents perceived them as having individual agency only when they publicly proffered themselves as critics of the state, although they denied that such was the case in practice.[37] One Chinese instructor at a public high school CC, for instance, assured me that when students would ask her about Tibet or Taiwan, her responses depicted her authentic assessment of global affairs rather than a limit on her right to speak. In fact, she suggested, being able to encounter different opinions was a positive aspect of the Chinese program:

> I try to explain that this is what I learn in China, that this is the history the way I understand it and that we all have different opinions. Americans like to say it's a free country, but actually there are lots of stereotypes, lots of set ways of thinking about things. I always say whatever I wanted [about

China to students and parents]. "Yes, this is what I believe, that Taiwan is part of China." I would explain the history. That's part of the value of having real Chinese people here. People get different points of view. I try to explain that there's actually something that is good in Marxism, to see both sides of the process, of the story.[38]

Despite her awareness of US antipathy toward China's politics, this teacher genuinely believed that these politics might have something to offer US students striving to understand the human condition.[39] Her position thus offered a vision of a different kind of political agency, one visible not only through resistance to the communist state but also through recognizing the potential value of difference and alternative ways of thinking about what constitutes the free subject.[40]

Describing their various encounters with CI teachers and Hanban administrators, the students and parents I spoke with, like many other CI observers, understood freedom of speech as dwelling in the nature of speech itself, in this case with critiques of the state. In such a conception, however, what constitutes freedom of speech inheres in its reception rather than in the words themselves. By assuming teachers could be "free-thinking" individuals only if they agreed with Western perceptions of a repressive Chinese state, the audience for their speech denied the teachers the subjectivity of the modern self either when they agreed with the state, for then their speech was viewed as merely propaganda, or when they criticized the state, in which case they were perceived to be speaking as renegades rather than "appropriate" or "normal" Chinese citizens. The possibility for agency in this case, following Butler, is located within structures of discursive power that, through iteration, accumulate "the force of authority" that in fact conceals the conventions through which they are mobilized (1997, 51).

Ultimately, this analysis suggests, understanding speech as free only when it comes in the form of a critique of the nation-state and assuming a speaker has agency only through dissent diminishes the usefulness of freedom of speech as an analytical tool for examining human rights and undermines the true purpose of a liberal education. By establishing the Chinese Other, embodied here by CI representatives, as incapable of speaking freely and hence as less truly modern, this rhetorical effect reinforces global hierarchies of power based upon an individual's or nation's relationship to a specific and arguably limited notion of modernity.[41] Constructing a litmus test for free speech through limiting conceptions of what counts for modernity serves to foreclose a more expansive conceptualization of individual agency that crosses political and national borders and perhaps works against academic freedom by constraining students' exposure to alternative forms of knowledge and ways of being. What might constitute "real" freedom of speech in this case is an acknowledgment of the limiting nature of our own discourses of power and recognition of others' ability to speak as equally human and modern subjects when their politics diverge from those of our own social and political worlds.

CHAPTER 7

The Sites and Struggles
of Global Belonging

Political and economic anxiety in the United States can often be traced through the dilemmas and antics of its Hollywood heroes. During the Cold War, Patrick Swayze and Charlie Sheen battled the Soviet Union and its communist allies who had invaded Colorado, and in the 1980s, when Japan appeared to be on the verge of eclipsing the United States' economic dominance, the xenophobic *Rising Sun* featured Sean Connery conquering Japanese corporate depravity. Likewise, in the 1990s, as China's growing economic ascendency became harder to ignore, Brad Pitt saved Tibet over the course of seven years, and in *Pacific Rim,* America rescued Hong Kong from regionally dominant giant monsters—metaphoric representations of an unnamed mainland China—that sought control over the South China Sea.

Yet lately, filmic images of China, the nation that arguably poses the biggest threat to US political and economic global hegemony in the contemporary era, increasingly intimate a different narrative. In the last few years, China has begun to form strategic alliances with Western film companies and producers, going on a buying spree in Hollywood that has included purchasing outright or amassing controlling shares in Voltage Pictures, producer of such smash hits as *The Hurt Locker* and *Dallas Buyers Club,* and Legendary Entertainment, the studio that, ironically, produced *Pacific Rim.* Chinese financiers have also set up partnerships with the likes of Hollywood giant DreamWorks Animation and now own the AMC movie theater chain and its massive distribution network. Through such repositioning, private Chinese entities have moved into a new realm of soft power production, clearly anticipating that Hollywood will assist the government's efforts to convince the world that China's rise to power is a peaceful one and to transform cultural influence into political power.

If recent film productions that are linked to these investments are any indication, it appears that these investments are beginning to succeed, if nothing else, in improving the visualizations of China that populate Hollywood film.[1] The blockbuster *The Great Wall*, for example, starring Matt Damon and backed by the Chinese entertainment conglomerate Dalian Wanda, has the famous star paying homage to Chinese culture and sending Western audiences the message that China values harmony and peace. And in *Arrival*, Chinese scientists save an American linguist. More subtly, Hollywood films, confronting the stagnation of domestic box office receipts and hoping to cash in on China's market, have taken care not to offend Chinese censors who might reject their films on the basis of anti-Chinese content. Chinese actors were inserted into scenes in *Iron Man 3*, including one who successfully performs surgery on the main character Tony Stark; a Tibetan character was excised from *Doctor Strange*; and *Rogue One: A Star Wars Story* includes Chinese characters in central scenes, one of whom intones at a crucial moment, "May the force be with you."

Members of the US Congress have expressed concern over China's foray into Hollywood, calling for increased scrutiny of Chinese investments into the movie industry; eighteen congressional representatives sent a letter to the US Government Accountability Office warning of "China's efforts to censor topics and exert propaganda controls on American media" (quoted in Wong 2016). When one considers box office receipts and critical receptions, however, one might question both whether these often maladroit efforts actually produced any soft power or, if soft power is indeed produced, whether its accrues to China or to the United States, where soft power is valued more when culture is distant from the state rather than intimate with it.[2] *The Great Wall* was a flop, losing $75 million at the box office, and many of the major Chinese studios have experienced market devaluations of 60 to 80 percent over the last few years (Pomfret 2017). Moreover, despite these efforts to advance Chinese culture globally, Chinese popular culture, in the words of one *Foreign Policy* analyst, remains "uncool" as a global commodity or marker of global cultural value (Gao 2017).[3]

Despite these roadblocks to successful cultural export, the CCP clearly remains committed to a soft power policy that relies on culture to smooth China's path to global power status. What *China in the World* has revealed about the workings of soft power, through the study of Confucius Institutes, is that it clearly takes more than financial wherewithal and official resolve to turn cultural presence into power even as these soft power efforts are central to a nation's place in the world. In this sense, Confucius Institutes can help us to understand these recent Hollywood incursions, the government's future efforts to win friends and neutralize enemies, and ultimately the nature of US-China relations that are embedded within the reception of these soft power efforts.

As a scholar of soft power—Olympics, world's fairs, Confucius Institutes—I am frequently asked about the potential threats that China's soft power efforts pose to US well-being and whether our schools should host the Chinese language programs.[4] My answers to that question sometimes frustrate the audience as I stray from a straightforward yes/no answer, for that question assumes that power remains at the geopolitical level of the state and operates through a zero-sum logic; it associates global interest in Chinese—as evidenced by students enrolling in Chinese language classes at CIs—as necessarily marking a shift in power from the United States to China. To truly answer yes or no involves making assumptions about power that are not necessarily warranted, for the implemented-in-the-real-world policy may not bear its desired fruit. As Phillip Huang notes of the broader field of China studies, and of relevance to any form of scholarship: "Our sense of problem—the central question we ask in our research—is arguably the most important and determinative part of any work of scholarship. It sets the agenda for what we want to know and determines what we ask and do not ask. It points our searchlight in a particular direction, and hence determines to a great extent what we will find" (2016, 116). Thus, while other scholars have explored the question of hosting CIs from a perspective of official policy aims that has provided a critical evaluation of state goals and their potential ramifications for shifting global hierarchies of power, I have responded, as does *China in the World*, through considering policy as envisioned, implemented, and consumed by policy makers *and* policy targets and, most important, by asking the reader to consider a different set of questions about power, global modernity, and policy practice.

First, rather than focus predominantly on whether the "culture" of the CIs is propaganda and presume that the globalization of Chinese culture accordingly denotes a zero-sum power play, this book asks how and whose culture matters to the production and consumption of power. Second, rather than assume an instrumental cause-and-effect model of policy, this book asks how policy as a space of encounter gets enacted and experienced by different actors, thus disrupting both assurances and meanings of policy practice. Last, *China in the World* asks how CIs illuminate shifting and often contradictory ideas of global modernity, with China simultaneously emerging as a source of global value and as a reflection of the perceived power, significance, and moral authority of its global Others. These are the questions asked by *China in the World,* and how they are answered allows us to complicate perceptions of a China threat and to comprehend how China's soft power language globalization project is not only an attempt at transforming the nation's place in the world but also a mechanism for shaping individual and institutional futures in the United States itself through their relationships with China.

Producing Power: How and Whose Culture Matters

While policy makers and policy targets rely on different cultural logics to ascertain and establish significance, both forms of culture—patriotic state culture and the public culture in which it is embedded—matter to the goals and processes of constituting power. Where most current analysis of soft power ends with the abstract, patriotic, state-sponsored culture of the CIs, *China in the World* begins in the spaces where that configuration of culture confronts soft power's policy targets. This is where policy is engaged and power produced and contested, and where the global order and its discontents are revealed in all their complexity. These are the spaces of social relations where culture operates and entangles, where China's policy targets in the United States negotiate their own experiences to interpret China's image management efforts, where culture is the terrain for engaging questions of power.

This ethnographic study of CIs thus shows us how culture remains a central ingredient for the production and dissemination of power and indicates that if the relationship between culture and power has any immutable features, they are that culture is dialogical in nature and that the power derived from it is rarely to be taken for granted; while Chinese CI culture may build upon nationalist formulations, it gets consumed in a particular cultural context that deconstructs and reconstructs its meaning. Culture here is revealed in all of its complexity, fluidity, and contradictions; its meaning remains an emergent phenomenon that integrates the educational, historical, political, and social frameworks in which it is embedded, both in China and in the United States. Thus, it is not only that there is a dialogical relationship between China and the United States but also that competing ideas about Chinese culture are embodied in the distinctive practices, images, and institutions of both China and the United States, each of which indexes and contributes to different formulations of power. Although anthropology rarely employs the term "soft power," anthropologists understand how power works through the integration of norms and common sense that constitute these practices, images, institutions, and relationships. Soft power theorists call these norms and commonsense "attraction"; anthropologists call them "culture." This vision then has important implications for power that preclude the possibility of seeing it inevitably as a zero-sum game, asking us to consider how different actors might claim culture as a means of promoting their own power (US students for individual mobility; US institutions for systemic resources; the Chinese government for global image production), and pushing us to think more critically about the nature of the "attraction" assumed to inhere in soft power endeavors.

While policy makers may seek to project culture toward nationalist ends—to improve the nation's global image and value—those efforts remain poor indicators of national power because they remain at the macrolevel of policy imagination. Although we may have the ability to locate the original seat of power, we cannot assume that the resources intended to produce power actually mutate into power for China.[5] China is pumping significant amounts of money into its CI program, money that former secretary of state Hillary Clinton wistfully compared to US diplomatic efforts, noting, "We don't have that kind of money in the budget" (quoted in Jensen 2012, 274). Nonetheless, this does not guarantee that the investment is solving China's image problem, as the controversies over CIs clearly indicate. As this research has shown, for example, Hanban tours bus students through Chinese cities with an agenda designed to push foreigners to rethink global assumptions about space. These tours confront students with a packaged narrative about Chinese culture that critiques the commonsensical "norm" of the West as the object of desire and the subject of globalization and the peripheral East as the parochial local, but that does not necessarily convince students that China is a source of universal value and practice. Although the tours position the students and the resource-hungry US educational system as the presumed objects of tutelage, as students look out the window, their cultural expectations for modernity and globalization reveal a different picture: they see poverty, they complain that the bus tours feel like incarceration, and they ask to stop at McDonald's. At the same time, while the potential effectiveness of Chinese culture as a form of power is subsumed here by China's perceived inability to embody the global modernity that students recognize as authentic, neither are the students operating as fully determining and unassailable subjects of control. Again, their expectations for future success and their strategies for mitigating risk suggest continuing the study of Chinese despite their less-than-satisfactory trips to China. Or they may indeed find China cool, as Hanban hopes, but because it empowers them through social norms at home rather than political and cultural narratives the CIs promote. In this case, while China itself may or may not be the initial object of desire, it still may accrue power because it ends up becoming a source of symbolic capital for students as the foundation upon which they assemble their own forms of power.

Accordingly, *China in the World* concludes that it is not only Chinese culture that matters for the success of soft power endeavors, but Western culture as well. While Hanban may offer CI students what it perceives to be a perfectly crafted product designed to sell the more harmonious aspects of Chinese culture, the official project, as Mosse reminds us in the context of international development missions, cannot decree its own reality (2005, 157), for that reality is always contingent on outside judgments borne of embedded cultural expectations for value and practice.[6] What US state culture may perceive as threat in its packaged form may be anything but at the level of consumption. Conversely, project "misfires" may, in the face of cultural predilections, accrue power to the host nation instead. For example, in the face of both expectations of censorship and cultural ideals for modernity that are fashioned through normative comprehensions of human rights, students and parents defined the absence of explicit politics in the classroom as the very epitome of censorship and control. References to Tiananmen Square as a tourist site were interpreted as attempts to cover up national repression rather than expressions of interest in national monuments. In this way, given China's poor record on human rights, including those of freedom of speech and freedom of inquiry, "China" in the CI classroom can come to represent the outer limits of expectations for liberal humanism and the United States as its relative embodiment.[7]

Yet when teachers became better acquainted with students and parents and began to have discussions about Chinese politics with them, policy targets often revised their conceptions of China, a process that re-interpolated the teachers into frameworks of individual rights. Students and parents began to perceive teachers as independent citizens, a view that could accrue soft power for a China thus identified as having the nascent potential for a universal modernity defined in part through its willingness to permit free speech. "China" accordingly emerges through multiple locations and on different scales of engagement and is imagined and challenged through assorted encounters among a diverse range of policy actors. While understanding CIs requires thinking about how culture and power shape policy goals, it also requires thinking about the particular cultural context in which these efforts unfold and the ways in which how culture is perceived there have the potential to disrupt and realign those power effects.

Policy Encounters, Policy Practices

Ultimately, to pay attention to culture and its effect on power reveals how policy effects are a complicated amalgamation of conflicting interests and subjectivities that rarely follow a smooth or linear trajectory between intention and application. What *China in the World* offers is not an assessment of whether China is a threat but an analysis of soft power and its contested efficacy. As Shore has noted, state policy, such as the CCP's soft power policy, as a political technology and tool of governance is "an instrument for the operation of state power" (2011, 169). Yet it is also a "lens for analyzing the operation of state power" (Shore 2011, 169) that when subjugated to scrutiny reveals a "power" that, my research suggests, is anything but ineluctably efficacious. While at the most obvious level, this conceptual unpacking exposes how people interpret policy differently as they view and experience it from distinctive vantage points and with sometimes conflicting visions of its constitution and value. More broadly, it also pushes us to denaturalize policy and the nature of the state and to understand how the collusions and conflicts between China and the United States are intimately linked to the manner in which policy is implemented and consumed, rather than merely envisioned.

In late December 2013, Xi Jinping gave a speech in Beijing that linked the attainment of the "China Dream" to the global production of Chinese soft power. The China Dream is a slogan Xi popularized a year earlier that expresses hope for "the great rejuvenation of the Chinese nation" and a "moderately well-off society" (quoted in Kuhn 2013) in which citizens enjoy a high standard of living, the air is clean, social classes exist in harmony, and culture flourishes. In this address, Xi depicted soft power—"showing the charm of Chinese culture to the world"—as central to the dream's realization (Mu 2014). It was through soft power productions around the world that China would be portrayed as a "civilized country featuring rich history, ethnic unity and cultural diversity, and as an oriental power with good government, developed economy, cultural prosperity, national unity and beautiful mountains and rivers" (quoted in Mu 2014), a portrayal that would facilitate China's emergence as a "qualified" world power (Zhang 2014) and hence smooth the progress of its rejuvenation.

Governments such as China's, as Xi's speech reveals, have turned to soft power policy, Ian Hall and Frank Smith argue, because they believe in the efficacy of exporting culture and cultural values as a means of image management (2013, 10) and hence of augmenting national power. In turn, analysts of soft power have often *assumed* a certain policy efficacy, which in the case of the CIs has led to concerns about a loss of local control over educational institutions and theories of a China threat. Yet as this book has shown, CIs—the centerpiece of China's soft power policy and the spaces of policy actualization—are not self-evident institutions, despite dominant public protestations to the contrary, but rather provisional outcomes of specific encounters and entanglements that need to be analyzed critically. As such, neither can we take their outcomes for granted. As CIs show us, power is produced and consumed, *and* modified and challenged, on multiple scales of engagement, from the hallowed halls of central government and the tour buses in China packed with high school students learning Chinese, to the school lunchrooms with Chinese teachers who struggle with how to teach Chinese and embody China most effectively. Therefore, while the CCP is explicit about leveraging soft power policy as an exercise in power, understanding policy effect in practice requires unmooring it from its official origins. As policy "moves," it is always translated—unsettled, taken apart, and reassembled (Clarke et al. 2015)—in ways that frustrate and defy attempts to determine its practice and meaning.

This study of soft power, through focusing on the experiences of a multitude of stakeholders and actors in an equally broad array of settings and scales of engagement in which these stakeholders engage with China, has provided new insight into how policy works in practice. The CI classroom is a site where diverse categories of actors—nation-states, teachers, administrators, students, and parents—each embodying different cultural norms and institutional imperatives, as well as distinctive knowledge sets about China and different ways of adjudicating knowledge claims, come together and negotiate new meanings concerning "China" and "Chinese culture/language" as forms of soft power. These meanings are asserted, impugned, and altered in the classroom. No one constituency controls these meanings, although each attempts to exercise control over them. Soft power policies are an expression of historical and institutional legacies: centrally coordinated by state policy makers, yet, as the stories in this book reveal, their implementation and reception are forever negotiated by those they are designed to address. It is this recognition that allows us to move beyond the dominant concern with whether CIs constitute a threat at the level of the state to consider how China and Chinese culture/language, and by association the United States, are negotiated as forms of value and expression through the production, implementation, and consumption of policy.

China in the World thus pushes us to think about policy as an analytical framework rather than as a mere aftereffect of what to take away from the Confucius Institute story, for this study of CIs disrupts the questions we ask about policy through expanding *how* we see policy and *where* we locate it. In the halls of Congress, with House representatives and human rights activists, this research reveals the cultural expectations for what constitutes moral authority as much as it reveals that China threatens liberal educational practices in the United States. When Congressman Smith introduced the panel of experts, for example, he cited their reputations as "true game changers when it comes to human rights" rather than their professional expertise on or academic experience with the CIs. In this case, a policy designed to win the hearts and minds of the global population emerges instead as a way to formulate China's symbolic place in the world as a human rights violator rather than as the source of linguistic pedagogy. And rather than establish power for China, soft power policy in that site becomes a method through which Chinese practices are contrasted with a Western moral authority that stresses the value of global human rights.

In the CI training sessions, conversations with students and parents, and interviews with me, teachers exposed their concerns with the language programs and their inconstant identification with the Chinese state. The motivations and engagements of the teachers, the very agents of policy and embodiments of the state, their projections of China, and their relationships with students and parents have unintended (by policy standards) but important effects that challenge perceptions of a monolithic, unified Chinese state and, as such, have the potential to improve how local populations perceive China and its attractiveness.[8] This suggests that the effects of policy are often contingent upon the kinds of relationships that students and parents create with teachers and upon the particular pedagogical practices in the classroom. At the same time, despite what we might call the unintentional "ineptitude" of policy, these same teachers—who sometimes offer stringent criticisms of the very state that exports them as its policy representatives—are forthright about their intentions to transform US citizens' perceptions about China in ways that remind us that caution is warranted when any ideologically motivated external funding comes into play.

On the one hand, then, we have to take seriously the real, material effects of these policies. As I write this final chapter, recent incidents underscore how cultural exchange projects, when accompanied even by "suggestions" of consequences for "misrepresentations" of China or disagreements with its official policies, are anything but "soft."[9] In May 2017, in consultation with the Los Angeles Chinese consulate, the Chinese Students and Scholars Association at the University of California, San Diego (UCSD) threatened "tough measures to resolutely resist [UCSD's] unreasonable behavior" in response to the university's announcement of the Dalai Lama as its commencement speaker (Saul 2017). And Monash University in Australia suspended a professor who was accused by a Chinese student of insulting Chinese officials (Ives 2017).

On the other hand, the students featured in this study—the main policy targets of CIs—were attuned to the politics of the CCP's soft power policy goals and how the CIs sought to reproduce them. Teachers' efforts to downplay the more problematic features of contemporary Chinese life, its human rights record, for example, were often read by students as censorship, indeed as a pointed example of China's unwillingness to prioritize civil liberties and constitutional rights. Similarly, while Hanban hoped that the increased number of students studying Chinese would come to correlate with the nation's growing power, students made clear that participation in Chinese language classes was as much a result of their own competitive struggles to get into college and obtain professional positions as it was of any specific embodiment in the teachers and texts that projected China and/or the Chinese state in a particular and loaded manner. In doing so, they disrupted what might be perceived as Chinese state policy goals, turning the CIs into a vehicle for their own upward mobility.

Challenging Global Modernities: China's Place in the World

What does reframing policy as an analytical lens in and of itself, and scrutinizing how and whose culture matters to its implementation and effect, ultimately tell us about China and its global relations in the contemporary era? The third of my questions concerns the link between perceptions and standards of global modernity, international relations, and a nation's place in the world. China has the world's largest economy, when measured in terms of purchasing power parity, and is the world's largest exporter of language and culture exchange programs. While Thomas Friedman may elucidate a Western model of globalization that resonates with my US interlocutors, CIs challenge the current model of globalization. For these and other reasons, China is arguably the only serious threat to US hegemony, and a study of CIs can also provide important insights into the relationship between the United States and China. Together the research presented in this book sheds light on the ambivalent relations that America has with China, a nation seen as necessary to the United States for economic security and regional stability but also feared for what its growing power suggests about the changing international hierarchy of nation-states. As Kenneth Pomeranz argues, "China, more than any other place . . . has served as the 'other' for the modern West's stories about itself" (Pomeranz 2000, 25).[10] And no history of modernity, as Hayot suggests, is complete without accounting for how China has long existed in the West as a sign of difference (2009, 8).[11] It is within this context that China's export of language programs in the interests of soft power falls easy prey to assumptions about zero-sum policy engagements in which the rise of China mandates that the power of other nations must fall in tandem.

As suggested by its title, *China in the World* is an analysis of how a cultural exchange program has come to embody the seemingly fraught and challenged position of China's shifting "place in the world," for a nation's place in the world is both a discursive process and an empirical reality. Perceptions about place in the world do not merely misunderstand or reflect global realities but come to constitute them (Ching 2000; Ferguson 2006).[12] And how governments and their policy actors and policy targets emplot, or locate nations relative to each other, affects the relations between them. In his study of what the "good life" connotes in different cultural and political contexts, Edward Fisher explains, anthropology prides itself on taking a critical stance toward the "dominant conceptions in the world, making sure that social constructions are not misconstrued as being natural or predetermined" (Fisher 2014, 214–215). Modernity and globalization are two such dominant conceptions that affect the discursive improvisations and empirical placements of a nation in the world, and discerning how policy targets and policy makers understand these concepts is central to realizing how CIs emerge as a product of and paradigm for international relations.

CIs reflect China's efforts to rewrite the rules of engagement in the characterizations, processes, and practices of globalization and modernity. Through exporting teachers and language institutes, teaching the world rather than being taught, and highlighting its cultural practices and histories, the CCP attempts to reposition China as the subject rather than the object of globalization and to suggest itself as a model for a different form of modernity. Yet, the controversial reception and debates over the programs (are they positive forms of global communication or bastions of communist propaganda?) indicate that "knowledge" about the CIs comes not only from what happens in the classroom but also through the very discursive conceptions of what counts for appropriate globalization and legitimate modernity. While Hanban offers CIs as an index of its ascendant global status and a new form of globalization that originates in China, students often dispute that assertion, conceiving of themselves as the locus of globalization in their travels to China, where they consume Chinese difference (exotic foodstuffs and bargain shopping) as markers of their own cosmopolitan identities. The program offered China as a model of the global but in the process paradoxically produced the US students as managing the global. In conquering the deep-fried silkworms and the shopkeepers who assume foreign students can (ought to?) pay inflated prices for their counterfeit goods, rather than dethroning the West as the locus of the global, the students conquer its risky "margins" and compose the self as the intrepid and innovative adventurer.[13] Similarly, while classroom textbooks and videos reveal the avant-garde spectacle of China's newly built architectural wonders and publicize the luxury of its rapidly sprouting shopping venues, the CIs' incessant stress on the nation's "five thousand years of history and culture" as the "real China" has the potential to suggest stagnation rather than rejuvenation and global display.

The nature and efficacy of CIs similarly revolve around concepts of modernity, not only what constitutes a proper modernity, but also who "owns" the definition and practice. Chinese language teachers in this case questioned parent and student representations of teachers' ability to embody modernity, both in how parents and students defined modernity as the practice of speaking against the state and in what parents and students assumed about the teachers' relationship to this form of modernity—that they did not have the freedom to do so. Yet these same teachers can also challenge Western expectations for modernity through their ability to oppose common US-based perceptions of the Chinese state and its capacity to be "modern." Although CI teachers may have shared Hanban's soft power policy intentions to create a different vision of China, their critical engagements with official pedagogical and curricular guidelines and their criticisms of the state, among other actions, allow us to reconsider the perceptions and depictions of the Chinese state as a monolithic entity that feature prominently in global accounts of Chinese difference and exception. CIs reflect China's material power and efforts to produce new ideas about and relationships to China, both in concept and in the classroom; yet they also illuminate tensions between China's conception of itself and that of its global Others. *China in the World* thus demonstrates that CIs have become a potent symbol of challenges to ideals and ideologies of globalization, modernity, and the global order, but at the same time constitute a potent set of practices through which different forms of globalization and modernity are realized—uncomfortable bedfellows, one might say, of both representation and realpolitik.

Each of these encounters, and the many others featured within these pages, bares the gaps between policy imaginations, Chinese nationalism, and the production of power. The experiences of teachers, parents, administrators, and students bring to light that power is rarely produced or transferred in a linear manner, that when CI culture is appropriated by policy targets it only sometimes provides value to China, and that when China or Chinese is found attractive, power is not necessarily accrued by China. This analytical approach to the study of power thus allows us to see the multilayered and often contradictory effects of policy in a manner that remaining at the level of global geopolitics struggles to perceive. These experiences thus allow us to examine CIs not only as state policy tools in and of themselves, but also as contingent outcomes of relations between nation-states whose very ontologies and epistemologies are equally contingent upon the cultural norms through which they are constructed.

Notes

Chapter 1: An Anthropology of International Relations

1. This definition of soft power is borrowed from Nye 2004.
2. In this context, China and the Chinese nation refer to the People's Republic of China (PRC). While the PRC concept of "One China" encompasses the reach of Chinese civilization more broadly, it does not legitimize any other claims to Chinese nationality (Taiwan, for example). As such, the "Chinese" language that the CIs promote is specifically Mandarin. This is especially important in the United States since early Chinese immigrants into the country and first-generation Chinese Americans were largely Cantonese speakers. The predominance of Mandarin among Chinese speakers in the United States is a fairly recent phenomenon and reinforcing this is arguably an unstated goal of the CI language programs apart from their cultural soft power projections.
3. In the United States, the controversy over Chinese language programs has been apparent at both the most local level of experience, where newspaper commentary in my hometown compared Chinese language instruction to "teaching communism" and "brainwashing," and the most national level of experience—the halls of Congress—as is discussed in the following paragraph.
4. Barr (2011) similarly argues that debates over CIs reflect as much upon the values and ideologies of those making the arguments as they do upon the language programs themselves.
5. I draw upon Nielsen's call for scholars to "people" policy "with multi-dimensional actors whose subjectivities are created in the intersections or assemblages of different rationalities, technologies, norms and values" rather than reducing policy to a "mentality of rule or a practice of thinking" (2011, 70, 69).
6. See also Gil 2017, for a discussion of CIs as a form of globalization.
7. Hanban is short for the Chinese equivalent of Office of the Chinese Language Council International.
8. The specific numbers, as of June 2018, are 511 Confucius Institutes at colleges and universities and 1,074 Confucius Classrooms at K–12 schools. This study is also the first research conducted at China's CI language programs in the middle and high school setting, even though these secondary programs constitute more than two-thirds of the Hanban

Chinese programs worldwide and three-quarters of the programs in the United States and thus arguably have the most potential impact on US students. Throughout the book, I use the term "Confucius Institute" while describing Hanban's general Chinese language program or referencing specific university and college institutions and "Confucius Classroom" when describing a specific CC located in a K–12 school.

9. Hanban provides these data each year in its annual development report. These figures are drawn from the 2016 report (Hanban 2016).

10. The claims on the CI Web page are slightly misleading because there is a difference between students studying at CIs and students studying Chinese at other institutions, but the visual image on the Hanban Web page seems to conflate the two. Other Hanban and government sites list this figure at one hundred million students and two hundred thousand language teachers (e.g., Ziguangge 2014). As of July 2017, the United States had 161 CIs and 554 CCs.

11. This period of globalization roughly corresponds to that of Deng Xiaoping's rule and influence, from 1978 until his death in 1997, although he no longer held a high-level official post during the final decade.

12. While this growing global engagement was accompanied by consistent increases in standards of living across broad portions of the Chinese population, it also occasioned intense public debate in China over the nation's role and position in the global hierarchy of nation-states and the forms and practices of globalization that might best augment its power and authority. Many scholars, citizens, and politicians advocated a model of globalization that equated it with Westernization, while others invoked a more skeptical and telling phrase I heard frequently in the late 1980s and early 1990s: "When you open the window, the flies also enter." I explore the debates over Westernization in Hubbert 2003.

13. The term "comprehensive national power" (*zonghe guoli*) is a Chinese measure that includes military, economic, and cultural power. For more detailed information, see Li 2008; Shambaugh 2014; Zhang 2010. Fiscal imperative, diversification, and urbanization provided additional rationales for going out.

14. In less fortunate ways, China's rise as an international player has mirrored that of other historically rising great powers in its exploitation and consumption of raw materials around the world in the interest of supplying domestic industries with the necessary primary products to fuel its massive growth. See, for example, Brautigam's work on Africa (2009) for one case study.

15. Domestic rhetoric in China often frames engagement with global multilateral institutions as befitting the status of a superpower. As one

Renmin University international relations textbook explains, "As a great power in the world, China has gradually become an important force in the international society, therefore we must intimately cooperate and coordinate with the United Nations and other international organizations, and play an active role in these organizations" (cited in Xie 2011, 89).

16. For more on the significance of China's hosting the Olympics for its stature as a global power, see Hubbert 2013 and 2014b.

17. Marjorie Ferguson (2005) calls these expectations for globalization a "myth" that consists not merely of physical "facts," but more fundamentally of a conception of what *ought* to constitute the global order. Ong calls this configuration of globalization a "conceptual terra firma" (2011, 2). Likewise, James Ferguson notes that the "globally oriented" social sciences often begin with a series of predictive assumptions about what globalized nations of the modern era ought to be: democracies, respectful of human rights and the rule of law, at peace with their neighbors (Schouten 2009, 1). Kornprobst and colleagues (2008) rightfully alert us to the ways in which the "oughts" of globalization include an ideational state of mind as well as a material state of affairs.

18. See, for example, much of the work of Arjun Appadurai, James Watson, and James Ferguson.

19. Excellent discussions are found in Comaroff and Comaroff 2012; Ferguson 2006; Roy and Ong 2011; Tsing 2005; and Zhan 2009.

20. Put another way, how do we understand the CIs and the changing global order not only as "an interesting empirical phenomenon but also as an imperative theoretical question" (Zhang 2008, 13)?

21. This is not meant to suggest that the manner in which CIs propose China as a model for global modernity offers a viable alternative to Western-dominated modernization schemes. Indeed, much of the "multiple modernities" or "alternative modernities" discourse, as Dirlik astutely points out, reifies such conceptualizations of difference "in order to render manageable cultural and political incoherence" (2003, 284). He thus adds, "There is good reason to question ideas of 'multiple' or 'alternative' modernities as expressions of an improved, genuinely democratic approach to global modernity; rather than simply a new mode of managing conflict by containing it when Eurocentric notions of modernity have lost their hegemony (but not their dominance)" (Dirlik 2003, 288). In a similar vein, Jean and John Comaroff question the conception of alternative identity to a globalized West as it preserves global assumptions about source and directionality (2012). What this approach does suggest is that we take seriously the CIs' practices and representations of modernity for what they reveal about China's perceptions of its place in the world and for what they reveal about modernity as a Eurocentric teleology,

to examine what Dirlik calls the globalization of modernity rather than the end of modernity (2003, 286).

22. Osburg's study of China's new rich provides an excellent examination of the permeability of these categories of state actors in China (2013).

23. This poses syntactical dilemmas for how one talks about an institution that oftentimes seems to act as a monolith, but whose acts can only transpire through the endeavors of tangible actors. While this is addressed at length in chapter 5, "the state," as Abrams argues, can be considered "a spurious object of sociological concern" (1988, 63), and in this book, I strive to use terminology that reflects the disaggregated nature of the state, to speak specifically about who constitutes the state and acts under, through, and against its direction, to locate it in identifiable actors and places. Sometimes this is possible, but I offer this caveat because many times it is not. And I consequently find myself forced to revert to a vernacular of the Chinese state that negates specificity when policies and mechanisms of the state remain immune to distinctive representation, for perceptions of the state are of political actions that may not be locatable in embodied form. At the same time, in China's case, there is little functional distinction between the "government" and the Communist Party, although they are technically discrete institutions. I therefore use the terms interchangeably. Like other scholars, I ponder how to avoid scare quotes each time I invoke the concept of the state, but also how to prevent prefacing each sentence with ponderous disclaimers about its disjointed and inconsistent nature. Mitchell (2006) explains how scholars have struggled over this dilemma both conceptually and linguistically, in the 1950s attempting to eliminate the term "state" from their vocabulary in favor of a focus on political systems, and then later in the 1960s being obliged to "return to the state" through neo-Marxist critiques of modernization theory. The task of the reader then is to read with an eye toward understanding the complex and imprecise nature of the state and empathy for the linguistic hegemonies required of writing, as well as an eye toward the complex and contingent positionalities of "agents" of the state and its very constitution.

24. In response to these concerns, various educational institutions around the world have closed their CI programs and severed links with Hanban. These include the University of Chicago, the Toronto School District, Stockholm University, McMaster University, and the University of Lyon, among others. Some of these closures are discussed later in the book. In the face of similar concerns, although not linked directly to the Confucius Institutes, the University of Texas recently rejected funding from the China–United States Exchange Foundation, a Hong Kong–based foundation whose leader is closely aligned with the Chinese Communist Party.

25. In so doing, *China in the World* engages in conversation with other scholars who critically consider how human rights are configured within dominant Western conceptions of modernity (Bornstein 2012; Butler 1997; Yeh 2013; Zigon 2013) to offer both a methodological and an ethnographic contribution to questions about universal values, questioning not the value of human rights per se, but the effects of how they are invoked in relation to governance and power.

26. This is often called the Thucydides trap, a metaphor for the potential violent dangers attendant when a rising power threatens a ruling power's ascendency.

27. While the phrase initially referred to geopolitical military stability, it has come to reference broader realms of engagement including those of the environment, human rights, democracy, and academic innovation, among others, in which China's rapid economic growth and increased global political power are perceived to threaten human rights, democracy, and material well-being through its destruction of the environment, for example, or its downward pressure on wages. Nonetheless, Shambaugh argues that despite China's extensive global reach, it lacks close friends and possesses no allies (2014, 7), leading the Chinese Academy of Social Sciences, China's foremost academic research organization, to describe neighboring countries in its 2014 *Pacific Blue Book* as "near but not dear" (Liu 2013). China's Blue Books are official government references on specific topics that are provided to domestic departments and sold in Chinese bookstores. For more detailed information on theories of the China threat, see Al-Rodhan 2007; Callahan 2004; Ding 2008; Gertz 2000; Roy 1996; and Wishnick 2005. While "China threat" arguments originated in Japan and the United States in the 1990s following the rise of China's relative post–Cold War power (Ueki 2006), in many ways the China threat can be most immediately felt by its Asian neighbors, who have been increasingly intimidated by China's unilateral annexation of regions of the South China Sea.

28. China's turn to soft power in response to perceptions of threat reflects a recognition that, as Joseph Nye argues, "soft co-optive power is just as important as hard command power. If a state can make its power seem legitimate in the eyes of others, it will encounter less resistance to its wishes. If its culture and ideology are attractive, others will more willingly follow" (1990, 167). Nye and other scholars have also argued that increased globalization has given soft power a more prominent role and greater importance in international relations; given that no single country has global sovereignty, a nation's ability to maintain and project power through noncoercive means has become crucial to the maintenance of global order (Nye 2004; see also Aysha 2005).

29. Flew (2016, 279) notes that while the concept of soft power originally emanated from the United States, the central place where the discussion about the concept has flourished is China. In addition to developing a comprehensive soft power policy, China has responded to the perception of threat by changing the terminology in its political discourse, from classifying China's growth as a "peaceful rise" to that of a "peaceful development," a move intended to subdue insinuations that the term "rise" might indicate an attempt to "rise over." Guo (2008) provides a more comprehensive discussion of these terminological changes.

30. Former PRC president Hu Jintao claimed that soft power is "a basic requirement for realizing scientific development and social harmony" and "necessary for satisfying rising demands for spiritual culture and national development strategy" (cited in Jian Wang 2011b, 8). It is important to remark here on the differential benefits that accrue from the fruits of soft power policy endeavors. While national governments potentially benefit from the ability to shape the preferences of global others, the costs of doing so are often borne on the shoulders of a dispossessed citizenry. Certainly, in the case of the Shanghai Expo and the Beijing Olympics, two of China's most massive soft power engagements, the costs of physical displacement from the production sites were equally massive, with 1.5 million people evicted from their homes in Beijing and eighteen thousand families from their households in Shanghai. Similarly, as some CI teachers and administrators complained to me, the amount of money the Chinese government was spending on promoting Chinese education abroad might have been more productively spent on a domestic rural educational system that struggles to educate its local citizens. At the same time, the "scientific development" and "national development strategy" that Chinese officials suggest soft power will advance have produced highly disparate levels of economic and social benefits for rural and urban citizens.

31. These comments were never intended to suggest that some monolithic Chinese or Western view of the nation exists, but that many of those I interviewed perceived that dominant Western representations of China tend to focus on its authoritarian politics and how its rise to power poses a threat to global well-being, and they wished to have more positive aspects of everyday Chinese experience portrayed to a global audience. Hartig (2015) argues that the widespread concerns about CIs as a form of Chinese propaganda arise from the gap between the vision of what he calls the "correct" version of China (the one promoted in CI materials and classrooms) and what the West perceives to be the "real" China, which may or may not be coterminous with this "correct" vision. See also Lai 2012;

Lahtinen 2015; and Wang and Adamson 2015 for similar arguments. The same caveat about the "real" China is true for Hartig's argument as well. For the teachers, the gap was between their own experiences of China (which were frequently positive) and the more critical representations found elsewhere.

32. The State Council Information Office has also interviewed Western public relations firms to enlist their help in telling what it sees as the "real" story in an appropriate way to foreigners (Tham and Miller 2016). Nyiri's study of Chinese media correspondents (2014) explains how Chinese news sources seek not only to attract a foreign audience, but also to define China and render its version of events credible.

33. China's Xinhua News reported that the Times Square video presented "Americans [with] a multi-dimensional and vivid image of Chinese people" (Guanqun Wang 2011). In case Times Square viewers were unclear on how to respond emotionally or how to understand this new China, many of the individual pictures suggested interpretation in English language titles. For example, a photo of a famous athlete in front of the Olympics Bird's Nest stadium included the subtitle "Thrilling Chinese Athletics," while an image of two technology entrepreneurs was captioned "Chinese Wealth." For a discussion of public opinion toward such image making as in this video, see Xie and Page 2013.

34. The volume of contemporary Western academic scholarship on China's global soft power projections has exploded in the last decade. This burgeoning literature has largely been dominated by international relations and political science studies that focus on macrolevel theories and quantitative measurement and has provided us with a productive sense of China's soft power intentions and their potential implication for global relations and hierarchies of power, producing, among others, several book-length studies and edited volumes (Callahan and Barabantseva 2011; Barr 2011; Lai and Lu 2012; Li 2009a; Ding 2008; Jian Wang 2011a) and numerous article-length analyses (Breslin 2010; Cho and Jeong 2008; Deng and Zhang 2009; Ding 2011, 2012; Gill and Huang 2006; Glaser and Murphy 2009; Houlden and Schmidt 2014; Hsiao 2009; Hunter 2009; Jensen 2012; Kalathil 2011; Nordin 2012; Wuthnow 2008; Yan 2006; Zhang 2010). The topic is not limited to academic debate; journalistic outlets from the *New York Times* and the *Economist* to the *Wall Street Journal* have employed the concept of soft power to frame Chinese resources and global projects as diverse as former NBA player Yao Ming and the attempted purchase of *Newsweek* by a Chinese media conglomerate. Within this context, Joshua Kurlantzick's (2007) book-length analysis, *Charm Offensive: How China's Soft Power Is Transforming the World,* is notable for

broadening the definition of soft power, highlighting specific cultural initiatives, and capturing popular perceptions about China's rise. The scholarship on soft power and Confucius Institutes mirrors that of soft power analyses in general in its domination by international relations and political science scholars (with a few exceptions) and its focus on the Chinese state's policy goals, political intentions, and global geopolitical implications. See, for example, Albro 2015; Chey 2008; Ding and Saunders 2006; Gil 2009, 2017; Gill and Huang 2006; Glaser and Murphy 2009; Hartig 2015; Hsiao and Yang 2009; Hughes 2014; Kluver 2014; Lahtinen 2015; Lai 2012; Lo and Pan 2016; Paradise 2009; Wang and Adamson 2015; Yang 2010; Zhe 2010, 2012; Zhou and Luk 2016. This literature is discussed at greater length throughout the book.

35. See, for example, Albro 2015; Hayden 2012; Kalathil 2011.
36. This is not to argue that youth are uncritical consumers of the nationalist ideologies presented in their textbooks or by their teachers (see, for example, Lukose 2009), but to acknowledge that as individuals age, they become less susceptible to attitude change (Krosnick and Alwin 1989). Hughes (2014) makes a similar argument about the potential impact of CIs on younger children. In addition, at the middle and high school levels, parents remain more involved in their children's education than they do at the collegiate level, and, as many of this book's interviews suggest, they become the critical voice of "appropriate" ideology, helping to frame the meaning of the classroom experiences for their children.
37. These "official" first openings followed a pilot program established in Tashkent, Uzbekistan, in June 2004.
38. Park places this growth in the context of China's GDP, nothing that the CI growth rate has been around ten times more rapid than the growth rate of the nation's GDP (2013, 1). Hanban was clearly not expecting this rapid growth (Zhe 2012), which led quickly to problems of staffing and teaching quality, the latter of which, according to several CI directors I interviewed, has afflicted the programs since their inception. Several teachers described to me the process of establishing CIs as "crossing the river by feeling for stones," a phrase coined by Deng Xiaoping to describe China's post-Mao economic liberalization process but since used to explain any number of experimental Chinese engagements and activities for which there are few historical precedents and which require continuous testing and modification. Hanban has since become even more ambitious, with a current goal of one thousand CIs by 2020 (Volodzko 2015). This figure does not include Confucius Classrooms.
39. See Hartig 2016; Redden 2012; and Starr 2009 for more information on funding.

40. Most commonly, the contracts that include these bylaws and requirements are not accessible to the public. They frequently incorporate explicit provisions for upholding certain CCP ideologies and practices. For example, they initially contained a clause that forbade schools from presenting Taiwan as a separate country, although this was later removed (this example is discussed in chapter 6). They also include ambiguous phrases about barring CIs from being involved in "activities that are not consistent with the missions of Confucius Institutes" or contravening in the "laws and regulations of China," which for teachers includes participating in organizations such as Falun Gong that are banned in China. Such conditions, were they to be made public, and when they have been made public, have met with both criticism and concern that CIs are engaging in actions that hamper freedom of speech in the classroom and encourage broader self-censorship on campuses that host the programs. The CI constitution explains that a Chinese agency can "pursue legal action" against any foreign education institution that "damages or tarnishes the reputation of the Confucius Institutes" (Hanban n.d., "Constitution").

41. This rising antipathy can be seen in opinion polls such as the Pew Global Attitudes Project (Kohut 2007).

42. In general, the developing world holds more positive views of China's rise to power (Wike, Stokes, and Poushter 2015). On the United States as a target of China's soft power efforts, see Hongying Wang (2011).

43. For information on programming at specific CIs, see Kluver 2017 and Peterson 2017.

44. At the college level, the credit situation is mixed. While Hanban-sponsored classes at university and college CIs are generally non–credit bearing, and attended by the wider public rather than by students matriculated at the university, some universities have incorporated the classes into their degree-granting programs. In those cases, course attendance and participation in these programs is mandatory to obtain credit and fulfill Chinese language department major or minor requirements.

45. While these are typical arrangements, Hanban has also established CIs dedicated to particular themes. The University of California, Davis, for example, hosts a CI focused on Chinese food and beverage culture; the United Kingdom's London South Bank University CI concentrates on traditional Chinese medicine; and the London School of Economics hosts a Confucius Institute for Business to promote Chinese specifically for trade and economic engagements. Zhe (2012) provides a more extensive description of the different types of CI associations, including those associated with universities, public organizations (such as school districts), and foreign corporations.

46. In a defensive response to criticisms of CIs, Xinhua News, China's central official press agency in China, argued, "Perhaps no one will label Goethe Institutes, Alliances Françaises or Cervantes Institutes as propaganda vehicles or tools of cultural invasion, so why all the fuss over China's Confucius Institutes, an identical organization?" (Liu 2010).

47. Hartig explains that although the "joint venture" model of education exchange is cost-effective for China, the host school's expenses typically exceed Hanban's (2016, 167; see also Starr 2009). An example of the financial breakdown for 2013 can be found in the annual development report (http://www.hanban.edu.cn/report/pdf/2013.pdf).

48. As one Confucius Institute director noted, "If you sign a contract, you know the limits" (quoted in Hartig 2016, 159). These are limits that former Australian diplomat Jocelyn Chey suggests could at best "result in dumbing down of research and, at worst, could produce propaganda" (Chey 2008, 44). Critics have also expressed concern that universities that host CIs, many of which have also come to depend upon full-tuition-paying students from China, will suffer if they offend Hanban and lose access to these students. (Chinese students now comprise more than 30 percent of international students in the United States [Institute of International Education 2015].) Indeed, Schiller calls soft power "cultural imperialism with a semantic twist" (1991, 18).

49. Several CI teachers and Chinese Hanban administrators explained to me that it was Hanban's ultimate intention to hire teachers from the local communities who were fluent in Chinese but that there were yet to be sufficient numbers of qualified teachers available. An explicit policy to appoint only PRC teachers and exclude from consideration academically qualified citizens from the host country would violate US employment laws. DeHart (2017) provides an example of the CI hiring of a local Chinese-speaking citizen in Costa Rica. I came across only one non-PRC Chinese teacher in my five years of research at various CIs and CCs.

50. I have chosen to retain the term "soft power," rather than use "sharp power," in the interests of consistency, as most scholars and journalists continue to use the original term. Sharp power is also a much more ideologically laden term whose usage makes assumptions about policy successes.

51. Rather than appeasing their detractors through becoming what Liu Yandong, vice-premier of the State Council of China, has called a "spiritual express train using culture as a track" (Hanban 2015), the language programs have often fostered perceptions that they are a threat to the central tenets of a liberal education and, ultimately, to US power itself. Consequently, as Ien Ang et al. have suggested within the broader context of international relations, the "race" for soft power, because it can be easily

understood as promoting national ascendance, has the potential to impede rather than enhance global relations (2015, 374). According to such a view, "China is assembling the resources to eclipse the US in many essential areas of international affairs and constructing an environment that will make US hegemonic action more difficult" (Ramo 2004, 3).

52. Indeed, as Heather Schmidt has noted, very little of the research on CIs concerns "what CIs actually do" or the influence "they actually garner" (2013, 650). Hartig (2012) and Hsiao and Yang (2009) offer similar assessments.

53. Gill and Huang, for example, suggest examining polling data about China's growing "popularity" to measure whether global citizens see "China's influence as positive" (Gill and Huang 2006, 24). Yet, within the context of CIs specifically, Paradise admits how difficult this can be, due to the complexity of separating the influence of CIs from that of other soft power cultural programs (2009, 662). Similarly, Hartig (2016, 65) explains that measuring impact is inherently difficult because cultural exchanges are intangible experiences and cultural diplomacy is a long-term undertaking not given to short-term impact assessment.

54. Scholars critical of this mode of policy analysis as it pertains to soft power policy, CIs, or both include Houlden and Schmidt 2014; Kluver 2017; Zhou and Luk 2016. Ang et al. (2015) advocate for a more ethnographic approach to studies of soft power and cultural diplomacy in general to reveal how policy is shaped in the accidental encounters rather than in the planning itself.

55. Chapter 2 takes "culture" up in detail, examining its constitution and the nature and rationale of its definition and deployment.

56. As Lukose points out, schools can therefore be key sites "for understanding how . . . politics are being struggled over and redefined" (2009, 162).

57. Hughes similarly contends that, "while older students might be able to see through such attempts at indoctrination, their impact on younger children may have less certain long-term consequences" (2014, 70).

Chapter 2: The Culture of Cultures

1. This letter and another similarly congratulatory one from Premier Li Keqiang are featured at the front of the 2014 Hanban annual development report (Hanban 2014).

2. In honor of the event, Hanban claims that more than twelve hundred CIs around the world held more than thirty-nine hundred cultural activities attended by more than 10 million participants (Hanban 2014, 6).

3. The decision to shutter the CI was in response to an "unflattering" letter in the Chinese press that insinuated that the University of Chicago had ceded to the demands of the "toughness" of Confucius Institutes director Xu Lin (Redden 2014; Sahlins 2015).

4. In the case of the CIs, "culture" arrives in myriad forms. The deployment and soft power effects of culture as language are discussed more specifically in chapter 3. This chapter primarily discusses culture as the set of material objects and practices and philosophies.

5. These invocations of "culture" render evident, as is discussed throughout the book, the differences between Chinese culture as everyday lived experience and the Chinese culture that I am calling "patriotic state ritual," which is appropriated and deployed by the CI programs for the purposes of soft power.

6. In his case study of a Confucius Institute in Britain, Pérez-Milans similarly notes that concerns about the program derive from the overlapping of what he calls "orders of indexicality" that reference the frictional spaces of foreign language learning and Hanban requirements and expectations (2014, 21).

7. For further discussions of China's instrumentalization of culture, see Albro 2015 and Glaser and Murphy 2009. While studies of Confucius Institutes that focus on soft power rarely scrutinize culture, other studies have increasingly begun to do so, most commonly through a focus on language and curriculum. See, for example, Churchman 2011; Fallon 2015; Gil 2009; Hua and Wei 2014; Pérez-Milans 2014; Stambach 2014; Starr 2009; Zhao and Huang 2010. While these scholars have employed various aspects of language as an analytical framework to make sense of the growth of CIs around the world, taken as a whole they also remind the reader that policy implementation remains highly place-specific and that language per se, despite Hanban's goals for its promotion and expansion, remains firmly embedded within local networks of exchange and value that defy easy categorization.

8. To do justice to the debates over the definition and analytical efficacy of the culture concept would require more space than this book can provide. Kuper (1999) provides an excellent assessment.

9. I draw here on Michael David-Fox's concept and phrasing. China's soft power engagements, such as the Shanghai Expo and the Olympics, provide an example of what David-Fox, in his study of Soviet-Western cultural exchanges in the interwar period, describes as culture "elevated into a virtual secular religion." In the Soviet case, this move was to counteract European notions of Russian backwardness (2011, 13), and we see a similar instrumentalization process at work in these and other soft power promotions of Chinese culture.

10. This strategy borrowed heavily from decades of effective use and refinement in the Soviet Union. See Dobrenko and Naiman 2003 for a discussion of the conjunctions of Soviet art, culture, and political ideology.

11. As discussed later in this chapter, ironically—given that Confucius is now the namesake of the CCP's most expansive strategy for international soft

power projection—during the Maoist years Confucius was attacked as counterrevolutionary and statues of Confucius and Confucian temples were destroyed along with other artifacts of "feudal" culture.

12. This revival is occurring in the midst of and as a constituent part of a "national studies craze" (*guoxuere*) that represents "efforts to construct . . . a past that would bolster claims to a uniquely Chinese national identity" (Dirlik 2011, 2) and includes not only the establishment of official national studies colleges and research centers at prestigious universities but also popular Web sites, blogs, televised lectures series, and summer camps, among others (Makeham 2011, 14).

13. See Barabantseva 2009; Gil 2017; Lahtinen 2015; Page 2015; Schmidt 2014; Stambach 2014; Yan 2007; Yao 2014; Zhou and Luk 2016.

14. Wuthnow summarizes it as "an amalgam of Confucian social and political values, folk and high customs and art, and the Chinese language" (2008, 9).

15. In Chinese culture, the dove is associated with fidelity and long life because the birds form lifelong relations and are known for taking care of their young. Jade scepters that were historically bestowed when someone reached seventy years of age were also known as "dove staffs." While the fire-breathing dragon often connotes fear and threat when depicted in these Western images, it has a long history in China as an auspicious symbol of potency and good fortune, a marker of benevolence rather than evil, and is ubiquitous throughout Chinese artistic and other representations. The dragon is one of the twelve animals on the Chinese zodiac, and China, Taiwan, and Singapore typically experience a baby boom during the year of the dragon (Lim 2012), as it is considered a promising year in which to have a child.

16. For a fuller discussion of *laozihao* and their role in the Olympics, see Hubbert 2010.

17. High-level politicians have been explicit about their support for this instrumentalization of culture for national power. On numerous occasions, President Hu Jintao, for example, whose political tenure included the Summer Olympics, equated culture's ability to establish power in the global arena with that of hard power tools such as defense, science and technology, and the economy (Li 2009b, 23).

18. For a fuller discussion of the Shanghai Expo and the myth of sustainability, see Hubbert 2015.

19. Readers might be tempted to take such commentary as mere regurgitation of official expo dogma, yet I caution against this. While researching the Shanghai Expo and other official soft power endeavors in China, including the Confucius Institutes, I have come across an equal number of people who are ardent critics and people who are supporters of the state's messaging.

This is covered in much greater detail in chapter 6, through a discussion of the constitution of free speech. Assuming that agreement with the state is necessarily an example of either false consciousness or purposeful misinformation strikes me at best as disingenuous and at worst as a reproduction of hierarchies of power that anthropology seeks consciously to deconstruct. Through providing examples of both critiques and concurrences with soft power messaging, I hope to provide readers with a broader range of potential subject positions.

20. Yao calls it a culture-rich approach that depoliticizes the CI power project (2014, 7).

21. In a different context, Rofel calls this "cosmopolitanism with Chinese characteristics," a "transcendence of locality, posited as a universal transcendence . . . and a domestication of cosmopolitanism by way of renegotiating China's place in the world" (2007, 111).

22. Yet it must be acknowledged that one would be hard-pressed to find state-sponsored soft power projects from any country that did not promote the most positive features of that nation.

23. In the case of CIs in Africa, Liang has argued, Western and Islamic civilizations have greater impact and "the fact that China has to rely on Confucian social and political values as the standard-bearer of its soft-power projection is an admission that it lacks an attractive contemporary culture" (2012, 684–685).

24. For more on this topic see Hayden 2012 and Houlden and Schmidt 2014.

25. For an examination of China's invocation of Confucian ideals of harmony as a model for global citizenship, see Albro 2015; Hayden 2012; Hubbert 2014b; and Niquet 2012.

26. Dirlik also argues that this pushes analysis of globalization to move beyond the concept of globalization as a Eurocentric teleology, to examine what he calls the globalization of modernity rather than the end of modernity (2003, 286).

27. For example, while visitors to the Shanghai Expo and the Olympics referred to and promoted traditional culture as a potential solution to the problems besetting China and the world, they just as frequently expressed skepticism at the government's ability and desire to enact the kinds of legislation and policies that must necessarily accompany philosophical musings if they are to have concrete effect. "The expo is only a face project," one visitor cynically informed me. It is all about the state wanting "to make China seem great, to get everyone to think that the Chinese are brilliant." Similarly, as a reporter explained to me, "These big 'green' events [the expo and the Olympics] are just ceremonies through which the Chinese government promotes the slogan because it is a concern to the outside world. . . . Green is just a concept. I never believed that it was a primary goal

of the government." This commentary foreshadows the experiences of the CI classroom, both as students navigate the self-portraits that China promulgates in the interests of image management and smoothing its rise to power, and as teachers, whose identification with the state is partial at best and frequently contentious, negotiate their sometimes conflicting roles as representatives of the state and independent citizens of the world.

28. Van Norden argues that Confucius's influence on Chinese society is the combined equivalent of that of Jesus and Socrates on Western traditions (2002, 3). The 2006 Hanban annual report provides a long explanation for the selection of Confucius as the symbol of the language programs that includes his historical significance, pedagogical practices, philosophical brilliance, and relevance to contemporary life. The report also includes a series of Confucian quotations and stresses that the "sayings have been the standard of self-cultivation for the Chinese people for generations." This report, originally available at http://www.hanban.edu.cn/report/2014.pdf, is no longer accessible. Sections of it are cited in Gil (2017, chap. 2).

29. "Criticize Lin, Criticize Confucius" was a political propaganda campaign that was launched in 1973 as a denunciation of Confucius and broadened in 1974 to merge with an attack on Lin Biao, vice chairman of the CCP, who allegedly attempted to instigate a coup and assassinate Mao.

30. The reference to thrift reflects China's initial post-Mao development strategies, which encouraged individual savings to finance state investment in support of economic growth.

31. In 2007, Beijing officials formalized the growing interest through sponsoring Confucian worship ceremonies on the anniversary of his birth.

32. I explore these exhibitions in more depth in earlier publications on the Olympics and the expo. See, for example, Hubbert 2017 and 2013. Of course, another central tenet of Confucian teachings, that there is no harmony without strict social order and respect for hierarchy, has received far less attention in the contemporary promotion of Confucian thought, although its practice remains important in state-society relations.

33. These appeals to tradition and its relevance to modernity were highlighted at the time in a September 1994 *People's Daily* (*Renmin ribao*) cosponsored conference on Confucianism that "revealed" the commonalities between Confucian values and the current regime's political and cultural agenda (Smith 1997).

34. Osnos (2014) makes a similar point about the contemporary Confucius campaigns.

35. See also Billioud and Thoraval 2014 and Hammond and Richey 2015.

36. Similarly, Tu Wei-ming draws direct links between Confucian ethics and capitalist economic growth throughout East Asia (1989).

37. The English-language edition of the Chinese *Economic Observer* reports that "according to officials with the National Museum," the statue's placement in Tiananmen Square was always intended to be temporary (Economic Observer Online 2011). When the Central Propaganda Department forbade Chinese journalists from reporting on the statue's removal, Chinese netizens joked that "Confucius" had been ejected from Beijing due to lack of a proper residence permit (Osnos 2014), referring to the fraught position of Chinese rural-to-urban migrants who labor in urban areas without official residency papers.

38. Yu Ying-shih defines this contradictory ethos as a division between "Confucianists who were oppressed" and "Confucianists who oppressed others," arguing that the CCP's promotion of Confucius is akin to oppressing others. The other Confucianists were "truly learned individuals" and encouraged criticism of social superiors (Yu 2015).

39. Billioud and Thoraval (2014) provide a thorough assessment of this Confucian revival as lived rather than as only conceived in contemporary China.

40. See Wu (2005) on the symbolic importance of Tiananmen Square.

41. The massive influx of Chinese students into high schools, colleges, and universities in other parts of the world, particular in England, Australia, and the United States, is a direct consequence of the fiercely competitive and sometimes psychologically brutal nature of the Chinese educational system. Nearly one in three international students in the United States is now Chinese (Waldmeir 2014).

42. This attitude, from PRC promoters of CIs, may speak volumes on the cultural influence of capitalism and consumerism, which has risen so dramatically in the last few decades and which is such a departure from the Mao years.

Chapter 3: Coolness and Magic Bullets

1. See also Hua and Wei 2014 and Pérez-Milans 2014.

2. Aside from the quotation from Mao, this décor was standard in all the classrooms I visited. As part of their curricular materials, Hanban provides supplies to decorate classrooms and teachers routinely availed themselves of these resources, particularly when the CIs and CCs were initially established. Over the years, as is discussed later in this chapter, I noticed successive teachers changing the decorations in the rooms, for example, featuring student work and images of scenic spots in China on the walls rather than the state-sanctioned maps, which, in their inclusion of Taiwan and Tibet as provinces, had the potential to spark conversations about China's controversial politics in regard to those places.

3. Outside of the dedicated classroom, there were several other places around the school campus that reflected China's presence. In the middle of the library were several large bookcases filled with books and visual materials donated by Hanban. On top of the central bookshelf, a prominent sign read "Gift Books." Hanban made its benefactor role clear inside the donated materials as well. Textbooks in the CI classrooms and materials in the library were all prominently stamped "Donated by Hanban" on the inside cover.

4. The term "fever" is a translation of the Chinese character *re,* which indicates a fad or a fervor for a practice, philosophy, or person. The term has been used frequently in China over the last several decades to explain a variety of popular fads, from the "culture fever" of the 1980s, which manifested in a fascination with a broad range of Western philosophies, particularly those concerned with issues of culture, modernity, and tradition, following the abrupt change in political climate following Mao Zedong's death (see Wang 1996), and the 1990s "Mao Zedong fever," which signposted a resurgence of interest in the late chairman and manifested in the popular consumption of iconographic paraphernalia (see Hubbert 2006), to the "stock fever" that led ordinary Chinese citizens, from students to retirees, to buy equities in unprecedented numbers (see Hertz 1998). This particular configuration of desire for China can also be seen elsewhere in Chinese media commentary regarding the ostensible China fevers occurring around the world. For example, various Chinese media reports described both President Xi Jinping's 2014 visit to Latin American and the Seattle population's tolerance of disruptions caused by Xi's 2015 visit to that city as evidence of a "China fever."

5. Nielsen argues that a focus on the peopling of policy helps us to avoid assuming that targets are mere effects of political rationality, which has been a tendency of governmentality studies of policy implementation (2011, 69).

6. By the end of my five years of research in the programs, many teachers had become aware of the cool factor of Chinese character tattoos and offered class lessons on the subject. However, rather than extolling the virtues of the practice, they showed students pictures of Chinese characters gone wrong on American bodies. One high school teacher, who was having a difficult time containing her mirth as she recounted the story, told students about swimming in a local pool in the United States and coming across a [presumably American] Caucasian man with two Chinese characters tattooed on his back. One was the character for fish and the other a poorly done character that most closely resembled the character for dead but was likely meant to be something else. Twenty minutes later, a very short student in the class burst out laughing and said, "That dead fish story is really funny. I think I'm going to get a tattoo that says *di* [short]." In her telling of the story, it is the gullible, noncomprehending American who is the equivalent

of the noncosmopolitan rube and China the marker and object of modernity. On Chinese as cool, see also Zhou 2011, 95.

7. That this form of power is recognized by others beyond their specific locality is part of the practical appeal with regard to college admissions and career prospects, as discussed later in the chapter.

8. Other students noted that studying Chinese made them "special" or "different." As one high school student explained, "One of my sisters does German, the other did Spanish, so I chose Chinese, to do something different, to be different."

9. This is similar to what Hua and Wei find in their study, arguing that student motivation for learning Chinese is "primarily local and more immediate to their personal circumstances" (2014, 332) rather than a result of broader geopolitical factors pertinent to China.

10. These summer programs are discussed at more length in chapter 4.

11. The dean of admissions quoted was not the only administrator I heard making this comment. A few years later, a principal at a high school with a CI would tell me, "The magic bullet thing, at first maybe it might have stood out more, for the first kids Chinese was [a magic bullet] for them, but not anymore. Look, even Obama's kids are taking Chinese."

12. In her study of job-seeking US undergraduate students, Gershon defines corporate personhood as akin to corporations' efforts to "represent complex social organizations as a single unity fashioned along the lines of a historically specific legal Euro-American vision of an individual" (2014, 282; see also Gershon 2017).

13. Multiple times over the years, as I visited various CIs, administrative staff paraded parents and other guests through the classrooms to publicize the programs, often relating these Chinese language success stories to attract students.

14. Others have similarly explored how Mandarin is perceived as a source of career opportunities, commercial potential, and upward social mobility. See, for example, Barabantseva 2009; Gil 2008; Park 2013; Wheeler 2014; Zhou and Luk 2016.

15. Gershon argues that this neoliberal student, soon-to-be-employed self differs from the kinds of personhood constructed during other periods of capitalism, in which one's self was metaphorically "rented" as a form of labor to an employer, akin to the ways in which property might be rented, rather than as a set of managed skills and assets that must continually undergo improvement and augmentation (2014; 2017).

16. As in this quote, and as discussed in the following paragraphs, it was clear in many of these conversations that parents played a role in students' decisions to take Chinese. Many students referenced parental perceptions about the

utility of the language. As one student explained, "My dad is in business. He says that the United States is doing more business with Chinese these days. Now Chinese language is rising, so better to learn Chinese than Japanese." Another noted, "My dad said it would look good on college résumés." At the same time as parents suggested that Chinese would be a potent résumé builder, they remained wary of the nation itself and routinely warned their children that China was "taking over the world." For these parents, Chinese emerged as a way of competing *with* China rather than a paean to its cultural glories and rapid development. Over the years, as the program became more established and normalized, I heard this remark less often.

17. And Hanban recognizes and spotlights this potential for Chinese. Hanban's Web site that describes its summer program explains it as follows: "As a pivotal world power, China is a nation that students must know about in order to raise their awareness about multiculturalism on their path to becoming world leaders in the future. This 'Chinese Bridge' Summer Camp offers the students a perfect opportunity to find out more about the world, understand the history, expand their horizon and improve themselves" (Xie 2015). This also certainly mirrors conversations I have had with Chinese middle and high school teachers and Chinese students, in which studying English, a trend enthusiastically encouraged by the PRC government, is similarly undertaken to mitigate risk and enhance career prospects.

18. Churchman (2011) argues that the mandated singular use of simplified characters and Mandarin in the CIs plays directly to this strategy to enhance nation-state power through marginalizing minority languages and dialects other than Mandarin. It also, he argues, demotes the importance of Taiwan's and Hong Kong's political claims to power and cultural applications to "Chineseness" as they continue to use complex characters and renders it difficult for students who have not learned complex characters to comprehend dissident and/or popular material from other places that have legitimate claims to represent Chinese history and culture.

19. Hanban defines HSK as an "international standardized exam that tests and rates Chinese language proficiency . . . to service Chinese language learners" (Hanban n.d., "HSK").

20. The YCT is for younger students and beginners. It includes pinyin and characters to facilitate comprehension.

21. I also watched them, as they rejected Hanban's standard cultural fare, increasingly conflate culture and modernization in the classroom in ways that were perceived as speaking to Hanban's focus on culture. For example, as one teacher explained, "The government wants us to get culture out, and

this I think is working. I barely get the 'do you have TV' question any longer. Or as one substitute teacher at the school asked me, 'It must be nice that you can have a car and drive.' She assumed that we can't drive in China. Where does she think all the bad traffic comes from? I had to explain to her that all my siblings have cars in China too."

22. This contrasts with Yao's (2014) findings that language learning is only a secondary activity in the CI classroom, in which activities about Chinese culture dominate, but dovetails with the ennui students experienced with the cultural messaging and activities on the summer Chinese Bridge program, which is the focus of the following chapter.

23. In her study of CIs in Nairobi, Wheeler realized that despite initial interest in Chinese, there were significant problems with retention (2014). I found a similar phenomenon in the CIs I studied. While Gil notes that the appeal of learning Chinese would likely decrease as students familiarized themselves with "China's problems . . . pollution, organized crime and support for authoritarian regimes in other nations" (2009, 120), students never expressed that to me as a reason for quitting. When I tracked students who went to college and quit Chinese studies at that point, they more often than not explained that Chinese had "served its purposes" by helping them achieve admission to college and was no longer necessary. Students who dropped out of the language while still in high school, particularly in the early years of the program, often targeted its negative effect on their grade point average or the perceived excessive amount of work required to attain fluency.

24. Chinese is frequently understood to be a far more difficult language to learn, relative to European languages. While part of this concerns the added level of difficulty faced by learning characters, one could also argue that teaching methods play an important role. Teachers at the CIs stressed learning characters from the beginning, as characters are oftentimes privileged because of their representation as a form of cultural knowledge. Chinese grammar is quite easy, as there are no verb tenses and some scholars argue that alternative pedagogical methods that first stress sounds and grammatical constructions and later proceed to learning characters are more successful (Everson 1998).

25. These practices have a contradictory effect. In a discussion with a school administrator at a high school CI, he explained how classroom leniency affects how the school labels the classes. Despite pressure from students and parents at this particular school, the fourth-year level of Chinese was not called AP Chinese (as it was with other languages) because it did not reach the level of academic difficulty of other AP language classes, precisely because the teachers did not push the students as hard.

26. Several teachers also mentioned that their hesitation to enforce discipline in the classroom was motivated by a fear that they would reinforce perceptions of Chinese authoritarianism.

27. This reflects what Starr calls insider and outsider concerns. He divides critics of Confucius Institutes into two categories, insiders and outsiders. Insiders largely address practical concerns about the institutes, including those of long-term support, inexperienced teachers, and academic viability, while outsiders, generally not associated with the institutes themselves, raise the specter of potential military and industrial espionage, surveillance, and propaganda dissemination (2009, 78–79).

28. The apolitical nature of the curriculum is discussed in greater detail in chapter 5.

29. Teachers' attempts to normalize historical China were not always successful. As is discussed in chapter 4, despite a curriculum designed to represent China as an example of the new global, students on the Chinese Bridge summer program spent much effort seeking examples of China as bizarre and different. Similarly, when I gave CI students an opportunity to ask me about my experiences in China, someone inevitably asked about the "weirdest food" I have ever eaten in China.

30. I use the term "orientalist" specifically in reference to Said's (1978) discussion of the derogatory and essentializing productions of value about "the Orient."

Chapter 4: Conjuring Commensurability and Particularity

1. Such sponsored trips explain some of the enthusiasm of cash-strapped US school administrators, for they can bolster the students' study abroad and cultural enrichment opportunities at no cost to the school budget.

2. I focus in this chapter on the disparities between policy intention and policy actualization to highlight the more common results of soft power policy effects, in this case. Of our group of twenty-six students, there were two or three who reacted far more positively than the rest to the program's soft power intentions. These students tended to be those who received special validation for their language proficiency or who found themselves the target of attention they were not used to receiving at home because they specifically sought the company of the guides and teachers while other students tended to gather among themselves.

3. My conversations with CI teachers and administrators also revealed that CIs were intended to enhance China's own globalization process, for example, through fostering business connections that would promote economic development and academic exchanges that would enhance domestic university reputations as "global" universities.

4. Taylor (2014, 219) invokes the felicitously phrased concept of the "pity of modernity" to illustrate the disappointment of tourists who discover signs of global modernization in the very places they are hoping to find local difference, and this describes succinctly the frustrations of the students who went to China predominantly seeking exoticism and distinction, not commensurability.

5. See Lozada 2005 and Yan 1997 on Westernization and the consumption of Western fast food in China.

6. This reflects a belief that, as one Chinese college president declared, "Many westerners' biases toward China result from their lack of understanding of the essence of the Chinese culture" and that "promotion of the Chinese culture is a good remedy for dissolving the 'China threat' argument" (cited in Lai 2012, 85).

7. CI teachers I interviewed in the United States who had acted as chaperones on these Chinese Bridge summer trips sometimes expressed frustration with the lack of appreciation expressed by the American students and chaperones. One invoked a comparison with gift giving to express his sense that this behavior was inappropriate. "When you receive a gift, even if you don't like it, you don't criticize it."

8. In contrast, CI teachers I interviewed in the United States who had been posted to smaller cities and towns around the country unfavorably compared the commercial opportunities, public transportation systems, and nighttime entertainment venues in the United States with those of their own Chinese cities. Similarly, on his excursion through Europe with a Chinese tour group, Osnos (2011) found the Chinese tourists reflecting favorably on China's economic growth and development relative to what they were seeing in Europe.

9. The presence of such markers of the global, such as the McDonald's that dot the landscape and internationally lauded contemporary architecture, reveals an environment ripe for the global production of soft power; indeed it is globalization that enables the production of soft power and demands it assume a prominent role in international relations (Nye 2004). Yet, as Kalathil argues (2011), this same environment is also the one that has the potential to reveal the gaps between soft power narratives and perceptions of "reality": the contiguous modernity and poverty and the cold French fries became instead experiences through which students refuted efforts to equate globalization with being a model of or for the global.

10. The students were clearly either ignoring or blissfully unaware of how their own historical textbooks engaged in similar practices.

11. Schmidt's 2014 essay provides an extensive description and analysis of the Exploratorium.

12. Several years later, I was reminded of this incident of misinterpretation while observing a CI class at a high school. While discussing the AP Chinese test's culture section, the teacher reminded the students that the exam always included questions about China's dynastic history and then sang them a song that listed all the emperors as a mnemonic device. This time, the song included Mao Zedong.

13. Albro explains how oftentimes cultural diplomacy fails as a strategy for effective intercultural dialogue because the intended audience "watches the show but is seldom an active participant in it" (2015, 385). Through directly engaging the students in such activities, Hanban attempted to promote a more embodied mimetic experience, calling literally upon students, in their reenactments of the past, to "understand" China through rehearsing a select form of cultural practice. This is meant, as Schmidt explains, to "elicit a feeling, a happy feeling which makes the PRC happy by association [and] . . . in which China is a 'good' and happy, and most importantly, benign place" (2014, 372). Schmidt's analysis ends at the level of potential, and she warns us in her conclusion, citing Berlant (2010, 116), that "shifts in affective atmosphere are not equal to changing the world" (Schmidt 2014, 373), a cautionary but prescient speculation that, as we move through policy analysis into the realm of engagement, becomes apparent.

14. Hua and Wei offer similar analysis from their research in a CI in the United Kingdom. Students confronted with these forms of traditional culture in the classroom similarly assessed them as inauthentic and felt that only when they could visit China itself would they encounter "authentic Chinese" culture (2014, 333).

15. See, for example, Gladney 1994; Litzinger 2000; and Schein 2000.

16. Thus, as hooks suggests, locating value in the body of the "eater" of the Other ([1992] 2006).

17. See Clifford 1992 for a related discussion of traveling, cosmopolitanism, and assumptions of difference.

18. Earlier and later conversations with CI teachers in the United States reinforced this recognition that Chinese Bridge programming was not achieving its intended results. One Chinese teacher who chaperoned a group a year after I attended was quite frank with me in his assessment:

> The students had no interest. When we went to Hanban headquarters it was pointless. Students just laid on the floor, some actually slept. Hanban is stupid. Hanban wants communication and conversation but I couldn't really see what the goal or the point of the visits to places like headquarters would accomplish. It got better when we left Beijing and students were allowed to go out with Chinese students. Really what this

all does though is help the American students treasure their own lives in
the United States. . . . They complain about the United States a lot and
then they realize there is this whole other reality to the world that makes
the United States look really good. I had students actually say this to me.
It makes them feel really lucky and then they stop complaining.

This first sentiment, that the programs were not enticing to an American
student audience, was also invoked at a 2012 House of Representatives
hearing on public diplomacy and China that frequently addressed the CIs.
One of the panelists, Robert Daly, then director of the Maryland China
Initiative at the University of Maryland, College Park, noted that the
language programs "tend to deal in culture as decoration, culture as
celebration, culture as friendship ritual. If we are going to criticize their
programs, one of the things we can throw at them is that they are
often, actually, can be sort of dull and uninteresting in those ways"
(US Congress 2012, 37).

19. At lunch, our leaders explained the history behind the unusual name of the
restaurant's feature dish. According to local lore, *goubuli* is said to derive
from the childhood name of the dish's creator, who had been nicknamed
"Doggy" (Gouzi) by his parents to protect him from bad luck, for why
would evil gods desire to harm a child named for a dog? When the child
grew up to become a renowned chef, his steamed buns were so popular that
customers had difficulty placing orders. They hence joked that Gou does not
pay attention (*bu li*) and the buns became known as *goubuli*.

20. Hongying Wang argues that China's government promotes global soft power
projects, such as the CIs, largely to bolster domestic legitimacy (2011, 52).
Michael Barr in fact argues that soft power deployment at home is as critical
as its projections abroad for national development (2012).

21. CI teachers in the United States frequently complained to me about the
expense of the language programs when, as they argued, rural education in
China was so deficient. Graan argues that nation-branding efforts, similar to
soft power projections, also allow the state to respond to domestic challenges
to its authority (2013, 165).

22. Barr, for example, argues that Chinese soft power engagements are
important for its drive to instill loyalty to the party and strengthen its
legitimacy (2012, 81).

23. This perspective attempts to reaffirm the program's constitution, which
declares that CIs "devote themselves to satisfying the demands of people
from different countries and regions in the world who learn the Chinese
language." The constitution and bylaws can be found at http://english
.hanban.org/node_7880.htm.

24. In a later conversation with the director of this particular CI, she explained to me that her program turned down the teachers offered by Hanban, agreeing to take the money under the conditions that the university hire its own faculty. She also noted that her organization has taken three hundred American students to China but has avoided the Chinese Bridge program, traveling independently instead. Calling her program a "square peg in a round hole," she shared that an upcoming CI-sponsored film festival at her school was showing a series of films that introduced China in a less-than-flattering light. Her point was to affirm that while the Chinese government funded the CI, the programming at her institution was solely under the purview of the American directors.

25. Beyond Hanban headquarters, Chinese media frequently cite what they describe as a global demand for learning the Chinese language as evidence of the world's attraction to China and the rationale for the spread of CIs. Reporting on this supposed international demand for Chinese instruction, an article in China.org, a Chinese government-authorized Internet portal, stated that "Nancy Jervis, vice president of the China Institute in New York . . . spoke of her disbelief that the 'Chinese language could become so popular'" and that "France, exhorted by its China-loving President Jacques Chirac, has seen 110 of its top universities open Chinese departments." This interest had also spread far beyond the West, according to the article, which claimed that "Chinese teaching is also a pillar of Sino-African cooperation," as illustrated by a group of African universities and student organizations that had "addressed a letter to the Chinese ambassador to Liberia wishing to soon be able to learn Chinese language and culture" and "sent up a clamor asking for a Confucius Institute" (Li 2007). According to one author, even the Swedes, who are "normally keen on protecting their own language . . . have shown great enthusiasm in learning Chinese and have admirably opened their arms to the Confucius Institute" (Guo 2008, 33) (although the Swedish CI discussed by this author has since been shut down). The underlying assumption of these claims is that the popularity of a nation's native language corresponds to global desire for that nation. These assertions of desire mirror the protestations of a China fever discussed in chapter 3.

26. Stambach notes a similar experience at a CI in the American Midwest, in which Chinese students were recruited to attend a CI cooking class but excluded from the "series of photographs" chronicling the event that were "a means of documenting the work of the Confucius Institutes to Hanban administrators" (2014, 81).

27. This was a line spoken by one of the American students in the video. Fallon (2014) offers an interesting analysis of a Hanban-sponsored Chinese language skit performed by foreigners very similar to the one featured in this film. She

argues that in featuring the Caucasian students wearing traditional Chinese clothing, it is as if China "absorbs" them into its culture, thus challenging typical racial hierarchies, while the African student in traditional native African dress, and the only foreigner not in Chinese clothing, sings about how learning Chinese will provide opportunities for her future, thus placing China in a superior position as the benevolent provider.

28. Ebron (2000) analyzes similar processes in homeland tours for African Americans.

29. Li makes a similar point (2009b, 28).

30. See also Zhang and Li 2010. Indeed, domestically, the Chinese government portrays the global spread of CIs as a national cause, designed to strengthen China's sense of self-esteem (Wang and Adamson 2015).

31. Zhou and Luk, for example, see the CIs as playing a role in "strengthening national identity, national dignity and national cohesiveness" (2016, 7). The presentation of national culture thus emerges as a resource for the national solidarity of the domestic audience.

Chapter 5: Imagining the State

1. Radcliffe-Brown, for example, suggested that, "the State . . . does not exist in the phenomenal world; it is a fiction of the philosophers" (1940, xxiii). Abrams labeled this fiction the "state idea," defined as "an ideological artifact attributing unity, morality and independence to the disunited, amoral and dependent workings of the practice of government" (1988, 81).

2. Steinmetz's 1999 edited volume is characteristic of this turn.

3. On the imagined state, see Aretxaga 2003; Ferguson and Gupta 2002; Gupta 2006; Taussig 1992. Precisely because this chapter focuses on the ways in which people experience and imagine an entity or entities they understand to represent and embody the state, I have chosen to retain the terminology of the state despite its admittedly problematic nature. For a longer discussion of this issue, see chapter 1, note 23.

4. An article on the Web site of the Chinese Academy of Social Sciences responded satirically to Stewart's lampooning of the Hacienda Height's CI: "To hear such remarks you might think that the US is still in the Cultural Revolution era" of ideological struggle, the author remarked, adding, "It's necessary for the West to gradually learn from the East." The link (http://www.cass.net.cn/file/20100701274848.html) is no longer active. I initially accessed it March 3, 2012.

5. Quotations from the board meeting come from footage included in the documentary *Mass Confucian* (Chung 2014).

6. CI hiring committees closely scrutinize potential language teachers and bar those who have participated in "illegal" organizations, such as banned

political parties or alliances like Falun Gong, although the parents likely had no way of knowing these specifics. The Toronto District School Board terminated its agreement with Hanban and closed its CI program in part because a teacher sent by Hanban revealed that she had to hide her beliefs in Falun Gong during her CI job interview.

7. It was also clear to teachers that many parents' suspicions about the programs had lessened over the years. As one CI teacher noted, "Parents now don't really care any more about the China part. They are more concerned with continuity and ask me if I'm going to be here next year. It's no longer so much the 'anti-China thing' but 'My kids like you and want to make sure there is going to be a good teacher here to teach them,' because there has been a lot of turnover with the program. Parents' attitude is better than before. . . . Studying Chinese gets normalized. The parents see the benefits of learning Chinese the longer the program is here. Kids tell parents what they see on videos. For example, I show them the Chinese New Year videos and send the links home with the kids and the parents see how much more modern China is than they expected."

8. The students showed little awareness that these policies were characteristic of authoritarianism rather than communism specifically.

9. Although their rationale for these questions about communism might vary. One student snickered as she explained that one of her fellow students would frequently ask the teacher "about the Chinese government and how it works, and whether or not they have an elected government," although she suspected that "he does it to take up class time. [Before class] he is in the hallway outside of class encouraging us to come up with questions to distract her and get her off track."

10. This is further explored at the end of the chapter.

11. Hanban clearly has high hopes for the diffusion of these texts. Xu Lin, the director general of Hanban, explained that she intended that Hanban textbooks would reach 80 percent of the world's educational markets, which she described as "a difficult but glorious task" (cited in Nguyen 2014, 103).

12. Chapter 6 analyzes similar avoidance strategies by the teachers. I have also written about Chinese culture and its perceived role in modernization in the context of the 2008 Summer Olympics in Hubbert 2013.

13. The article is evocatively called "So Long, Dalai Lama: Google Adapts to China." The contrast in these images was summoned in the congressional hearings I attended in 2014, discussed in Chapter 1.

14. I discuss the role of the iconic Tank Man photo in US politics in Hubbert 2014a.

15. The Chinese government has done a thorough job of erasing knowledge about 1989 from public memory. Over the years, I have encountered

numerous Chinese students and CI teachers who were unaware of what had happened in Tiananmen Square, although several CI teachers over the years mentioned it to me in passing, one to inform me that her father had participated. Nonetheless, there was always a bit of a furtive quality to these conversations, the teachers' unease a palpable reflection of their awareness of this government repression.

16. One CI teacher recounted an amusing story about her attempt to discuss Mao Zedong in the language classroom, thus introducing more of these "absent" politics but in a manner that deflected attention from the more brutal aspects of his reign in favor of a discussion about linguistic practices. When a student asked about the former chairman, the teacher wrote the name on the board in Chinese characters, noting that his surname, Mao, also sounds like the character for cat. As she told me, "I explained that his surname is actually the character for fur, which they think is even funnier. But I try to explain that when it is a name, it has no meaning, and compare it to names in English. When someone's name is Grossman, it doesn't mean that he is a gross man." Her point in relating the story was to reinforce how the unintended effect of one of the few potentially political classroom conversations was to make Chinese culture seem more incomprehensible.

17. I also wondered if she was playing against the association of red with communism.

18. The fieldwork portion of this research began in 2011 and ended in mid-2016. I point out these dates because both journalists and scholars have begun to note the ideological tightening that has taken place under the Xi Jinping regime during the last two years, including increasing detentions of human rights and labor advocates, more robust censoring of social media, and demands that media accommodate CCP perspectives and dictates. I do not know this to be the case, but teachers during the years 2011–2016 may have felt more comfortable with some of the critiques that they shared with me.

19. Thanks to Richard Handler for pushing me on this point.

20. It should be noted that this particular incident occurred at a highly monocultural, rural high school in which students had very little access to cultural difference. Hanban-sponsored Chinese was the only foreign language offered in this district's middle school.

21. Similarly, Wang Jisi argues that a central component of soft power is Chinese citizens' communicating to a global audience their sense of general well-being (cited in Wang 2011a, 9).

22. Albro (2015) similarly notes that soft power efforts are more effective when targets perceive a separation between state and society.

23. It is important to note that the "progressive China" proffered by the teachers strips away the complexities of what constitutes "China" across different

social and economic realms, such as in rural areas and among the uneducated and others excluded from contemporary development schemes. Special thanks to Jennifer Hsu for pointing this out to me.

24. I play here upon the idea of the "economy of moral disagreement," a theoretical feature of deliberative democracy in which citizens and their political representatives justify the minimization of political difference (Gutmann and Thompson 2004).

Chapter 6: Rethinking "Free" Speech

1. Scholars and reporters have expressed similar concerns about the CCP's potential repression of information globally as it extends its reach into media and entertainment industries around the world. When, for example, Dalian Wanda invested $3.5 billion in AMC and Legendary Entertainment and signed an agreement with Sony Pictures, US lawmakers and film analysts were outspoken about their misgivings about possible Chinese censorship of American movies and the promotion of content intended to further Chinese interests. According to film scholar Wheeler Winston Dixon, "The ideological consequences of these deals cannot be overlooked. . . . Now we're selling out to this country, and they're not exactly our pals" (quoted in Faughnder and Pierson 2016). In a similar vein, Western academic publishers have been pressured (and some have succumbed) to remove articles from their China-accessible databases that reference issues the CCP perceives as deleterious to its image (for example, articles on the 1989 massacre or on repression in Tibet) and an Australian publisher recently backed away from an agreement to publish a scholarly book that documented the CCP's growing influence in the Australian education system and media. The book in question, *Silent Invasion: China's Influence in Australia,* was authored by Clive Hamilton, professor of public ethics at Charles Sturt University.

2. One of the more well-cited and extensive of these debates occurred in June and July 2014, on the *ChinaFile* Web site. *ChinaFile* is an online magazine, published by the Asia Society, that provides original reporting and analysis about contemporary China. Participants in the debate included well-known scholars, journalists, politicians, and political consultants.

3. Within this context, the AAUP noted that globalization has led American educational institutions to welcome the "involvement of foreign governments, corporations, foundations, and donors." Similarly, a number of scholars have expressed mounting anxiety over how the corporatization of higher education threatens freedom of speech and job security for scholars who dissent from dominant political and ideological approaches or who feel compelled to shape research endeavors around commercial interests (see Deeb and Winegar 2015; Shore and Wright 1999; Stambach 2014).

4. See, for example, the debate between Sahlins and McCord, carried out in part on the *Savage Minds: Notes and Queries in Anthropology* (now published as *anthro{dendum}*) blog: http://savageminds.org/2014/03/25/on-the-defense-of-confucius-institutes-at-the-university-of-chicago-for-example/.

5. Freedom of speech is often understood as both a key precursor to successful globalization and a symbol of what it means to be a cosmopolitan, global nation. Thomas Friedman, for example, sees freedom of speech as crucial to successful globalization. After spending time in Asia, marveling at its ultramodern airports and transportation systems and returning stateside to be greeted by US infrastructural decay, he compared the two in terms of freedom of speech: "China may have great airports but last week it went back to censoring *The New York Times* and other western news sites. Censorship restricts your people's imaginations. That's really, really dumb. And that's why for all our missteps, the 21st century is still up for grabs" (Friedman 2008). Here Friedman suggests that even though China has bested the United States hands down in its twenty-first-century infrastructural development, it will not continue to globalize successfully if it continues to repress its citizens' rights of expression and neither will it truly count for a global, cosmopolitan nation (i.e., be able to "grab" the twenty-first century) until it unfetters domestic speech and access to information.

6. For a discussion of the use of ethnography to speak back to normative liberal assumptions about human nature, see Mahmood (2006).

7. These include Hartig (2016) and Sahlins (2013). Kluver admitted that he was "a bit chagrined that much of the analysis is driven by those who have limited, or at the most, arms-length experience with the CI" and suggested "that rather than relying on 'thought experiments' . . . we examine the actual activities of the CIs. . . . I would certainly encourage specific examples, rather than blanket assertions. . . . Until we know exactly which compromises have been made, let's avoid the insults to our colleagues, who are doing their best to help US students understand one of the most geopolitical important developments in recent years" (*ChinaFile* 2014).

8. This exploration thus builds upon a rich body of research that examines narratives of human rights and their links to liberal ideals for global belonging (see Adunbi 2016; Bornstein 2012; Butler 1997; Merry 2006a; Zigon 2013) and extends this analysis to address the case of China, a nation whose state apparatus remains ideologically opposed to the universalizing expectations of dominant Western human rights discourses.

9. Some of this material is also examined in the discussion of the imagined nature of the Chinese state in chapter 5.

10. There is a fundamental conflict at work here in terms of the CCP's soft power efforts abroad and at home. The historical record in China, which includes analyses of the Korean War, highlights a "century of humiliation" narrative that locates the onset of China's modernity in episodes of humiliation and tragedy rather than in moments of triumph (Schell and Delury 2013; see also Callahan 2004). This century of humiliation discourse frequently appeared in our CI tours of the various museums that showcased Chinese history, offering both concrete history lessons and the ideological context for how the students were to understand contemporary China. During our visit to a local history museum, the guide halted our tour in front of specific displays that reinforced the global oppression of China, comparing, for example, weaponry of China and Britain during the Opium War (bows and arrows for the subjugated Chinese and massive guns for the European conqueror). As our docent explained this history he noted, "It was a pitiable past, this part of Chinese history. It explains a lot about China today." The oppression was all the more severe, for prior to foreign invasion, he added, the city was a "thriving business and industrial center," not a center of economic stagnation that needed saving by the West. The CCP has used this narrative to foment a nationalism that will rally the population around its governance. Yet while it seeks simultaneously to augment its soft power globally, these kinds of narratives sometimes prove to be the undoing of that goal when foreign audiences, such as the students and chaperones on the Chinese Bridge summer program, "misrecognize" the intended messaging, as discussed in chapter 4.

11. Most critiques of propaganda in Chinese textbooks ignore similar compositions of history found in texts about other places. Scholars have chronicled narratives in US history textbooks that might similarly be understood as propaganda (e.g., Loewen 2007), which indicates the different expectations that the Chinese language programs often encounter. Though not a justification of these practices, such examples challenge the exceptionalism that often accompanies discussions of Chinese state practice.

12. One scholar originally from China who gave a CI-sponsored public talk in the United States that I attended argued that this focus on national rejuvenation was "used to justify dictatorship, civil rights limitations, and limits on freedom of speech. People are told all these limitations are necessary in order to achieve the grand mission of rejuvenation."

13. Matteo Mecacci, Italian parliament member and president of the International Campaign for Tibet, has similarly criticized the partial nature of CI's published materials. In the *ChinaFile* debate, he cited his organization's request for information about Tibet from a Washington, DC-based CI. He noted that in response, they received books that provided

what he considered to be a propagandistic "Chinese narrative on Tibet" rather than "scholarly materials published by credible American authors" that would presumably have offered a more critical perspective (*ChinaFile* 2014).

14. While I did not directly observe nor was I told by my informants of any overt Hanban interference into CI and/or host institutions' activities and engagements, these have been chronicled at length elsewhere. Sahlins's pamphlet (2015) and extensive contributions to the *ChinaFile* debate have enumerated several such issues, including Tel Aviv University's closing of an art exhibit on Falun Gong, which is banned in China, because of CCP coercion and successful Hanban pressure on North Carolina State University to cancel a visit by the Dalai Lama. One of the most well-known and egregious examples of overt Hanban pressure to suppress information occurred shortly after the *ChinaFile* debates during the biennial European Association for Chinese Studies conference in Braga, Portugal. The host university's CI had provided partial sponsorship of the conference that included funds to offset costs of printing the abstracts. When Hanban discovered that the conference bulletin included information about Taiwan's Chiang Ching-kuo Foundation and a book exhibit sponsored by the Taiwan National Central Library, CI director Xu Lin ordered her staff to gather the bulletins and tear out what she perceived to be the "offensive" pages. See Hughes 2014 for more information.

15. See "Guidelines for Establishing Confucius Institutes Abroad," June 12, 2006, http://www.china-embassy.or.jp/chn/jyylxsjl/hyjx/t257515.htm. Zhou and Luk provide a more complete discussion of this clause (2016, 10). McCord explains that this clause was quickly removed from the agreements because of partnering institutions' objections but remains fodder for the debates (n.d., 11).

16. Maps, as Callahan and others have explored, "constitute a symbolic discourse that can mobilize the masses. In this way, maps not only tell us about the geopolitics of international borders; when they inscribe space as a geobody, maps also tell us about the biopolitics of national identity practices" (2009, 144).

17. Given the political goals of the CI programs, critics have been worried that, as Link has noted, CI teachers may suffer negative consequences at home if they are critical of China while abroad and are thus motivated, even if not actively forced, to repress censure and promote optimistic visions of their nation-state (*ChinaFile* 2014). Multiple participants in the *ChinaFile* debate expressed qualms about other forms of self-censorship. Link presented the example of schools with CIs choosing to not publicly memorialize the twenty-fifth anniversary of 1989, although one might not necessarily expect

schools, even those without a CI, to do so either. Several others in the debate, while unable to offer concrete examples, similarly mentioned self-censorship as a problem of the programs. Former ambassador to China Winston Lord mentioned the possibility of academics and business executives refraining from critiques of China in the interest of procuring visas, and professor Mary Gallagher, from the University of Michigan, explained that while she could not "give specific examples of interference or self-censorship," she took seriously "the insidiousness of self-censorship."

18. See Hubbert (2014a) for a discussion of the symbolic importance of the 1989 Tiananmen violence in the US imagination.

19. Red of course is also a color associated with good luck and happiness in Chinese culture and is often used in celebrations.

20. I am reminded here of Geertz's famous point about perceiving the difference between a wink and a twitch. In discussing this point, Herzfeld noted, "Some details strike us only retrospectively, through a sudden realization of our own initial failure to recognize them" (Herzfeld 2015, 21).

21. Esarey, Stockmann, and Zhang's interesting research on propaganda in China reveals that Chinese citizens tend to read what many Americans would label as "propaganda" quite differently, supporting rather than lamenting the government's capacity to "guide public opinion" (2017).

22. I was also missing, as discussed later in the chapter, the implications of my overly narrow expectations for the constitution of free speech.

23. The topic of curriculum and teacher choices is discussed at greater length in chapter 5.

24. Most of the material from my own research on CI teacher training that has been cited by other scholars concerns CI teachers' revelations that they were explicitly instructed by Hanban during their pre-posting training to present a glorious picture of the nation and avoid discussing controversial topics, which confirms critics' suspicions that the soft power image management goals of the programs are being implemented in the language classrooms.

25. These teacher training conferences also frequently offered comparisons of US and Chinese students that were unfavorable to US students, as in the following remarks by a Hanban administrator at a training session I attended: "American students are really lacking. They are difficult to teach. Every five to ten minutes they have need to drink water, get up and go to the bathroom. Chinese students are really great in comparison. They do things really fast. It's much more intense. Learning goes faster. Here they just want to have fun." Chinese teachers frequently made similar remarks to me, contrasting the discipline and productivity of classrooms in China to what they saw as chaotic and unproductive US classrooms.

26. See also Albro 2015 and Nye 2002.

27. For an examination of media representations of China, see Broomfield 2003.

28. The references to these topics were mixed in their level of critique. The guide mentioned the Dalai Lama as an important spiritual leader without characterizing him, as the official PRC position would, as an agitator with no legitimacy. And the passing reference to the 1989 demonstrations was certainly not the same as acknowledging a large-scale government-ordered massacre of unarmed protestors. One could argue that these references were merely a sanitized method of broaching sensitive topics that allowed the speaker to conform to Western expectations of what was important in China and quickly move on to other more approved topics of conversation. Regardless, that the topics were broached at all was what emerged as central to how the US audience reacted.

29. Those to whom I reported the tour guide's open references to "forbidden" issues when I returned to the United States also expressed surprise that people in China could "speak so freely," similarly underscoring a perception of a "real" China that is understood only as negative and repressive.

30. These are comments from a variety of different teachers.

31. Indeed, at a 2016 talk I gave in Europe that advocated for a broader definition of freedom of speech, the first question from the audience was by an American scholar who asked, "If a parent asks, 'Should we have CIs or not? Are they good or bad?' how would you answer?"

32. See, for instance, Habermas 1991; Lee and LiPuma 2002; Taylor 2002. As Merry points out, these assumptions are also used on the global stage to augment a nation-state's claims to credibility and challenge and demoralize those of other states (1996). Anthropologists have long been engaged with issues of human rights, including as critics of assumptions about the universal nature of human rights—what Billaud calls the "ethos of 'universal human rights'" (2016)—and of its emergence as a discursive form of power. The debate over universal versus relative human rights has been well conceptualized, with universalists arguing that the principles of human rights, as laid out in the Universal Declaration of Human Rights, for example, apply to all cultures, while relativists argue that cultural differences need to be respected and that human rights must be understood as relative to the culture in which they are embedded. This latter argument has been articulated in many places in Asia through a conversation about "Asian values" that prioritizes economic development over political rights such as the freedom to vote and freedom of speech (Sen 1997). My point here is not a critique of freedom of speech as a practical concept or an argument about the validity or invalidity of the concept of Asian values, but to argue that if freedom of speech, and human rights in general, provide a dominant theoretical and rhetorical framework for thinking about the world,

stipulating the moral language that grounds the political status quo, we ought to examine the concepts analytically.

33. On Chinese citizens' appeals to freedom of speech, in the context of the 2008 Olympics as a marker of global citizenship, see Hubbert 2010.

34. Despite the extensive psychological literature that characterizes the Chinese as conflict avoidant and excessively concerned with preserving "face," I have not yet encountered an analysis of avoiding sensitive topics in the classroom described in those terms rather than in terms of politics and propaganda. In addition to rethinking the constitution of free speech, we might also examine, in this instance, how culturally appropriate forms of speech exchange might lead teachers to avoid conflict with members of the host countries rather than only assuming that they are merely avoiding contentious politics.

35. In a rejoinder to Sahlins, McCord makes a similar argument, noting, "Any statement of support by CI teachers . . . at odds with the sympathies of the CI detractors on topics such as Tibetan or Taiwan independence is somehow taken to be a threat to free expression" (McCord n.d., 13). He sees this as a "no-win" situation in which CIs are expected to offer programing on contentious issues but are accused of propaganda if they present PRC perspectives. This is not to imply that people in China do not wish to have greater freedom of speech (see Davies 2012), but to suggest that not all forms of freedom must be the same. Rutz (1999) and Dominguez (2011) discuss similar cases in which free speech is constrained under the guise of liberalism and in the name of modernity.

36. See also Anagnost 1997 on Chinese citizens' "speaking the state" as a form of alternative politics.

37. This process mirrors Mahmood's discussion (2006) of how feminist analyses of Islamic religious traditions and gender invoke a form of human agency that is located in the political autonomy of the subject, similarly foreclosing alternative forms of agency.

38. In a mix of both English and Chinese, she used both the phrase *bianzheng zhuyi*, which refers to the Marxist dialectic and "both sides of the process, of the story." Other teachers have made similar points. As one explained to me, "I know that some people say that it's about free speech, that it's diminishing freedom of speech, that a teacher might not talk about Tibet, Taiwan. These conversations are still happening, but the CI teachers might have different opinions. So it's still free speech, but everyone should have a voice, not just one voice."

39. Her point strikes me as recognizing what Boyer and Yurchak (2010) argue in their analysis of media practices in late socialism and the contemporary West. They suggest that Western responses to socialism say as much about the West's own philosophical production as about socialism itself.

40. Dutton's analysis of the art exhibit *Venice's Rent Collection Courtyard,* a partial reproduction of a famous Cultural Revolution sculptural series, offers a similar conundrum. Dutton describes a form of art that would be easily classified as propaganda in the West but that through a Marxist analysis of class created a different, but equally valid, kind of political subject and offered another way of apprehending politics (Dutton 2012).

41. As Pierre Bourdieu argues, "authority comes to language from outside" (1991, 109); it is not the words themselves that are instruments of action and power.

Chapter 7: The Sites and Struggles of Global Belonging

1. This is not, of course, to argue that earlier films consistently presented an antagonistic perspective. Bernardo Bertolucci's *The Last Emperor* (Columbia Pictures, 1987), the first major Western film authorized by the PRC to film inside the Forbidden City, led to the creation of "Last Emperor Tours" for Western travelers and contributed to an increase in Western interest in Chinese civilization and culture (Zhang, 1989).

2. Flew argues that such "generic" blockbusters do little to promote Chinese culture globally even though they "enhance the economic standing of Chinese media and creative industries" (2016, 288).

3. Deng and Zhang provide a quantitative assessment of the US-China gap in exports of cultural productions. Drawing upon UNESCO statistics, they show that when Western consumers choose what to acquire they rarely opt for Chinese cultural exports: China's imports of books are nearly two and a half times its exports, and its audio and visual production imports are nearly seventeen times as high (Deng and Zhang 2009, 149).

4. Only once have I been asked a similar question from a counterperspective. At a talk I gave at a large, state-run university with a CI, after I had chronicled the problems confronting the language programs, a member of the audience asked, in effect, how the programs could improve and more effectively serve our students. Recently, another report on the CIs has been publicly issued in the United States, this one by the conservative-leaning National Association of Scholars, that at almost two hundred pages is the longest assessment of the programs thus far and that has dominated a renewed online debate on the presence of CIs at US educational institutions. This report, too, is focused on answering this question about whether the United States should admit CIs. Its policy recommendation to close all Confucius Institutes is based upon case studies at twelve CIs in New York and New Jersey that focus primarily on hiring policies, funding arrangements, university-Hanban contracts, and whether faculty were pressured by Hanban (Peterson 2017, 9). The debates over these reports often

cause me to wonder why the ethnographic scholarly literature on the subject rarely makes an appearance. Where, I ask, is Stambach's (2014) nuanced discussion of the dialectic nature of language as it constitutes the everyday practices and interactions in Confucius Institutes? Where are Schmidt's discussions of the importance of affect (2014) or race (2013)?

5. Michael Barr calls this the "vehicle fallacy" (2012, 48): the confusion of resources with output.
6. Albro's examination of US public diplomacy similarly reveals how project practitioners assumed that the cultural expressions they were offering to a foreign audience were "unproblematic and effective vehicles for national values" (2015, 384).
7. Eng, Ruskola, and Shen (2012) explore the role of human rights discourses in locating China in relation to concepts of the human.
8. This also contradicts theories of soft power in China as exceptional because of the presence of a perceived authoritarian state, thus challenging perceptions of the way in which power is presumed to operate through soft power.
9. Chun argues similarly that the manner in which Hanban influences "all matters pertaining to China" should be conceived not as soft power but as "hard sell" (2017, 183).
10. China has never been a standard Other to Western power. While prior to the nineteenth century, Western colonial authorities, missionaries, explorers, and traders encountered forms of difference in other places that confirmed evolutionary perspectives on global hierarchies, in contrast, in their "curious and exotic encounters" with China (Zhang 2013, 55), rather than an object in need of reform, they found a contemporaneous competing civilization, a source of European desires and "of economic and technological advantage" (Hayot 2009, 9). At the same time, as many scholars have explored, China historically neither perceived itself as a deficient Other to Western power, nor desired its material presence. China thus remains a bit of an uncomfortable Other to the Western standard self, with one history as a contemporaneous equivalent and/or superior and another more recent history as a subjugated periphery.
11. Precisely because of this relationship, Laurel Kendall (2014) argues that anthropology's early lack of engagement with China may in fact have changed the face of anthropology as we know it. In a fascinating exploration of lesser-known intellectual history, Kendall explores the travels of Berthold Laufer, one of Franz Boas's early protégés, who under direction from Boas (who himself envisioned a major role for East Asian studies within anthropology) spent a significant amount of time in China during the early part of the twentieth century. For a variety of reasons, although Boas's plan

for Laufer's research "reflected an appreciation of the historical depth, complexity, technological sophistication, and sheer enormity of 'China'" (Kendall 2014, 12), unlike the similarly Boas-directed research excursions among the North American native populations that provided the comparative foundations for early American anthropology, the China program was ultimately sidelined. The significance of this sidelining, Kendall argues, lies in "what might have been," an anthropology of an equivalent civilizational Other that might have "sidestepped its now very dated (but in popular culture tenacious) association with the study of 'simple societies' and 'primitive peoples'" (Kendall 2014, 2).

12. Or as Tate argues, "Policy narratives play a role in making politics legible; that is, coherent and comprehensible" (2015, 4).

13. I draw the term "margins" from Orta's 2013 discussion of MBA students who work to "manage the margins" of the global through their short-term study abroad trips to Mexico, where they convert the risks of social and cultural differences into social capital for the self.

References

AAUP. 2014. "On Partnerships with Foreign Governments: The Case of Confucius Institutes." Accessed July 1, 2014. https://www.aaup.org/report /confucius-institutes.

Abrams, Philip. 1988. "Notes on the Difficulty of Studying the State." *Journal of Historical Sociology* 1 (1): 58–89.

Adunbi, Omolade. 2016. "Embodying the Modern: Neoliberalism, NGOs and the Culture of Human Rights Practices in Nigeria." *Anthropological Quarterly* 89 (2): 397–430.

Albro, Robert. 2015. "The Disjunction of Image and Word in US and Chinese Soft Power Projection." *International Journal of Cultural Policy* 21 (4): 382–399.

Aldrich, John, Jie Lu, and Liu Kang. 2015. "How Do Americans View the Rising China?" *Journal of Contemporary China* 24 (92): 203–221.

Al-Rodhan, Khalid. 2007. "A Critique of the China Threat Theory: A Systematic Analysis." *Asian Perspective* 31 (3): 41–66.

Anagnost, Ann. 1997. *National Past-Times: Narrative, Representation, and Power in Modern China.* Durham, NC: Duke University Press.

———. 2013. "Introduction: Life-Making in Neoliberal Times." In *Global Futures in East Asia: Youth, Nation, and the New Economy in Uncertain Times,* edited by Ann Anagnost, Andrea Arai, and Hai Ren, 1–27. Stanford, CA: Stanford University Press.

Ang, Ien, Yudhishthir Raj Isar, and Phillip Mar. 2015. "Cultural Diplomacy: Beyond the National Interest?" *International Journal of Cultural Policy* 21 (4): 365–381.

Aretxaga, Begoña. 2003. "Maddening States." *Annual Review of Anthropology* 32:393–410.

Arnason, Johann. 2000. "Communism and Modernity." *Daedalus* 129 (1): 61–90.

Austin, April. 2004. "Where Are the Chinese-Speakers of the Future?" *Christian Science Monitor,* February 10, 11.

Aysha, Emad El-Din. 2005. "September 11 and the Middle East Failure of US 'Soft Power': Globalisation Contra Americanisation in the 'New' US Century." *International Relations* 19 (2): 193–210.

Bandurski, David. 2016. "Supervising Supervision." *China Media Project,* June 17. Accessed January 15, 2017. http://www.cmp.hku.hk/?p=39775.

Barabantseva, Elana. 2009. *"Shijie* Meets *Tianxia* in China's Interactions with the World." *Alternatives: Global, Local, Political* 34 (2): 129–155.

Barmé, Geremie. 2008. "Olympic Art & Artifice." *American Interest* 3 (6), July 1. https://www.the-american-interest.com/2008/07/01/olympic-art-artifice/.

Barr, Michael. 2011. *Who's Afraid of China? The Challenge of Chinese Soft Power.* London: Zed Books.

———. 2012. "Nation Branding as Nation Building: China's Image Campaign." *East Asia* 29:81–94.

Beck, Ulrich. 1992. *Risk Society: Towards a New Modernity.* London: Sage Publications.

Beck, Ulrich, and Elisabeth Beck-Gernsheim. 2002. *Individualization: Institutionalized Individualism and Its Social and Political Consequences.* London: Sage Publications.

Bell, Daniel. 2006. "China's Leaders Rediscover Confucianism." *New York Times,* September 14. Accessed December 17, 2017. http://www.nytimes .com/2006/09/14/opinion/14iht-edbell.2807200.html.

———. 2009. "What Can We Learn from Confucianism?" *Guardian,* July 26. Accessed December 17, 2017. https://www.theguardian.com/commentisfree /belief/2009/jul/26/confucianism-china.

Berlant, Lauren. 2010. "Thinking about Feeling Historical." In *Political Emotions,* edited by Janet Staiger, Ann Cvetkovich, and Ann Reynolds, 229–245. Florence, KY: Routledge.

Bhabha, Homi. 1984. "Of Mimicry and Man: The Ambivalence of Colonial Discourse." *October* 28:125–133.

Billaud, Julie. 2016. "Afterword: A Post–Human Rights Anthropology of Human Rights?" *PoLAR: Political and Legal Anthropology Review.* Accessed December 3, 2016. https://polarjournal.org/a-post-human-rights -anthropology-of-human-rights/.

Billioud, Sébastien, and Joël Thoraval. 2014. *The Sage and the People: The Confucian Revival in China.* Oxford: Oxford University Press.

Bornstein, Erica. 2012. *Disquieting Gifts: Humanitarianism in New Delhi.* Stanford, CA: Stanford University Press.

Bourdieu, Pierre. 1984. *Distinction: A Social Critique of the Judgement of Taste.* Translated by Richard Nice. Cambridge, MA: Harvard University Press.

———. 1991. *Language and Symbolic Power.* Edited by John Thompson; translated by Gino Raymond and Matthew Adamson. Malden: Polity Press.

Boyer, Dominic, and Alexei Yurchak. 2010. "American Stiob: Or, What Late Socialist Aesthetics of Parody Reveal about Contemporary Political Culture in the West." *Cultural Anthropology* 25 (2): 179–221.

Brady, Anne-Marie, ed. 2012. *China's Thought Management*. New York: Routledge.

Brautigam, Deborah. 2009. *The Dragon's Gift: The Real Story of China in Africa*. Oxford: Oxford University Press.

Breslin, Shaun. 2010. "China Engages Asia: The Notion of China's 'Soft Power.'" *Ethos* 8:5–11.

Broomfield, Emma. 2003. "Perceptions of Danger: The China Threat Theory." *Journal of Contemporary China* 12 (35): 265–284.

Bruckermann, Charlotte. 2016. "Trading on Tradition: Tourism, Ritual, and Capitalism in a Chinese Village." *Modern China* 42 (2): 188–224.

Butler, Judith. 1997. *Excitable Speech: A Politics of the Performative*. New York: Routledge.

Cai, Jianguo. 2010. "Shanghai shibohui he ahongguo wenhua ruanshili de goujian" (Constructing Chinese soft power at the Shanghai world expo). *Qiushi lilun* (Seeking truth theory), May 10. Accessed November 12, 2012. http://www.qstheory.cn/hqwg/2010/201009/201005/t20100510_29280 .htm.

Callahan, William. 2004. "National Insecurities: Humiliation, Salvation, and Chinese Nationalism." *Alternatives* 29:199–218.

———. 2009. "The Cartography of National Humiliation and the Emergence of China's Geobody." *Public Culture* 21 (1): 141–173.

———. 2012. "Sino-Speak: Chinese Exceptionalism and the Politics of History." *Journal of Asian Studies* 71 (1): 33–55.

Callahan, William, and Elena Barabantseva, eds. 2011. *China Orders the World: Normative Soft Power and Foreign Policy*. Baltimore, MD: Johns Hopkins University Press.

Camicia, Steven, and Barry Franklin. 2011. "What Type of Global Community and Citizenship? Tangled Discourses of Neoliberalism and Critical Democracy in Curriculum and Its Reform." *Globalisation, Societies and Education* 9 (3–4): 311–322.

Canaves, Sky. 2009. "Global Times Breaches China's Official Media Silence on Tiananmen." *Wall Street Journal,* June 4. Accessed June 5, 2009. https:// blogs.wsj.com/chinarealtime/2009/06/04/global-times-breaches-chinas -official-media-silence-on-tiananmen/.

Chang, Anita. 2011. "Confucius Shows up in China's Tiananmen Square." MSNBC.com. Accessed May 15, 2013. http://www.nbcnews.com/id /41061323/ns/world_news-asia_pacific/t/confucius-shows-chinas -tiananmen-square/.

Chang, Jung-A. 2016. "From Folk Culture to Great Cultural Heritage of China: The Aporia of the Quest for the Essence of Chinese Culture." In *Intangible Cultural Heritage in Contemporary China: The Participation of Local*

Communities, edited by Khun Eng Kuah and Zhaohui Liu, 112–136. New York: Routledge.

Chen, Chen. 2010. "Finding Support for Confucius Institutes." *CPD Blog,* USC Center on Public Diplomacy, April 27. Accessed May 8, 2016. https:// uscpublicdiplomacy.org/blog/finding-support-confucius-institutes.

Chen Jie. 2016. "Xi: Build China's Cultural Confidence." *ChinaDaily.com,* December 1. Accessed May 25, 2017. http://www.chinadaily.com.cn/china /2016-12/01/content_27532284.htm.

Chey, Jocelyn. 2008. "Chinese 'Soft Power': Cultural Diplomacy and the Confucius Institutes." *Sydney Papers* 20 (1): 32–46.

ChinaFile. 2014. "Debate over Confucius Institutes: A *ChinaFile* Conversation." *ChinaFile.com.* Accessed July 1, 2014. https://www.chinafile.com/conversation /debate-over-confucius-institutes.

Ching, Leo. 2000. "Globalizing the Regional, Regionalizing the Global: Mass Culture and Asianism in the Age of Late Capital." *Public Culture* 12 (1): 233–257.

Cho, Young Nam, and Jong Ho Jeong. 2008. "China's Soft Power: Discussions, Resources, and Prospects." *Asian Survey* 48 (3): 453–472.

Chu, Julie. 2014. "When Infrastructures Attack: The Workings of Disrepair in China." *American Ethnologist* 41 (2): 351–367.

Chun, Allen. 2017. *Forget Chineseness: On the Geopolitics of Cultural Identification.* Albany: State University of New York Press.

Chung, Philip, director. 2014. *Mass Confucian: Language Learning or Communist Propaganda?* Produced by Clyde Kusatsu, Tony Lam, Tim Lounibos, and Nancy Wang Yuen.

Churchman, Michael. 2011. "Confucius Institutes and Controlling Chinese Languages." *China Heritage Quarterly* 26. Accessed February 12, 2012. http://www.chinaheritagequarterly.org/articles.php?searchterm=026_ confucius.inc&issue=026.

Clarke, John, Dave Bainton, Noémi Lendvai, and Paul Stubbs, eds. 2015. *Making Policy Move: Toward a Politics of Translation and Assemblage.* Chicago: Policy Press.

Clifford, James. 1992. "Travelling Cultures." In *Cultural Studies,* edited by Lawrence Grossberg, Cary Nelson, and Paula Treichler, 96–116. New York: Routledge.

Cobb, Russell. 2014. "Introduction: The Artifice of Authenticity in the Age of Digital Reproduction." In *The Paradox of Authenticity in a Globalized World,* edited by Russell Cobb, 1–9. New York: Palgrave Macmillan.

Cole, Jennifer, and Deborah Durham. 2008. "Introduction: Globalization and the Temporality of Children and Youth." In *Figuring the Future: Globalization and the Temporalities of Youth,* edited by Jennifer Cole and

Deborah Durham, 3–23. Santa Fe, NM: School for Advanced Research Press.

Comaroff, Jean, and John L. Comaroff. 1999. "Occult Economies and the Violence of Abstraction: Notes from the South African Postcolony." *American Ethnologist* 26 (2): 279–303.

———. 2012. *Theory from the South: Or, How Euro-America Is Evolving toward Africa.* New York: Taylor & Francis.

David-Fox, Michael. 2011. *Showcasing the Great Experiment: Cultural Diplomacy and Western Visitors to the Soviet Union, 1921–1941.* New York: Oxford University Press.

Davies, Gloria. 2012. "*Homo Dissensum Significans,* or The Perils of Taking a Stand in China." *Social Text* 29 (4): 29–56.

Deeb, Lara, and Jessica Winegar. 2015. *Anthropology's Politics: Disciplining the Middle East.* Stanford, CA: Stanford University Press.

DeHart, Monica. 2017. "Who Speaks for China? Translating Geopolitics through Language Institutes in Costa Rica." Special edition. *Journal of Chinese Overseas* 13 (2).

Deng, Xiaogang, and Lening Zhang. 2009. "China's Cultural Exports and Its Growing Cultural Power in the World." In *Soft Power: China's Emerging Strategy in International Politics,* edited by Mingjiang Li, 143–162. Lanham, MD: Lexington Books.

d'Hooghe, Ingrid. 2011. "The Expansion of China's Public Diplomacy System." In *Soft Power in China: Public Diplomacy through Communication,* edited by Jian Wang, 19–35. New York: Palgrave Macmillan.

———. 2014. *China's Public Diplomacy.* Boston, MA: Brill Hijhoff.

Ding Feng. 2014. "Xi Jinping: Kongzi xueyuan shuyu zhongguo ye shuyu shijie" (Xi Jinping: Confucius Institute belongs to China and belongs to the world). Xinhua News, September 27. Accessed May 14, 2017. http://news.xinhuanet.com/politics/2014-09/27/c_1112652079.htm.

Ding, Sheng. 2008. *The Dragon's Hidden Wings: How China Rises with Its Soft Power.* Lanham, MD: Lexington Books.

———. 2011. "Branding a Rising China: An Analysis of Beijing's National Image Management in the Age of China's Rise." *Journal of Asian and African Studies* 46 (3): 293–306.

———. 2012. "Is Human Rights the Achilles' Heel of Chinese Soft Power? A New Perspective on Its Appeal." *Asian Perspective* 36:641–665.

Ding, Sheng, and Robert Saunders. 2006. "Talking Up China: An Analysis of China's Rising Cultural Power and Global Promotion of the Chinese Language." *East Asia* 23 (2): 3-33.

Dirlik, Arif. 1995. "Confucius in the Borderlands: Global Capitalism and the Reinvention of Confucianism." *Boundary 2* 22 (3): 229–273.

———. 2003. "Global Modernity? Modernity in an Age of Global Capitalism." *European Journal of Social Theory* 6 (3): 275–292.

———. 2011. "Introduction." *China Perspectives* 1:2–3.

Dobrenko, Evgeny, and Eric Naiman, eds. 2003. *The Landscape of Stalinism: The Art and Ideology of Soviet Space.* Seattle: University of Washington Press.

Dominguez, Virginia. 2011. "Discussants' Commentary: Antonio Lauria and 'An Anthropology of Critical Engagement.'" *Tranforming Anthropology* 19 (1): 59–61.

Dong Yan. 2014. "2014 Nian jiang zai quanqiu fanwei nei sheli 'kongzi xueyuan ri'" (The global Confucius Institute Day will be established in 2014). *Zhongguo jintian* (China today), March 10. Accessed February 2, 2017. http://www.chinatoday.com.cn/ctchinese/zhuanti/2014-03/10/content _604597.htm.

Dutton, Michael. 2012. "Fragments of the Political, or How We Dispose of Wonder." *Social Text* 30 (1): 109–141.

Ebron, Paula. 2000. "Tourists as Pilgrims: Commercial Fashioning of Transatlantic Politics." *American Ethnologist* 26 (4): 910–932.

Economic Observer Online. 2011. "Statue of Confucius Moved to Less Prominent Location." *Economic Observer,* April 21. Accessed June 28, 2017. http://www.eeo.com.cn/ens/homepage/haedlinescanner/2011/04/21/199530 .shtml.

Economist. 2006. "Selling the Sage of Qufu: China's Answer to the Alliance Française." *Economist,* July 6. Accessed November 15, 2016. http://www .economist.com/node/7141845.

———. 2009. "A Message from Confucius: New Ways of Projecting Soft Power." *Economist,* October 22. Accessed June 8, 2017. http://www. economist.com/node/14678507.

———. 2015. "Confucius Says, Xi Does." *Economist,* June 25. Accessed May 17, 2017. http://www.economist.com/news/china/21659753-communist-party -turns-ancient-philosophy-support-confucius-says-xi-does.

Eng, David, Teemu Ruskola, and Shuang Shen. 2012. "Introduction: China and the Human." *Social Text* 29 (4): 1–27.

Esarey, Ashley, Daniela Stockmann, and Jie Zhang. 2017. "Support for Propaganda: Chinese Perceptions of Public Service Advertising." *Journal of Contemporary China* 26 (103): 101–117.

Everson, Michael. 1998. "Word Recognition among Learners of Chinese as a Foreign Language: Investigating the Relationship between Naming and Knowing." *Modern Language Journal* 82 (2): 194–204.

Fallon, Tracey. 2014. "Chinese Fever and Cool Heads: Confucius Institutes and China's National Identities." *China Media Research* 10 (1): 35–46.

———. 2015. "Nationalism, National Identity and Politics in the Teaching of Chinese as a Foreign Language." PhD diss., University of Nottingham.

Fallows, James. 2016. "China's Great Leap Backward." *Atlantic,* December. Accessed January 8, 2017. http://www.theatlantic.com/magazine/archive /2016/12/chinas-great-leap-backward/505817/.

Faughnder, Ryan, and David Pierson. 2016. "Chinese Billionaire Wang Jianlin Makes Aggressive Moves in Hollywood." *Los Angeles Times,* September 30. Accessed May 3, 2017. http://www.latimes.com/entertainment/envelope /cotown/la-et-ct-wanda-hollywood-20160928-snap-story.html.

Ferguson, James. 2006. *Global Shadows: Africa in the Neoliberal World Order.* Durham, NC: Duke University Press.

Ferguson, James, and Akhil Gupta. 2002. "Spatializing States: Toward an Ethnography of Neoliberal Governmentality." *Cultural Anthropology* 29 (4): 981–1002.

Ferguson, Marjorie. 2005. "The Mythology about Globalization." In *Communication Theory and Research,* edited by Denis McQuail, 23–36. London: Sage Publications.

Fisher, Edward. 2014. *The Good Life: Aspiration, Dignity, and the Anthropology of Wellbeing.* Stanford, CA: Stanford University Press.

Flanagan, Constance. 2008. "Private Anxieties and Public Hopes: The Perils and Promise of Youth in the Context of Globalization." In *Figuring the Future: Globalization and the Temporalities of Youth,* edited by Jennifer Cole and Deborah Durham, 125–150. Santa Fe, NM: School for Advanced Research Press.

Flew, Terry. 2016. "Entertainment Media, Cultural Power, and Post-Globalization: The Case of China's International Media Expansion and the Discourse of Soft Power." *Global Media and China* 1 (4): 278–294.

Friedman, Thomas. 1999. *The Lexus and the Olive Tree.* New York: Picador.

———. 2007. *The World Is Flat: A Brief History of the Twentieth-First Century.* New York: Farrar, Straus and Giroux.

———. 2008. "Time to Reboot America." *New York Times,* December 23. Accessed December 24, 2008. http://www.nytimes.com/2008/12/24 /opinion/24friedman.html.

Frum, David. 2010. "The Recession Was Made in China." CNN.com, October 12. Accessed November 2, 2010. http://www.cnn.com/2010/OPINION/10 /11/frum.china.currency/.

Gao, George. 2017. "Why Is China So . . . Uncool?" *ForeignPolicy.com,* March 8. Accessed March 10, 2017. http://foreignpolicy.com/2017/03/08/why-is-china -so-uncool-soft-power-beijing-censorship-generation-gap/.

Garrett, Banning. 2001. "China Faces, Debates, the Contradictions of Globalization." *Asian Survey* 41 (3): 409–427.

Gershon, Ilana. 2014. "Willing Your Self in the United States." *PoLAR: Political and Legal Anthropology Review* 37 (2): 281–295.

———. 2017. *Down and Out in the New Economy*. Chicago: University of Chicago Press.

Gertz, Bill. 2000. *The China Threat: How the People's Republic Targets America*. Washington, DC: Regnery.

Giddens, Anthony. 1998. *Conversations with Anthony Giddens: Making Sense of Modernity*. Stanford, CA: Stanford University Press.

Gil, Jeffrey. 2008. "The Promotion of Chinese Language Learning and China's Soft Power." *Asian Social Science* 4 (10): 115–122.

———. 2009. "China's Confucius Institute Project: Language and Soft Power in World Politics." *Global Studies Journal* 2 (1): 59–72.

———. 2017. *Soft Power and the Worldwide Promotion of Chinese Language Learning: The Confucius Institute Project*. Kindle ed. Bristol, UK: Multilingual Matters.

Gill, Bates, and Yanzhong Huang. 2006. "Sources and Limits of Chinese 'Soft Power.'" *Survival* 48 (2): 17–36.

Gladney, Dru. 1994. "Representing Nationality in China: Refiguring Majority/Minority Identities." *Journal of Asian Studies* 53 (1): 92–123.

Glaser, Bonnie, and Melissa Murphy. 2009. "Soft Power with Chinese Characteristics: The Ongoing Debate." In *Chinese Soft Power and Its Implications for the United States: Competition and Cooperation in the Developing World*, edited by Carola McGiffert, 10–26. Washington, DC: Center for Strategic and International Studies.

Golden, Daniel. 2011. "China Says No Talking Tibet as Confucius Funds U.S. Universities." *Bloomberg News*, November 1. Accessed November 3, 2011. https://www.bloomberg.com/news/articles/2011-11-01/china-says-no-talking-tibet-as-confucius-funds-u-s-universities.

Graan, Andrew. 2013. "Counterfeiting the Nation? Skopje 2014 and the Politics of Nation Branding in Macedonia." *Cultural Anthropology* 28 (1): 161–179.

Groot, Gerry. 2016. "The Expansion of the United Front under Xi Jinping." In *Pollution*, edited by Gloria Davies, Jeremy Goldkorn, and Luigi Tomba, 167–178. Canberra: Australian National University Press.

Guo, Xiaolin. 2008. *Repackaging Confucius: PRC Public Diplomacy and the Rise of Soft Power*. Stockholm: Institute for Security and Development Policy.

Gupta, Akhil. 2006. "Blurred Boundaries: The Discourse of Corruption, the Culture of Politics, and the Imagined State." In *The Anthropology of the State: A Reader*, edited by Aradhana Sharma and Akhil Gupta, 211–242. Malden, MA: Blackwell Publishing.

———. 2012. *Red Tape: Bureaucracy, Structural Violence, and Poverty in India*. Durham, NC: Duke University Press.

Gutmann, Amy, and Dennis Thompson. 2004. *Why Deliberative Democracy?* Princeton, NJ: Princeton University Press.

Habermas, Jurgen. 1991. *The Structural Transformation of the Public Sphere: An Inquiry into a Category of Bourgeois Society.* Cambridge, MA: MIT Press.

Hall, Ian, and Frank Smith. 2013. "The Struggle for Soft Power in Asia: Public Diplomacy and Regional Competition." *Asian Security* 9 (1): 1–18.

Hammond, Kenneth, and Jeffrey Richey, eds. 2015. *The Sage Returns: Confucian Revival in Contemporary China.* New York: State University of New York Press.

Hanban. n.d. "Constitution and By-Laws of the Confucius Institutes." Accessed April 10, 2015. http://english.hanban.org/node_7880.htm.

———. n.d. "HSK." Accessed June 2, 2015. http://english.hanban.org/node_8002.htm.

———. 2014. *Confucius Institute Annual Development Report: 2014.* Confucius Institute Headquarters. Accessed June 29, 2017. http://www.hanban.edu.cn/report/2014.pdf.

———. 2015. "Telling the Story and Spreading the Voices of China—the Confucius Institute Builds a 'Spiritual Express Train' Connecting China with the People of the World." Accessed March 2, 2017. http://english.hanban.org/article/2015-12/30/content_628684.htm.

———. 2016. *Confucius Institute Annual Development Report: 2016.* Confucius Institute Headquarters. Accessed June 29, 2017. http://www.hanban.edu.cn/report/2016.pdf.

Handler, Richard. 2013. "Disciplinary Adaptation and Undergraduate Desire: Anthropology and Global Development Studies in the Liberal Arts Curriculum." *Cultural Anthropology* 28 (2): 181–203.

Hartig, Falk. 2012. "Confucius Institutes and the Rise of China." *Journal of Chinese Political Science* 17:53–76.

———. 2015. "Communicating China to the World: Confucius Institutes and China's Strategic Narratives." *Politics* 35 (3–4): 245–258.

———. 2016. *Chinese Public Diplomacy: The Rise of the Confucius Institute.* New York: Routledge.

Harvey, Penelope. 2005. "The Materiality of State-Effects: An Ethnography of a Road in the Peruvian Andes." In *State Formation: Anthropological Perspectives,* edited by Christian Krohn-Hansen and Knut Nustad, 123–141. London: Pluto Press.

Hayden, Craig. 2012. *The Rhetoric of Soft Power: Public Diplomacy in Global Contexts.* Lanham, MD: Lexington Books.

Hayot, Eric. 2009. *Hypothetical Mandarin: Sympathy, Modernity, and Chinese Pain.* New York: Oxford University Press.

Hertz, Ellen. 1998. *The Trading Crowd: An Ethnography of the Shanghai Stock Market.* New York: Cambridge University Press.

Herzfeld, Michael. 2015. "Anthropology and the Inchoate Intimacies of Power." *American Ethnologist* 42 (1): 18–32.

Ho, Karen. 2009. *Liquidated: An Ethnography of Wall Street.* Durham, NC: Duke University Press.

Hoag, Colin. 2010. "The Magic of the Populace: An Ethnography of Illegibility in the South African Immigration Bureaucracy." *PoLAR: Political and Legal Anthropology Review* 33 (1): 6–25.

hooks, bell. (1992) 2006. "Eating the Other: Desire and Resistance." In *Media and Cultural Studies: KeyWorks,* edited by Meenakshi Gigi Durham and Douglas M. Kellner, 366–380. Malden, MA: Blackwell Publishing.

Houlden, Gordon, and Heather Schmidt. 2014. "Rethinking China's Soft Power." *New Global Studies* 8 (3): 213–221.

Hsiao, Alan. 2009. "Soft Power: China on the Global Stage." *Chinese Journal of International Politics* 2:373–398.

Hsiao, H. H. Michael, and Alan Yang. 2009. *"Soft Power Politics in the Asia Pacific: Chinese and Japanese Quests for Regional Leadership." Asia-Pacific Journal 7 (8).* Accessed October 27, 2012. http://japanfocus.org /-A_-Yang/3054.

Hu Jintao. 2007. "Hold High the Great Banner of Socialism with Chinese Characteristics and Strive for New Victories in Building a Moderately Prosperous Society in All Respects." *Beijing Review.com,* November 20. http://www.bjreview.com.cn/document/txt/2007-11/20/content_86325.htm.

Hua, Zhu, and Li Wei. 2014. "Geopolitics and the Changing Hierarchies of the Chinese Language: Implications for Policy and Practice of Chinese Language Teaching in Britain." *Modern Language Journal* 98 (1): 326–339.

Huang, Phillip. 2016. "Our Sense of Problem: Rethinking China Studies in the United States." *Modern China* 42 (2): 115–161.

Hubbert, Jennifer. 2003. "Signs of the Modern: Intellectual Authority, Pain and Pleasure in Reform China." In *Trans-Pacific Relations: America, Europe, and Asia in the Twentieth Century,* edited by Richard Jensen, Jon Davidann, and Yoneyuki Sugita, 269–291. Westport, CT: Praeger Publishers.

———. 2006. "(Re)Collecting Mao: Memory and Fetish in Contemporary China." *American Ethnologist* 33 (2): 145–161.

———. 2010. "Spectacular Productions: Community and Commodity in the Beijing Olympics." *City & Society* 22 (1): 119–142.

———. 2013. "Of Menace and Mimicry: The 2008 Beijing Olympics." *Modern China* 39 (4): 408–437.

———. 2014a. "Appropriating Iconicity: Why Tank Man Still Matters." *Visual Anthropology Review* 30 (2): 114–126.

———. 2014b. "The Darfur Olympics: Global Citizenship and the 2008 Beijing Olympic Games." *Positions: East Asia Culture Critique* 22 (1): 203–236.

———. 2015. " 'We're Not *that* Kind of Developing Country': Environmental Awareness in Contemporary China." In *Sustainability as Myth and Practice,* edited by Gary McConogh, Melissa Checker, and Cindy Isenhour, 29–53. New York: Cambridge University Press.

———. 2017. "Back to the Future: The Politics of Culture at the Shanghai Expo." *International Journal of Cultural Studies* 20 (1): 48–64.

Hughes, Christopher. 2014. "Confucius Institutes and the University: Distinguishing the Political Mission from the Cultural." *Issues & Studies* 50 (4): 45–83.

Hunter, Alan. 2009. "Soft Power: China on the Global Stage." *Chinese Journal of International Politics* 2:373–398.

Institute of International Education. 2015. "International Students in the United States." Project Atlas, Institute of International Education. Accessed October 15, 2016. http://www.iie.org/Services/Project-Atlas/United-States /International-Students-In-US#.WIt2HPArKM8.

Ives, Mike. 2017. "Chinese Student, Graduating in Maryland, Sets Off a Furor by Praising the U.S." *New York Times,* May 24, A4.

Iwabuchi, Koichi. 2002. *Recentering Globalization, on Pop Cultural Traffic in East Asia.* Durham, NC: Duke University Press.

Jacobs, Andrew. 2011. "Confucius Statue Vanishes Near Tiananmen Square." *New York Times,* April 22. Accessed April 23, 2011. http://www.nytimes.com /2011/04/23/world/asia/23confucius.html.

Jensen, Lionel. 2012. "Culture Industry, Power and the Spectacle of China's 'Confucius Institutes.' " In *China in and Beyond the Headlines,* edited by Timothy Weston and Lionel Jensen, 271–299. Lanham, MD: Rowman & Littlefield.

Kahn, Joseph. 2006. "One Subject, Two Results: Tiananmen Square." *New York Times,* February 12. Accessed May 25, 2016. http://www .nytimes.com/imagepages/2006/02/12/weekinreview/20060212kahn_ graph.html.

Kalathil, Shanti. 2011. "China's Soft Power in the Information Age: Think Again." ISD Working Papers in New Diplomacy, Institute for the Study of Diplomacy, Georgetown University, Washington, DC, May. Accessed October 14, 2014. https://isd.georgetown.edu/sites/isd/files/Kalathil_ Chinas_Soft_Power.pdf.

Kamola, Isaac. 2013. "Why Global? Diagnosing the Globalization Literature within a Political Economy of Higher Education." *International Political Sociology* 7:41–58.

Kau, Michael Y. M., and John K. Leung, eds., 1986. *Mao Zedong: The Writings of Mao Zedong, 1949–1976,* vol. 1, *September 1949–December 1955.* Armonk, NY: M. E. Sharpe.

Kendall, Laurel. 2014. "'China to the Anthropologist': Franz Boas, Berthold Laufer, and a Road Not Taken in Early American Anthropology." In *Anthropologists and Their Traditions across National Borders,* edited by Regna Darnell and Frederic Gleach, 1–39. Lincoln: University of Nebraska Press.

Kluver, Randolph. 2014. "The Sage as Strategy: Nodes, Networks, and the Quest for Geopolitical Power in the Confucius Institute." *Communication, Culture & Critique* 7:192–209.

———. 2017. "Chinese Culture in a Global Context: The Confucius Institute as a Geo-Cultural Force." In *China's Global Engagement: The Twenty-First Century,* edited by Jacques deLisle and Avery Goldstein, 389–416. Washington, DC: Brookings Institution Press.

Kohut, Andrew. 2007. "How the World Sees China." Pew Research Center, December 11. Accessed December 15, 2007. http://www.pewglobal.org/2007/12/11/how-the-world-sees-china/.

Kornprobst, Markus, Vincent Pouliot, Nisha Shah, and Ruben Zaiotti. 2008. "Introduction: Mirrors, Magicians and Mutinies of Globalization." In *Metaphors of Globalization: Mirrors, Magicians and Mutinies,* edited by Markus Kornprobst, Vincent Pouliot, Nisha Shah, and Ruben Zaiotti, 1–16. New York: Palgrave Macmillan.

Krosnick, Jon, and Duane Alwin. 1989. "Aging and Susceptibility to Attitude Change." *Journal of Personality and Social Psychology* 57 (3): 416–425.

Kuhn, Robert Lawrence. 2013. "Xi Jinping's Chinese Dream." *New York Times,* June 5. Accessed June 6, 2013. http://www.nytimes.com/2013/06/05/opinion/global/xi-jinpings-chinese-dream.html.

Kuper, Adam. 1999. *Culture: The Anthropologists' Account.* Cambridge, MA: Harvard University Press.

Kurlantzick, Joshua. 2007. *Charm Offensive: How China's Soft Power Is Transforming the World.* New Haven, CT: Yale University Press.

Lahtinen, Anja. 2015. "China's Soft Power: Challenges of Confucianism and Confucius Institutes." *Journal of Comparative Asian Development* 14 (2): 200–226.

Lai, Hongyi. 2012. "China's Cultural Diplomacy: Going for Soft Power." In *China's Soft Power and International Relations,* edited by Hongyi Lai and Yiyi Lu, 83–103. New York: Routledge.

Lai, Hongyi, and Yiyi Lu, eds. 2012. *China's Soft Power and International Relations.* New York: Routledge.

Latour, Bruno. 1993. *We Have Never Been Modern.* Cambridge, MA: Harvard University Press.

Leavenworth, Stuart. 2014. "University of Chicago Pulls Out of Confucius Institute." McClatchy DC Bureau, September 26. Accessed April 29, 2017. http://www.mcclatchydc.com/news/nation-world/world/article24773845.html.

Lee, Benjamin, and Edward LiPuma. 2002. "Cultures of Circulation: The Imaginations of Modernity." *Public Culture* 14 (1): 191–213.

Lee, Chin-Chuan. 2010. "Bound to Rise: Chinese Media Discourses on the New Global Order." In *Reorienting Global Communication: Indian and Chinese Media Beyond Borders,* edited by Michael Curtin and Hemant Shah, 260–283. Urbana: University of Illinois Press.

Li, David C. S. 2017. *Multilingual Hong Kong: Languages, Literacies and Identities.* Berlin: Springer.

Li, Mingjiang. 2008. "China Debates Soft Power." *Chinese Journal of International Politics* 2:287–308.

———, ed. 2009a. *Soft Power: China's Emerging Strategy in International Politics.* Lanham, MD: Lexington Books.

———. 2009b. "Soft Power in Chinese Discourse: Popularity and Prospect." In *Soft Power: China's Emerging Strategy in International Politics,* edited by Li Mingjiang, 21–44. Lanham, MD: Lexington Books.

Li, Tania. 2005. "Beyond 'the State' and Failed Schemes." *American Anthropologist* 107 (3): 383–394.

Li Xiaohua. 2007. "Confucius Institutes Taking Chinese to the World." China. org.cn, March 23. Accessed March 23, 2007. http://www.china.org.cn /english/education/204196.htm.

Liang, Wei. 2012. "China's Soft Power in Africa: Is Economic Power Sufficient?" *Asian Perspective* 36:667–692.

Lim, Rebecca. 2012. "Enter the Dragons: A Baby Boom for Chinese across Asia." BBC, January 20. Accessed December 10, 2017. http://www.bbc.com/news /world-asia-16589052.

Litzinger, Ralph. 2000. *Other Chinas: The Yao and the Politics of National Belonging.* Durham, NC: Duke University Press.

Liu, Chang. 2010. "No Need to Fuss over Confucius Institutes." *China Daily,* August 14. Accessed June 11, 2018. http://www.chinadaily.com.cn /opinion/2010-08/14/content_11153143.htm.

Liu Fuhua, Wang Wei, Zhou Renan, and Li Dongmei. 2005. *Chinese Paradise Student Book 3B.* Beijing: Beijing Language and Culture University Press.

Liu, Guo-qiang. 2012. "Confucius Institutes and China's National Identity." In *ALAA 2012: Proceedings of the Applied Linguistics Association of Australia 2012 Conference,* 505–524. Perth, Western Australia: Curtin University.

Liu Kang. 2012. "Searching for a Cultural Identity: China's Soft Power and Media Culture Today." *Journal of Contemporary China* 21 (78): 915–931.

Liu Kun. 2013. "Shekeyuan baogao: Jueda bufen zhoubian guojia dui zhongguo jen er bu qin" (The majority of China's neighboring countries are near but not dear). *Huanqiu* (Global). December 26. Accessed December 10, 2015. http://mil.huanqiu.com/china/2013-12/4699725.html.

Lo, Joe Tin-yau, and Suyan *Pan. 2016.* "Confucius Institutes and China's Soft Power: Practices and Paradoxes." *Compare: A Journal of Comparative and International Education* 46 (4): 512–532.

Loewen, James. 2007. *Lies My Teacher Told Me: Everything Your American History Textbook Got Wrong.* New York: Touchstone.

Lozada, Eriberto P., Jr. 2005. "Globalized Childhood? Kentucky Fried Chicken in Beijing." In *The Cultural Politics of Food and Eating: A Reader,* edited by James Watson and Melissa Caldwell, 163–179. Oxford: Blackwell.

Lukose, Ritty. 2009. *Liberalization's Children: Gender, Youth, and Consumer Citizenship in Globalizing India.* Durham, NC: Duke University Press.

MacCannell, Dean. 1976. *The Tourist: A New Theory of the Leisure Class.* New York: Schocken Books.

Mahmood, Saba. 2006. "Feminist Theory, Agency, and the Liberatory Subject: Some Reflections on the Islamic Revival in Egypt." *Temenos* 42 (1): 31–71.

Mahoney, Josef Gregory. 2008. "On the Way to Harmony: Marxism, Confucianism, and Hu Jintao's *Hexie* Concept." In *China in Search of a Harmonious Society,* edited by Sujian Guo and Baogang Guo, 99–128. Lanham, MD: Lexington Books.

Makeham, John. 2011. "The Revival of *Guoxue:* Historical Antecedents and Contemporary Aspirations." *China Perspectives* 1:14–21.

Mao Tse-Tung. 1967. "Talks at the Yenan Forum on Literature and Art." *Selected Works of Mao Tse-tung.* Peking: Foreign Language Press.

Mathews, Gordon, Gustavo Lins Ribeiro, and Carlos Alba Vega, eds. 2012. *Globalization from Below: The World's Other Economy.* New York: Routledge.

Mattis, Peter. 2012. "Reexamining the Confucian Institutes." *Diplomat,* August 2. Accessed December 5, 2017. https://thediplomat.com/2012/08 /reexamining-the-confucian-institutes/.

McCord, Edward. n.d. "Confucius Institutes in the U.S.: Let a Hundred Flowers Bloom; Let a Hundred Schools of Thought Contend." lawprofessors. typepad.com/files/response-to-salins-6.pdf.

Merry, Sally Engle. 1996. "Legal Vernacularization and Ka Ho'okolokolonui Kanaka Maoli, The People's International Tribunal, Hawai'i 1993." *PoLAR: Political and Legal Anthropology Review* 19 (1): 67–82.

———. 2006a. *Human Rights and Gender Violence: Translating International Law into Local Justice.* Chicago: University Of Chicago Press.

———. 2006b. "Transnational Human Rights and Local Activism: Mapping the Middle." *American Anthropologist* 108 (1): 38–51.

Mitchell, Timothy. 1991. "The Limits of the State: Beyond Statist Approaches and their Critics." *American Political Science Review* 85 (1): 77–96.

———. 2006. "Society, Economy, and the State Effect." In *The Anthropology of the State: A Reader,* edited by Aradhana Sharma and Akhil Gupta, 169–186. Malden, MA: Blackwell Publishing.

Mosse, David. 2005. *Cultivating Development: An Ethnography of Aid Policy and Practice.* Ann Arbor, MI: Pluto Press.

Mu Xuequan. 2014. "Xi: China to Promote Cultural Soft Power." *China Daily,* February 1. Accessed June 11, 2018. http://www.chinadaily.com.cn/china /2014-01/01/content_17208354.htm.

Mueller, Gotelind. 2013. *Documentary, World History, and National Power in the PRC: Global Rise in Chinese Eyes.* New York: Routledge.

Murray, Julia. 2009. "The Global Rebranding of Confucius." In *China in 2008: A Year of Great Significance,* edited by Jeffrey Wasserstrom, Kate Merkel-Hess, and Kenneth Pomeranz, 263–270. Lanham, MD: Rowman & Littlefield.

NBC News. 2009. "China's 60th Anniversary Stirs Pride, Unease." NBC News, October 1. Accessed October 9, 2011. http://www.nbcnews.com/id/33108782 /ns/world_news-asia_pacific/t/chinas-th-anniversary-stirs-pride-unease /#.Ww2c2maZNkU.

Nelson, Diane. 2009. *Reckoning: The Ends of War in Guatemala.* Durham, NC: Duke University Press.

Nguyen, Van Chinh. 2014. "Confucius Institutes in the Mekong Region: China's Soft Power or Soft Border?" *Issues & Studies* 50 (4): 85–117.

Ni, Ching-Ching. 2007. "She Makes Confucius Cool Again." *Los Angeles Times,* May 7. Accessed July 2, 2014. http://articles.latimes.com/2007/may/07 /world/fg-confucius7.

———. 2010. "Chinese Government's Funding of Southland School's Language Program Fuels Controversy." *Los Angeles Times,* April 4. Accessed July 2, 2014. http://articles.latimes.com/2010/apr/04/local/la-me-confucius -school4-2010apr04.

Nielsen, Gritt. 2011. "Peopling Policy: On Conflicting Subjectivities of Fee-Paying Students." In *Policy Worlds: Anthropology and the Analysis of Contemporary Power,* edited by Cris Shore, Susan Wright, and Davide Però, 68–85. New York: Berghahn Books.

Niquet, Valerie. 2012. "Confu-talk: The Use of Confucian Concepts in Contemporary Chinese Foreign Policy." In *China's Thought Management,* edited by Anne-Marie Brady, 76–98. New York: Routledge.

Noack, Rick, and Lazaro Gamio. 2015. "The World's Languages, in 7 Maps and Charts." *Washington Post,* April 23. Accessed May 3, 2015. https://www .washingtonpost.com/news/worldviews/wp/2015/04/23/the-worlds -languages-in-7-maps-and-charts/?utm_term=.c7df511e9946.

Nordin, Astrid. 2012. "How Soft Is 'Soft Power'? Unstable Dichotomies at Expo 2010." *Asian Perspective* 36:591–613.

Nye, Joseph. 1990. "Soft Power." *Foreign Policy* 80:153–171.

———. 2002. *The Paradox of American Power. Why the World's Only Super-Power Can't Go It Alone.* New York: Oxford University Press.

———. 2004. *Soft Power: The Means to Success in World Politics.* New York: Public Affairs.

Nyiri, Pal. 2014. "Reporting for China: Cosmopolitan Attitudes and the 'Chinese Perspective' among Chinese Correspondents Abroad." *New Global Studies* 8 (3): 223–243.

Ong, Aihwa. 1999. *Flexible Citizenship: The Cultural Logics of Transnationality.* Durham, NC: Duke University Press.

———. 2011. "Introduction: Worlding Cities, or the Art of Being Global." In *Worlding Cities: Asian Experiments and the Art of Being Global,* edited by Ananya Roy and Aihwa Ong, 1–26. Oxford: Blackwell Publishing.

Orta, Andrew. 2013. "Managing the Margins: MBA Training, International Business, and 'the Value Chain of Culture.'" *American Ethnologist* 40 (4): 689–703.

Osburg, John. 2013. *Anxious Wealth: Money and Morality among China's New Rich.* Stanford, CA: Stanford University Press.

Osnos, Evan. 2011. "The Grand Tour: Europe on Fifteen Hundred Yuan a Day." *New Yorker* 87 (9): 50–60.

———. 2014. "Confucius Comes Home." *New Yorker* 89 (44): 30–35.

Overseas Chinese Affairs Office of the State Council. 2015. *Common Knowledge about Chinese History.* Beijing: Higher Education Press.

Page, Jeremy. 2015. "President Xi Jinping, Set to Arrive in U.S. Tuesday, Is Promoting Traditions His Party Once Reviled." *Wall Street Journal,* September 20. Accessed September 20, 2015. https://www.wsj.com/articles/why-china-is-turning-back-to-confucius-1442754000.

Paradise, James. 2009. "China and International Harmony: The Role of Confucius Institutes in Bolstering Beijing's Soft Power." *Asian Survey* 17 (4): 647–669.

Park, Jae. 2013. "Cultural Artefact, Ideology Export or Soft Power? Confucius Institute in Peru." *International Studies in Sociology of Education* 23 (1): 1–16.

Pérez-Milans, Miguel. 2014. "Mandarin Chinese in London Education: Language Aspirations in a Working-Class Secondary School." Working Papers in Urban Language & Literacies 129, Centre for Language Discourse & Communication, King's College London.

Perry, Elizabeth. 2013. "Cultural Governance in Contemporary China: Reorienting Party Propaganda." Harvard-Yenching Institute Working Paper Series. Harvard-Yenching Institute, Cambridge, MA.

Peters, Mike, and Chunyan Zhang. 2011. "Confucius Lives." *New York Times,* October 30, A8.

Peterson, Rachelle. 2017. "Outsourced to China: Confucius Institutes and Soft Power in American Higher Education." Report by the National Association of Scholars. https://www.nas.org/articles/outsourced_to_china_confucius _institutes_and_soft_power_in_american_higher.

Phillips, Tom. 2016. "China Universities Must Become Communist Party 'Strongholds,' Says Xi Jinping." *Guardian,* December 9. Accessed January 15, 2017. https://www.theguardian.com/world/2016/dec/09/china -universities-must-become-communist-party-strongholds-says-xi-jinping.

Pomeranz, Kenneth. 2000. *The Great Divergence: China, Europe, and the Making of the Modern World Economy.* Princeton, NJ: Princeton University Press.

Pomfret, John. 2017. "Don't Worry Hollywood. China's Not a Threat." *Los Angeles Times,* May 26. Accessed May 27, 2017. http://www.latimes.com /opinion/op-ed/la-oe-pomfret-hollywood-china-20170526-story.html.

Pun, Ngai. 2005. *Made in China: Women Factory Workers in a Global Workplace.* Durham, NC: Duke University Press.

Radcliffe-Brown, Alfred. 1940. "Preface." In *African Political Systems,* edited by Meyer Fortes and E. E. Evans-Pritchard, xi–xxiii. Oxford: Oxford University Press.

Rafael, Vincente. 2009. "Translation, American English, and the National Insecurities of Empire." *Social Text* 27 (4): 1–23.

Ramo, Joshua Cooper. 2004. *The Beijing Consensus: Notes on the New Physics of Chinese Power.* London: Foreign Policy Centre.

Rampell, Catherine. 2011. "Many with New College Degree Find the Job Market Humbling." *New York Times,* May 18. Accessed February 14, 2012. http://www.nytimes.com/2011/05/19/business/economy/19grads.html.

Redden, Elizabeth. 2012. "Confucius Says . . . Debate over Chinese-Funded Institutes at American Universities." *Inside Higher Ed,* January 4. Accessed January 5, 2012. http://www.insidehighered.com/news/2012/01/04 /debate-over-chinese-funded-institutes-american-universities.

———. 2014. "Chicago to Close Confucius Institute." *Inside Higher Ed,* September 26. Accessed October 1, 2014. https://www.insidehighered.com /news/2014/09/26/chicago-severs-ties-chinese-government-funded -confucius-institute.

Rofel, Lisa. 2007. *Desiring China: Experiments in Neoliberalism, Sexuality, and Public Culture.* Durham, NC: Duke University Press.

Ross, E. Wayne, and Kevin Vinson. 2013. "Resisting Neoliberal Education Reform: Insurrectionist Pedagogies and the Pursuit of Dangerous Citizenship." *Cultural Logic: Marxist Theory & Practice,* 17–45.

Roy, Ananya, and Aihwa Ong. 2011. *Worlding Cities: Asian Experiments and the Art of Being Global.* Oxford: Blackwell Publishing.

Roy, Denny. 1996. "The 'China Threat' Issue: Major Arguments." *Asian Survey* 36 (8): 758–771.

Ruan, Lotus. 2014. "Chinese Doubt Their Own Soft Power Venture." *Foreign Policy,* October 17. Accessed October 10, 2015. http://foreignpolicy .com/2014/10/17/chinese-doubt-their-own-soft-power-venture/.

Rutz, Henry. 1999. "The Rise and Demise of Imam-hatip Schools: Discourses of Islamic Belonging and Denial in the Construction of Turkish Civic Culture." *PoLAR: Political and Legal Anthropology Review* 22 (2): 93–103.

Sahlins, Marshall. 2013. "China U." *Nation,* October 30. Accessed October 31, 2013. https://www.thenation.com/article/china-u/.

———. 2015. *Confucius Institutes: Academic Malware.* Chicago: Prickly Pear Press.

Said, Edward. 1978. *Orientalism.* New York: Pantheon Books.

Saul, Stephanie. 2017. "On Campuses Far from China, Still under Beijing's Watchful Eye." *New York Times,* May 4. Accessed May 4, 2017. https:// www.nytimes.com/2017/05/04/us/chinese-students-western-campuses -china-influence.html?_r=0.

Schein, Louisa. 2000. *Minority Rules: The Miao and the Feminine in China's Cultural Politics.* Durham, NC: Duke University Press.

Schell, Orville, and John Delury. 2013. "A Rising China Needs a New National Story." *Wall Street Journal,* July 12. Accessed July 13, 2013. https://www.wsj.com/articles/SB10001424127887324425204578599633633 456090.

Schiller, Herbert. 1991. "Not Yet the Post-Imperialist Era." *Critical Studies in Mass Communication* 8:13–28.

Schmidt, Heather. 2013. "China's Confucius Institutes and the 'Necessary White Body.'" *Canadian Journal of Sociology* 38 (4): 647–668.

———. 2014. "The Politics of Affect in Confucius Institutes: Re-orienting Foreigners towards the PRC." *New Global Studies* 8 (3): 353–375.

Schmindle, Nicholas. 2010. "Inside the Knockoff-Tennis-Shoe Factory." *New York Times,* August 19. Accessed April 22, 2014. http://www.nytimes .com/2010/08/22/magazine/22fake-t.html?pagewanted=all.

Schouten, Peer. 2009. "Theory Talk #34: James Ferguson on Modernity, Development, and Reading Foucault in Lesotho." *Theory Talks.* Accessed February 1, 2015. http://www.theory-talks.org/2009/11/theory-talk-34.html.

Sen, Amartya. 1997. "Human Rights and Asian Values." *New Republic* 33–40 (July 14–21).

Shambaugh, David. 2014. *China Goes Global: The Partial Power.* New York: Oxford University Press.

Sharma, Aradhana, and Akhil Gupta. 2006. "Introduction: Rethinking Theories of the State in an Age of Globalization." In *The Anthropology of the*

State: A Reader, edited by Aradhana Sharma and Akhil Gupta, 1–41. Malden, MA: Blackwell Publishing.

Shore, Cris. 2011. "Espionage, Policy and the Art of Government: The British Secret Services and the War on Iraq." In *Policy Worlds: Anthropology and the Analysis of Contemporary Power,* edited by Cris Shore, Susan Wright, and Davide Però, 169–186. New York: Berghahn Books.

Shore, Cris, and Miri Davidson. 2014. "Beyond Collusion and Resistance: Academic-Management Relations with the Neoliberal University." *Learning and Teaching* 7 (1): 12–28.

Shore, Cris, and Susan Wright, eds. 1997. *Anthropology of Policy: Perspectives on Governance and Power.* New York: Routledge.

———. 1999. "Audit Culture and Anthropology: Neo-Liberalism in British Higher Education." *Journal of the Royal Anthropological Institute* 5 (4): 557–575.

Shore, Cris, Susan Wright, and Davide Però, eds. 2011. *Policy Worlds: Anthropology and the Analysis of Contemporary Power.* New York: Berghahn Books.

Shryock, Andrew. 2012. "Breaking Hospitality Apart: Bad Hosts, Bad Guests, and the Problem of Sovereignty." *Journal of the Royal Anthropological Institute* 18 (s1): S20–S33.

Simcox, Robin. 2009. *A Degree of Influence: The Funding of Strategically Important Subjects in UK Universities.* London: Centre for Social Cohesion.

Smith, Richard. 1997. "Flies and Fresh Air: Culture and Consumerism in Contemporary China." *Problems of Post-Communism* 44 (2): 3–13.

Stambach, Amy. 2014. *Confucius and Crisis in American Universities: Culture, Capital, and Diplomacy in U.S. Public Higher Education.* New York: Routledge.

Starr, Don. 2009. "Chinese Language Education in Europe: The Confucius Institutes." *European Journal of Education* 44 (1): 65–82.

Steffenhagen, Janet. 2008. "Has BCIT Sold Out to Chinese Propaganda?" *Vancouver Sun,* April 2. Accessed June 22, 2013. http://forums .canadiancontent.net/news/85292-close-confucius-insititute-bcit -vancouver.html.

Steinmetz, George, ed. 1999. *State/Culture: State-Formation after the Cultural Turn.* Ithaca, NY: Cornell University Press.

Tate, Winifred. 2015. *Drugs, Thugs, and Diplomats: U.S. Policymaking in Columbia.* Stanford, CA: Stanford University Press.

Taussig, Michael. 1992. *The Nervous System.* New York: Routledge.

Taylor, Charles. 2002. "Modern Social Imaginaries." *Public Culture* 14 (1): 91–124.

Taylor, Sarah. 2014. "Maya Cosmopolitans: Engaging Tactics and Strategies in the Performance of Tourism." *Identities: Global Studies in Culture and Power* 21 (2): 219–232.

Tham, Engen, and Matthew Miller. 2016. "Beijing Auditions Foreign Public Relations Firms to Polish China Brand." Reuters, April 22. Accessed April 30, 2016. http://www.reuters.com/article/us-china-pr-exclusive -idUSKCN0XJ007.

Trouillot, Michel-Rolph. 2001. "The Anthropology of the State in the Age of Globalization: Close Encounters of the Deceptive Kind." *Current Anthropology* 42 (1): 125–138.

Tsing, Anna. 2000a. "The Global Situation." *Cultural Anthropology* 15 (3): 327–360.

———. 2000b. "Inside the Economy of Appearances. *Public Culture* 12 (1): 115–144.

———. 2005. *Friction: An Ethnography of Global Connection.* Princeton, NJ: Princeton University Press.

Tsung, Linda, and Ken Cruikshank, eds. 2010. *Teaching and Learning Chinese in Global Contexts: Multimodality and Literacy in the New Media Age.* New York: Continuum.

Tu, Wei-ming. 1989. "The Confucian Dimension in the East Asian Development Model." Paper presented at the Confucianism and Economic Development in East Asia conference, Taipei, Taiwan, May 29–31.

Tylor, Edward Burnett. (1871) 1920. *Primitive Culture: Researches into the Development of Mythology, Philosophy, Religion, Language Art, and Custom.* London: John Murray.

Ueki, Chikako. 2006. "The Rise of 'China Threat' Arguments." PhD diss., Massachusetts Institute of Technology.

US Congress. House of Representatives. Committee on Foreign Affairs. 2012. *The Price of Public Diplomacy with China. Hearings before the Subcommittee on Oversight and Investigations of the Committee on Foreign Affairs, House of Representatives.* 112th Cong. (March 28).

US Congress. House of Representatives. Committee on Foreign Affairs. 2014. *Is Academic Freedom Threatened by China's Influence on U.S. Universities? Hearings before the Subcommittee on Africa, Global Health, Global Human Rights, and International Organizations.* 113th Cong. (December 4).

Van Norden, Bryan. 2002. "Introduction." In *Confucius and the Analects: New Essays,* edited by Bryan Van Norden, 3–36. New York: Oxford University Press.

Volodzko, David. 2015. "China's Confucius Institutes and the Soft War." *Diplomat,* July 8. Accessed August 10, 2015. https:// thediplomat.com/2015/07/chinas-confucius-institutes-and -the-soft-war/.

Von Mayrhauser, Melissa. 2011. "China-Funded Institute Tests Columbia's Commitment to Academic Integrity." *Columbia Spectator,* November 11.

Accessed November 1, 2012. https://www.columbiaspectator.com/2011
/11/11/china-funded-institute-tests-columbias-commitment-academic
-integrity/.

Waldmeir, Patti. 2014. "China's University System Faces Criticism for Being
Unfit for a Modern Economy." *Financial Times,* October 6. Accessed
December 2, 2017. https://www.ft.com/content/07c0aa44-283b-11e4-9ea9
-00144feabdc0.

Walker, Christopher, and Jessica Ludwig. 2017. "From 'Soft Power' to 'Sharp
Power': Rising Authoritarian Influence in the Democratic World." National
Endowment for Democracy. Accessed January 10, 2018. https://www.ned
.org/wp-content/uploads/2017/12/Introduction-Sharp-Power-Rising
-Authoritarian-Influence.pdf.

Walton, Linda. 2017. "The 'Spirit' of Confucian Education in Contemporary
China: Songyang Academy and Zhengzhou University." *Modern China*
44 (3): 313–342.

Wang, Danping, and Bob Adamson. 2015. "War and Peace: Perceptions of
Confucius Institutes in China and USA." *Asia-Pacific Education Researcher*
24 (1): 225–234.

Wang, Guanqun. 2011. "'Experience China' Debuts at New York City's Times
Square." *China Daily,* January 18. Accessed June 11, 2018. http://www
.chinadaily.com.cn/photo/2011-01/18/content_11872277.htm.

Wang, Hongying. 2011. "China's Image Projection and Its Impact." In *Soft
Power in China: Public Diplomacy through Communication,* edited by Jian
Wang, 37–56. New York: Palgrave Macmillan.

Wang, Jian, ed. 2011a. *Soft Power in China: Public Diplomacy through
Communication.* New York: Palgrave Macmillan.

———. 2011b. "Introduction: China's Search for Soft Power." In *Soft Power in
China: Public Diplomacy through Communication,* edited by Jian Wang,
1–18. New York: Palgrave Macmillan.

Wang, Jing. 1996. *High Culture Fever: Politics, Aesthetics, and Ideology in Deng's
China.* Berkeley: University of California Press.

Warren, Kay. 1998. *Indigenous Movements and Their Critics: Pan-Maya Activism
in Guatemala.* Princeton, NJ: Princeton University Press.

Wheeler, Anita. 2014. "Cultural Diplomacy, Language Planning, and the Case
of the University of Nairobi Confucius Institutes." *Journal of Asian and
African Studies* 49 (1): 49–63.

Wike, Richard, Bruce Stokes, and Jacob Poushter. 2015. "Views of China and the
Global Balance of Power." Pew Research Center: Global Attitudes & Trends.
Accessed May 20, 2017. http://www.pewglobal.org/2015/06/23/2-views-of
-china-and-the-global-balance-of-power/#china-receives-generally-positive
-ratings-from-global-publics.

Wishnick, Elizabeth. 2005. "China as a Risk Society." East-West Center Working Papers 12:1–50, Politics, Governance, and Security Series. East-West Center, Honolulu, HI.

Wong, Edward. 2016. "Chinese Purchases of U.S. Companies Have Some in Congress Raising Eyebrows." *New York Times,* September 30. Accessed May 15, 2017. https://www.nytimes.com/2016/10/01/world/asia/china -us-foreign-acquisition-dalian-wanda.html?_r=0.

World Bank. n.d. "GDP per Capita." Accessed January 19, 2018. http://data .worldbank.org/indicator/NY.GDP.PCAP.CD.

Woronov, Terry. 2016. *Class Work: Vocational Schools and China's Urban Youth.* Stanford, CA: Stanford University Press.

Wu, Hung. 2005. *Remaking Beijing: Tiananmen Square and the Creation of a Political Space.* Chicago: University of Chicago Press.

Wu, Ka-ming. 2015. *Reinventing Chinese Tradition: The Cultural Politics of Late Socialism.* Urbana: University of Illinois Press.

Wuthnow, Joel. 2008. "The Concept of Soft Power in China's Strategic Discourse." *Issues & Studies* 44 (2): 1–28.

Xie, Tao, and Benjamin Page. 2013. "What Affects China's National Image? A Cross-National Study of Public Opinion." *Journal of Contemporary China* 22 (83): 850–867.

Xie Yuling. 2015. "U.S. Congresswoman Marcia Fudge Supports 'Chinese Bridge' Summer Camp Hosted by Confucius Institutes at Cleveland State University." Confucius Institute at the Cleveland State University. July 14. Accessed January 20, 2016. http://english.hanban.org/article/2015-07/14 /content_609615.htm.

Xie, Zhihai. 2011. "The Rise of China and Its Growing Role in International Organizations." *ICCS Journal of Modern Chinese Studies* 4 (1): 85–96.

Yahuda, Michael. 2003. "China's Win-Win Globalization." *YaleGlobal Online* (February 19). Accessed March 14, 2015. http://yaleglobal.yale.edu/content /chinas-win-win-globalization.

Yan, Xuetong. 2006. "The Rise of China and Its Power Status." *Chinese Journal of International Politics* 1:5–33.

Yan, Yunxiang. 1997. "McDonald's in Beijing: The Localization of Americana." In *Golden Arches East,* edited by James Watson, 39–76. Stanford, CA: Stanford University Press.

———. 2007. "Managing Cultural Conflicts: State Power and Alternative Globalization in China." In *Conflicts and Tensions,* edited by Helmut Anheier and Yudhishthir Raj Isar, 172–184. Los Angeles: Sage Publications.

Yang, Fan. 2015. *Faked in China: Nation Branding, Counterfeit Culture, and Globalization.* Bloomington: Indiana University Press.

Yang, Rui. 2010. "Soft Power and Higher Education: An Examination of China's Confucius Institutes." *Globalisation, Societies and Education* 8 (2): 235–245.

Yao, Minji. 2011. "Businessmen Seek Confucian Chic." *Shanghai Daily,* December 13. Accessed December 14, 2011. http://www.shanghaidaily.com /feature/Businessmen-seek-Confucian-chic/shdaily.shtml.

Yao, Weiming. 2014. "The New Middle Kingdom: The Symbolic Power of the Confucius Institute's Pedagogical Approach." *China Media Research* 10 (1): 4–12.

Yeh, Emily. 2013. *Taming Tibet: Landscape Transformation and the Gift of Chinese Development.* Ithaca, NY: Cornell University Press.

Yu, Ying-shih. 2015. "The Chinese Communists Are Not Confucianists." *China Change,* July 1. Accessed January 10, 2018. https://chinachange.org/2015/07 /01/the-chinese-communists-are-not-confucianists/.

Zhan, Mei. 2005. "Civet Cats, Fried Grasshoppers, and David Beckham's Pajamas: Unruly Bodies after SARS." *American Anthropologist* 107 (1): 31–42.

———. 2009. *Other-Worldly: Making Chinese Medicine through Transnational Frames.* Durham, NC: Duke University Press.

Zhang, Guangrui. 1989. "Ten Years of Chinese Tourism: Profile and Assessment." *Tourism Management* 10 (1): 51–62.

Zhang, Li. 2008. "China's Ascent as a Theoretical Question." *Anthropology News* 49 (8): 13.

Zhang, Lihua. 2014. "Beijing Focuses on Soft Power." Carnegie-Tsinghua Center for Global Policy, April 28. Accessed May 13, 2017. http://carnegietsinghua .org/2014/04/28/beijing-focuses-on-soft-power-pub-55458.

Zhang, Weihong. 2010. "China's Cultural Future: From Soft Power to Comprehensive National Power." *International Journal of Cultural Policy* 16 (4): 383–402.

Zhang, Yongjin. 2013. "Curious and Exotic Encounters: Europeans as Supplicants in the Chinese Imperium, 1513–1793." In *International Orders in the Early Modern World: Before the Rise of the West,* edited by Shogo Suzuki, Joel Quirk, and Yongjin Zhang, 55–75. London: Routledge.

Zhang, Yuzhi, and Ying Li. 2010. "On the Necessity of the CPC's Construction in Soft Power." *International Journal of Business and Management* 5 (4): 204–207.

Zhao, Hongqin, and Jianbin Huang. 2010. "China's Policy of Chinese as a Foreign Language and the Use of Overseas Confucius Institutes." *Educational Research for Policy and Practice* 9:127–142.

Zhe, Ren. 2010. "Confucius Institutes: China's Soft Power?" Policy Commentary, Sigur Center for Asian Studies of George Washington University, Washington, DC, June, 1–3.

———. 2012. "The Confucius Institutes and China's Soft Power." IDE Discussion Paper 330, Institute of Developing Economies, Japan External Trade Organization, Chiba, Japan.

Zheng, Yongnian. 1999. *Discovering Chinese Nationalism in China: Modernization, Identity, and International Relations.* New York: Cambridge University Press.

Zhou, Muriel. 2011. "School-University Partnerships in Teaching the Mandarin Chinese Language: The Confucius Institute Experience." PhD diss., University of Pittsburgh.

Zhou, Ying, and Sabrina Luk. 2016. "Establishing Confucius Institutes: A Tool for Promoting China's Soft Power?" *Journal of Contemporary China* 25 (100): 628–642.

Zhu, Juanjuan. 2013. "Citizenship Education and Foreign Language Learning: Deconstructing the Concept of Good Citizenship Embedded in Foreign Language Curricula in China and America." PhD diss., Utah State University.

Zigon, Jarrett. 2013. "Human Rights as Moral Progress? A Critique." *Cultural Anthropology* 28 (4): 716–736.

Ziguangge. 2014. "Jiaoyubu kongzi xueyuan zongbu" (Confucius Institute Headquarters, Ministry of Education). Accessed November 8, 2016. http://www.zgg.gov.cn/cjwmjgxjjtpx/xjjtpx/201405/t20140509_439363.html.

Žižek, Slavoj. 2005. "Against Human Rights." *New Left Review* 34:119.

Index

61–62, 159n2, 177n18; tattoos with Chinese characters, 52, 175–176n6

Chinese language education: Advanced Placement program and exams, 15–16, 65–66, 71; Chinese Bridge summer classes, 86; competitions, 96; demand for, 13, 14–15, 95, 100–101, 183n25; Hanban exams, 64–65, 177nn19–20; Hanban programs, 13–14, 15–17; interest in United States, 47–49, 59–60; learning characters, 67, 178n24; linguistic differences perceived, 45–46; outcomes, 46; student motives, 46, 50–63, 64, 72–73, 150, 154; vocabulary translations, 113–114. *See also* Confucius Classrooms; Confucius Institutes; curricular materials; pedagogical practices

Chinese New Year Gala, 88

Chinese Paradise texts, 112–113

Chinese state, perceptions of: by American public and politicians, 9–10, 104–105, 110, 119, 120; authoritarianism, 117, 120; based on everyday encounters in CC classrooms, 103–104, 110–112, 120–123, 125; communism as frame, 104–112, 125; distinction from attitudes toward Chinese people, 109; imagined views, 103; misunderstandings, 120; by parents, 105–108, 109–110, 120–122, 124–125, 141–142, 150–151, 185n7; by students, 110–112, 114–115, 116–118, 120–123, 124–125, 126; as unified entity, 8. *See also* "China threat" theory; communism; image management; soft power policies, Chinese

CIs. *See* Confucius Institutes

classroom experiences: cultural and linguistic differences, 45–46; decor, 49–50, 174n2; discipline, 68–69, 71, 178–179nn25–26, 191n25; image management, 120, 129–134, 164–165n31; influences on, 46–47; in middle schools, 45–46, 49–50, 68; perceptions of China based on, 103–104, 110–112, 120–123, 125; political discussions, 111–112, 130, 133, 150–151, 186n16; political topics avoided, 112–116, 130, 132–135, 141–142, 150, 154; unique aspects, 45–46, 49–50. *See also* Chinese language education; pedagogical practices; students; teachers

Clinton, Hillary, 149

Cobb, Russell, 92

Cold War, 56, 81–82, 104, 125, 134, 145

Cole, Jennifer, 61

College Board, 15

colleges. *See* academic freedom; host institutions; universities

Columbia University, 15

Comaroff, Jean, 84–85, 161n21

Comaroff, John L., 84–85, 161n21

Common Knowledge about Chinese History, 131

communism: CC teachers on, 115–116; classroom discussions, 111–112; as frame, 104–112, 125; negative views in United States, 104–106, 159n3; red color associated with, 134; student understandings, 110–112, 134, 185nn8–9. *See also* Chinese Communist Party

concerns about Confucius Institutes:
academic freedom, 2, 15, 17,
128–129, 154, 190n14, 190–191n17;
Chinese government interference,
119, 154, 168n48, 190n14;
congressional hearings, 1–2, 109,
153; discrimination against Falun
Gong practitioners, 2, 167n40,
190n14; ethnographic evidence,
129–130, 140, 152–154; false
picture of China, 18, 71, 129–130,
133–134; free speech, 8–9, 24–25,
127–128, 129–130, 167n40;
ideological motivations, 104, 135,
140, 159n3; of insiders and
outsiders, 179n27; lessened by
exposure to program, 109–110;
normalization, 110; normative
expectations, 134–135; propaganda
in classrooms, 8–9, 18, 105–106,
130–134, 140, 141–142,
164–165n31, 193n35; self-
censorship by host institutions, 18,
167n40, 190–191n17; topics avoided
in classrooms, 17, 114, 130,
132–135, 141–142, 150, 154.
See also censorship
Confucianism: Communist views of,
35–36, 37, 38–40, 170–171n11,
173n29, 174n38; cultural
importance, 34, 35–41; curricular
materials on, 36–37, 40–42; dove as
symbol of peacefulness, 29, 171n15;
in East Asian culture, 34–35, 36–37,
38, 39, 173n36; economic
development and, 38, 173n30,
173n36; on education, 41, 42, 49;
evocations at Shanghai Expo, 31, 38;
harmony (*hexie*), 1, 11, 31, 38, 43,
131, 138; ideals and values, 29, 31,
34, 36–41, 43, 85–86, 131; imperial

civil service examinations, 26, 36;
revival, 28, 36, 37–40, 173n31,
173n33; rulers' relations with over
time, 36; temples, 37, 42–43, 85
Confucius: biographical film, 37, 39;
as brand, 35–44; choice of name for
Confucius Institutes, 35–36, 41,
43–44, 173n28; history textbooks
on, 131; life of, 36; portrait in
CI classrooms, 50; seen as villain
in Maoist period, 35–36, 37; statue
in Tiananmen Square, 37, 39, 40,
174n37
Confucius Classrooms (CCs): benefits
for host schools, 48–49, 60;
ethnographic research sites, 20–21;
extracurricular activities, 16–17;
language and culture lessons, 16,
66–67, 86, 178n22; middle and
high school levels, 15–16, 20,
166n36; number of, 5, 20,
159–160n8. *See also* Chinese
language education; classroom
experiences; pedagogical practices;
students; teachers
Confucius Institute Day (2014), 24,
169n2
Confucius Institutes (CIs):
administration, 13, 14, 18;
American administrators, 14,
48–49, 58, 95, 183n24; class
offerings, 16; closed by host
institutions, 24–25, 128, 162n24,
169n3, 184–185n6; Communist
Party links, 12, 122; constitution,
182n23; cultural education, 16, 29,
86, 181–182n18; description, 1;
enrollments in United States, 5;
establishment process, 14–15;
ethnographic research, 2–4, 7, 9,
18–22, 129–130, 134–135;

foods, Chinese, 89–90, 91–92,
182n19. *See also* restaurants
France, Confucius Institute programs,
162n24
Franklin, Barry, 47
freedom: in China, 123; of choice,
123–124; of press, 127; Western
perspectives, 141. *See also* academic
freedom; free speech
Freedom House, 127
free speech: in China, 43, 137–139,
192nn28–29; of CI teachers and
staff, 129, 134–140, 141–144,
150–151, 193n35, 193n38; concerns
expressed about Confucius
Institutes, 8–9, 24–25, 127–128,
129–130, 167n40; globalization and,
188n5; as modernity marker, 8, 141,
143–144, 188n5; questioning
usefulness of concept, 9, 129,
192–193n32; repression in China,
43, 127, 133–134, 138, 186n18;
Western perspectives, 8, 140–144.
See also academic freedom;
censorship
Friedman, Thomas, 6, 155, 188n5

Germany, Goethe-Institut, 13, 17
Gershon, Ilana, 58–59
Giddens, Anthony, 61
global and local: authenticity, 76, 90;
center and periphery, 76, 80; desire
for global, 61, 76, 94, 100; local as
Other, 100; negative view of local,
81; relationship, 79, 84–85, 92–93,
98–99; resistance to globalization, 7;
tourism, 90; traditional local
cultures, 76, 84
globalization: China as model, 4–6, 7,
76–77, 156; China's power, 5,
59–60, 62, 63, 98, 131, 145–146,

154–155; consumer products, 5,
80–81; cultural impact, 80, 84;
debates in China, 160n12; foreign
investment, 5, 145–146; free speech
and, 188n5; interest in foreign
languages, 47–49, 58, 59–60;
modernity and, 62, 76, 172n26; soft
power production and, 180n9; US
education policies in response to,
47–49; Western perspectives, 6–7,
76, 155, 161n17. *See also* "China
threat" theory; power
Goethe-Institut, 13, 17
Google, 115, 138–139
governance: democratic, 124; state,
108–109. *See also* communism
Great Wall, The, 146
Gupta, Akhil, 8, 108, 119, 126

Hacienda Heights, California, 102,
104–105, 184n4
Hall, Ian, 152
Hanban (Office of the Chinese
Language Council International):
books donated to CC schools, 14,
175n3; contracts with host
institutions, 14, 15, 133, 167n40,
168n48, 190n15; future goals,
166n38; headquarters, 15, 85,
94–95, 96, 181n18; language
exams, 64–65, 177nn19–20;
launching of CIs, 13, 14–15;
photos and videos highlighting
white students, 96–97,
183–184nn26–27; programs,
13–14, 15–17, 53. *See also* Chinese
Bridge summer program; Confucius
Classrooms; Confucius Institutes;
curricular materials
Hartig, Falk, 13, 164–165n31
Hayot, Eric, 109, 155

higher education. *See* Confucius
Institutes; host institutions;
universities
high schools. *See* Confucius
Classrooms; host institutions
high school students. *See* Chinese
Bridge summer program; students
history lessons: Advanced Placement
exams, 66; American teachers, 116;
in Chinese museums, 83–84,
189n10; Confucianism discussed,
37, 131; in Confucius Institute
classrooms, 69–71, 130–135;
textbooks, 37, 112–113, 130–132,
189n11
Hoag, Colin, 119
hospitality, 83
host institutions: books donated to, 14,
175n3; Chinese students, 168n48;
CI establishment process, 13, 14–15;
CIs closed by, 24–25, 128, 162n24,
169n3, 184–185n6; contracts with
Hanban, 14, 15, 133, 167n40,
168n48, 190n15; dependence on
Chinese funding, 18, 168n48;
expenses, 168n47; interest in
Confucius Institute program, 95,
183n25; rationales for CIs, 48–49,
128; self-censorship, 18, 167n40,
190–191n17; sister universities in
China, 14, 16, 77–78. *See also*
concerns about Confucius Institutes;
Confucius Classrooms; Confucius
Institutes
House of Representatives, 1–2, 109,
153, 181–182n18. *See also* Congress
HSK (Hanyu Shuiping Kaoshi
[Chinese Proficiency Test]), 64–65,
177n19
Hu Jintao, 26, 28, 34, 164n30, 171n17
Hu Youqing, 12

Huang, Phillip, 147
Hughes, Christopher, 48, 132
human rights, 9, 128, 140–141,
153, 186n18, 192n32. *See also*
free speech

image management: by China, 29,
55–56, 111–112, 130, 131–132,
151–152; in CI classrooms, 120,
129–134, 164–165n31; of Confucius
Institutes, 102–103; as soft power
policy, 12, 134–135, 152; in Soviet
Union, 81–82
Internet censorship, 115, 127,
138–139, 187n1, 188n5
Italian-style street, 78–79, 94
Iwabuchi, Koichi, 80

Japan: exports, 80; manga and
anime, 54; McDonald's, 74. *See also*
East Asia
Jiang Feng, 13
Jiang Zemin, 6–7

K–12 schools. *See* Confucius
Classrooms; host institutions
Kalathil, Shanti, 138
Kamola, Isaac, 34
Kendall, Laurel, 195–196n11
Koolhaas, Rem, 78
Korean War, 130, 131–132

language: as form of cultural power,
25; global, 61–62, 65; Western
European education programs, 13,
17, 168n46. *See also* Chinese
language
Latour, Bruno, 75
Laufer, Berthold, 195–196n11
Legendary Entertainment, 145, 187n1
Li, Tania, 126

About the Author

Jennifer Hubbert is chair of the Department of Sociology and Anthropology and associate professor of anthropology and Asian studies at Lewis & Clark College in Portland, Oregon. She has a BA in international relations and an MA in international policy studies from Stanford University and an MA and PhD in anthropology from Cornell University. Jennifer has published extensively on China's soft power projects, including the Olympics and the Shanghai Expo, and teaches courses on the anthropology of policy, power and resistance, Chinese culture and film, the anthropology of the news, and Pacific Rim cities.